Time and Photography

Edited by

Jan Baetens, Alexander Streitberger and Hilde Van Gelder

Leuven University Press

TIME AND PHOTOGRAPHY

The Lieven Gevaert Series is a major series of substantial and innovative books on photography. Launched in 2004, the Series takes into account the ubiquitous presence of photography within modern culture and, in particular, the visual arts. At the forefront of contemporary thinking on photography, the books offer new insights in the position of the photographic medium within the art historical, theoretical, social and institutional contexts.

The Series is produced by the Lieven Gevaert Research Centre for Photography (www.lievengevaertcentre.be) and covers four types of approaches: publication of outstanding monographic studies, proceedings of international conferences, book length projects with artists, translations and republications of classic material.

The Lieven Gevaert Series is published by Leuven University Press, and distributed in North America by Cornell University Press.

Contents

Introduction

Jan Baetens, Alexander Streitberger and Hilde Van Gelder

Time and space are the yin and yang of photography. Space was a preoccupation of the modernist era in photography studies, obsessed with medium-specific issues turned towards indexicality and (lacking or, on the contrary, renewed) aura. The more you press on space, the more the notion of time will return with a vengeance—and vice versa, as will become clear in most of the essays gathered in this collection. The traditional definition of the photographic image as a slice of time and space, which has long been used to foreground the idea of photography as spatial framing rather than as temporal reinterpretation of the pictured object, has been dramatically questioned by the encounter of, on the one hand, postmodern reflections on the importance of spectatorship and reading and, on the other hand, a better informed rereading of premodern photographic practices, devices, and cultures, in which the reduction of photography to a slice of time has rapidly become anachronistic. Photographic studies, in this sense, display and obey the same evolution as one can observe in other fields of visuality such as film studies or comics studies, in which comparable convergences between very contemporary interrogations on matters of (social) meaning and new approaches to the history of the medium, no longer as mere technology but as social practice, have similarly expanded the relevance of what is being studied.

The essays brought together in this book all testify to the ongoing project of redefining the photographic field as epitomized by the new interest in time. Yet, this notion of time escapes, in many senses, the merely technical mode that has played such a paramount role in the history of medium, where issues of time reduction have been instrumental in the production of the hegemonic view of photography as a slice of time: reduction of shutter time (a problem of optics), reduction of development time (a problem of chemistry), and reduction of processing time, between the taking of the picture and its social circulation in printed form (a problem of industrial management). The gradual speeding up of all these processes is undeniable, and their convergence has become (almost) complete in today's world of instant taking and global circulation of any image whatsoever. At least from a theoretical point of view, for in practice things are less clear-cut. There are now other elements, more specifically legal and copyright elements that produce an opposite phenomenon of slowing down, if not the social destruction of many images. However, the global feeling of such a speeding-up has formed a vision of photography that matched perfectly certain high-modernist views on the image as timeless or purely 'present'—all these words are heavily burdened with manifold connotations which many essays in this book carefully disentangle—that has lost today any real use value. It is the critical discussion of this blindness to the complexity of photography's temporalities, for it is no longer possible to use the word 'time' in singular, that is at the heart of this book.

However, the aim of these essays is less to criticize or to deconstruct the exclusive focus on spatiality and visuality in a now old-fashioned paradigm. Instead of simply questioning what went wrong in certain excesses of a narrowly defined medium-specific approach (which was also an exaggeratedly philosophical and pictorially art historical point of view), the authors share the common endeavor of laying bare the many forms of time and temporality that shape photography as a complex social process, which is not just a technique, an art, or a way of picture-making, but also a dream, an idea, a political device, in short an object that is by definition hybrid and networked: things, people, technology, and institutions, both synchronically and diachronically are intertwined and produce social meanings and interactions that evolve in time and through time. Moreover, the rediscovery of the temporal multilayeredness of the photographic image has made room for the new reading of time aspects within the photographic image itself, which is never just a slice of time, even if it is now possible to consider this duration in the almost non-duration of nanoseconds. Once again: the more one tries to put time between brackets, the more it will come back and occupy the whole field, both the whole field of vision and the field of photography studies in a more general sense.

The essays in this book discuss these issues in a wide range of photographic objects and practices, as well as from different perspectives. Some of them deal primarily, if not only with time, others demonstrate how time slowly emerges as an indispensable critical category for the analysis of specific images or specific ways of picturing. This diversity, which is part of the richness of the collection, does not prevent all authors from taking a similar stance on the central place of time in thinking photography. A first section, 'Time and Technology / Devices for Time', brings together three essays whose objects cover the whole history of the medium—from the emerging photographic experiments by Talbot and the 19th century craze of ghost photography to the digital reshaping of the world by postmodern artists such as David Claerbout and Jeff Wall. Each of them tackles however one and the same question: How to fix time? How to stop what is on the verge of disappearing? How to produce an image of the instantaneous? In her essay, 'Fixing Transience: Photography and other Images of Time in 1830s London', Chitra Ramalingam situates the early history of photography in Britain against the context of the contemporary scientific fascination with transience. She does so through the figure of William Henry Fox Talbot, whose ideas about the meaning of photographic instantaneity were shaped by his experience with non-photographic experimental imaging practices. These techniques all centered on causing a transient event to leave a fixed trace on a sensitive surface, and like photography were understood as providing a new means of visualizing, recording and representing time. Ramalingam argues that what we might consider to be distinctively photographic approaches to time—in particular the long exposure and the instantaneous image—had important analogues and predecessors in these inscription practices emerging from early 19th century experimental science. Drawing upon deconstruction and psychoanalysis, Louis Kaplan's 'Spooked Time: The Temporal Dimensions of Spirit Photography' (reprinted from *The Strange Case of William Mumler, Spirit Photographer*, Minneapolis: Minnesota UP, 2008) focuses on the temporal dimension of spirit photography. Stressing the untimeliness of the ghostly he analyses the complex temporal structure of spirit photographs as fixations of a past moment and a promise of future immortality by the depiction of a revenant. Therefore Kaplan speculates about Mumler's spirit photography in relationship to the uncanny (Sigmund Freud's haunted concept of the *unheimlich*), psychoanalytic discourses of mourning and bereavement, and haunting or *hauntology* (as articulated by Jacques Derrida in *Specters of Marx*). The strange case of William Mumler, who was the subject of a sensational trial in New York in spring 1869, is placed in the context of the religious doctrines of Spiritualism and against the historical backdrop of the American Civil War. In 'Modern Time: Revisiting the Tableau', Joanna Lowry discusses the device of the tableau, which has a long history in painting as a narrative construction for the representation of significant moments in time. The *photographic* tableau holds added complexity, based as it is upon technologies that have their own implicit relationship to the actual production of ideas about time. Through a discussion of selected examples of photographic works by Michael Snow, Jeff Wall and David Claerbout that are based upon the depiction of an instantaneous 'event'—as a moment of pure referentiality that threatens conventional discourses of pictorial representation—Lowry discusses the way in which these artists use the photographic tableau to comment upon our contemporary relationship to time itself.

The second part of the book, 'Returning Time / Memory / Order', turns toward the reading of the image, which ceases rapidly to be a simple reading and proves to be a process of rereading, if not of meditation. Essays in this section question the tension between fixed images, whose temporality seems to be reducible to one single moment, and the dizzying profusion of temporal layers that is being constructed through the photograph's proper content (images can 'show' time, both past and present), the montage of the image in larger series and in combination with other images (pictures are not only made for exhibitions, where they are seen in splendid isolation on white walls in white cubes, they can address different audiences in permanently shifting formats and contexts), or the clash between, for instance, production time and reception time (for the 'here and now' of the photographer is never that of the spectator). Beginning with Roland Barthes' observation that 'cameras...were clocks for seeing' Graham Smith examines 'Time and Memory in William Henry Fox Talbot's Calotypes of Oxford and David Octavius Hill and Robert Adamson's of St Andrews'. In consideration of Fox Talbot's interest in the function of time in the process of photography, Smith focuses on three photographs of Oxford revealing the manner in which time is either embedded or embodied in them. Hill and Adamson's depictions of St Andrews Cathedral ruins make time visible and offer a historical narrative of pre-Reformation Scotland. In 'Between Present and Past: Photographic Portugal of the 1950s' (an edited version, originally published in *Image [&] Narrative*, IX-3, 2008: http://www.imageandnarrative.be/Timeandphotography.be/martins.html), Susana S. Martins argues that the image of a place is always formed by a great variety of cultural mediations, where photographs play a crucial role. Considering photographic travel books on Portugal published during the 1950s and the 1960s, the author analyzes these cultural objects as 'time-structured' and 'time-proposing' devices, before examining their relevance in the building and spreading of national narratives. Departing from some visual examples, Martins investigates how photographs contribute to the creation, maintenance or denial of recurrent Portuguese historical fictions. Her essay clearly demonstrates how ideological frames can also be understood as a matter of time. Maren Polte's essay, 'Time and Order:

Self-reflective Strategies in Photo Essays', examines how, using the specific instruments of their profession, photographers have been exploring the role of pictures in our picture-ridden society. The essay discusses the auto-reflective strategies employed by five germanophone artists (Hans Peter Feldmann, Jens Hagen, Wiebke Loeper, Peter Fischli and David Weiss), Between them, they display a remarkable variety of narrative concepts—not inferior in precision, and superior in emotional impact, to word-based analysis.

The essays in the third section, 'Cinematic Time / Duration and Fragment', reconsider the notion of time and temporality from a more intermedial point of view. Already present in various other articles of this book, intermediality issues come to the fore when the photographic medium is analyzed in the light of its analogies and differences with other, both similar and dissimilar, media such as film, a medium that, like photography, is characterized by an inherent tension between stillness and movement. In this section, the authors take as their starting point a certain number of challenges posed by the contrast between the narrative and the nonnarrative. Inevitably, this perspective forces them to reconsider all major theoretical statements on the specificity of the medium that have been foregrounded since the rise of photography theory as an independent field—but not as a field theorized independently of other media such as film, painting, theater, performance, illustration, and narrative. Corollary, issues of fictionality and the documentary value of photography are also paramount in this section. Understanding the coda of Michelangelo Antonioni's film *The Eclipse* as an assemblage of photographs, Victor Burgin, in 'The Eclipse of Time', questions the distinction traditionally made between photographic time and filmic time, between clock time and subjective time. The complex temporal structure of photography, so Burgin argues, is not reducible to a specific quality which can be considered in opposition to the temporal character of other media such as film but depends always on socio-historical conventions within a society and the subjective use of a spectator. 'Suspended Relationships: The Montage Photography Books of Moshe Raviv Vorobeichic' by Andrea Nelson analyzes two photography books (*Paris* and *Wilna*) by Lithuanian photographer Moshe Raviv Vorobeichic, who often worked under the pseudonym Moï Ver. Nelson's essay investigates the manner in which the photography book's relation to time is suspended somewhere between that of the singular photograph and the projected filmstrip. Nelson argues that Vorobeichic's books are structured by the logic of montage: the individual page spreads comprised of juxtaposed images must be read in relation to one another, and the compelling sequencing of each book disrupts any sense of traditional narrative progression, presenting an alternative to standard constructions of history. In his contribution, David Green tackles time in and through photography during the heydays of Minimalist art, in which the discussion of time became an absolutely central issue, both aesthetic and ideological, in visual and performing arts. Commencing with a re-reading of Michael Fried's 'Art and Objecthood', David Green examines '"An image of an image': Photography and Robert Morris's *Continuous Project Altered Daily*'. He argues that Fried's notion of the modernist artwork as 'instantaneously present' is analogous to the photographic image and, for that very reason, antithetical to minimalist sculpture, which is characterized by endlessness and a preoccupation with duration. Robert Morris's 'The Present Tense of Space' and other projects of that period are presented in response to Fried. Green stipulates that despite Morris's attack on the photographic recording of site sculpture, Morris produced a number of earlier 'anti-form' works, which used photography in such a way that complicates a distinction between the work itself and its documentary recording. The frontier between images and images of images becomes blurred, and this complexity underscores the crucial importance of the debates on time and photography for the larger debates on art and temporality in general. Although devoted to a very limited, yet culturally and theoretically key corpus of contemporary art and thinking, David Green's essay is a fitting closing point to this volume in which we have tried to think time through the lens of temporality and vice versa, yet always with a strong emphasis on the cultural context and framing of the images under analysis.

part 1

Time and Technology / Devices for Time

1 Fixing Transience: Photography and other Images of Time in 1830s London

Chitra Ramalingam

Photography and the Science of Transience

This story about early photography takes place in the context of a scientific fascination with fixing transience. By the 1830s, London had long come to epitomize the destabilizing conditions of modern urban life: a bustling world city presenting endless change and variety, a sprawling, labyrinthine space for fugitive, fleeting interactions, and a hub for mechanized movement and the jarring dislocations of railway travel. Meanwhile, a new science of ephemera was emerging in the capital, a discipline of electric sparks, magnetic movements, and imperceptible vibrations. For the first time, scientists sought to see, represent, and analyze what occurred in tiny intervals of time. The central problem was how to take the flickering spectacle of moving reality and turn it into a static record for sober and steady analysis; that is, how to take a movement and turn it into an image. It is not a coincidence, I will argue, that photography—a new visual medium whose practitioners were deeply concerned with the passage of time and the capturing of the ephemeral—emerged at this moment.

Writers on photography have long wrestled with how the medium's origins in experimental science have figured its relationship to the traditional representational arts. As a prominent 'gentleman of science', photographic inventor, and influential early voice on photographic aesthetics, William Henry Fox Talbot represents an originary moment for this question. In Britain, photography emerged in and was first taken up by an informal circle of genteel amateurs like Talbot and his friend John Herschel, men of means who shared a fascination with the empirical study of the natural world (Schaaf, 1992; Tucker, 2005). Talbot was also involved in the new science of fixing transience, in part through his friendship with two less genteel London scientists, the renowned experimentalist Michael Faraday and the instrument-maker and future telegraphic inventor Charles Wheatstone. Talbot, Faraday, and Wheatstone were in close contact in the 1830s, and the three men shared an important preoccupation with a single problem: viewing and representing transience. Their efforts were linked by a shared strategy: a dynamic event was made to leave behind a fixed trace on a sensitive surface, through its action in time. I will describe their exploration of each of these sensitive surfaces in turn: first, a plate covered in fine dust; second, the retina of the human eye itself; and finally, in Talbot's case, a surface covered with a light-sensitive chemical emulsion. All of these imaging practices resulted in the production of an image understood to be 'drawn by nature', an image which could then be analyzed and interpreted in order to reveal the spatial and temporal structure of the invisibly quick movements that had inscribed it. Talbot's own ideas about the possibility of photographic instantaneity were filtered through the response of these London experimenters to the perceptual challenges of observing and recording the ephemeral.

Until the final section of this article I will not discuss photography at all, focusing instead on these other decidedly non-photographic experimental imaging techniques and how they were understood to capture and represent time. My aim is to highlight certain temporal qualities and possibilities that early photography may have shared with these imaging practices, when considered as a practice for recording and producing knowledge about the transient. In this approach I follow recent writers on photography who urge us to look beyond the idea that photographs are a particular class of images governed by specific graphic codes or visual characteristics, and instead to consider photographs as the result of a particular family of procedures: a way of producing markings on sensitized surfaces by the action of light through time (Brunet, 1996, 297; Maynard, 1997). Rather than press general claims about how photographs represent time, I will focus primarily on historical questions: how did certain influential individuals infer information about the physical world and its change through time from specific images 'drawn by nature' (whether photographic or non-photographic), and what assumptions, rhetorical resources and material practices did they draw upon to make those inferences? Perhaps we may glean some new insight by investigating how these now-forgotten alternative methods of fixing transience were understood to represent time.

Dust Figures

Since the late 18th century, dust had been the scientific visual medium of choice for naturally fixing transient events. German natural philosophers, seeking to uncover hidden symmetries in nature, caused electric sparks and acoustic vibrations to act upon a layer of fine powder, leaving behind surprisingly beautiful and often intricate symmetric patterns. In the case of sound, it had been known for a long time that sound was caused by vibrating bodies which transmitted their minute and rapid movements to the surrounding air. But the exact nature of this movement was challenging to observe, taking place at such rapid speeds and over such minute distances that the eye could not distinguish it in any detail. In 1785, Ernst Chladni took a square glass plate, clamped it at one end, and scattered the entire surface with fine sand. When he ran a violin bow across an edge of the plate, caus-

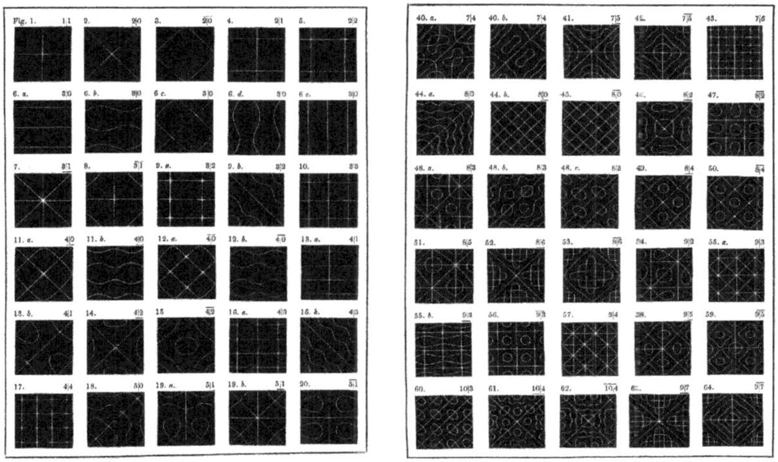

Fig. 1.1 Chladni's acoustic figures in dust (Wheatstone, 1833, 611, 615).

ing it to vibrate and emit a musical tone, the sand immediately gathered into symmetric figures, which remained on the plate after the sound ceased. The sand was shaken away from the areas of the plate that were the most violently agitated, and collected in straight and wavy lines (fig. 1.1). Chladni proposed that these stationary or 'nodal lines' where the sand gathered represented the parts of the plate that remained still throughout the complex vibration (Chladni, 1802).

These 'sound figures' converted sounds into sights, but they also converted a transient, spatiotemporal movement into a static, spatial pattern. This was one solution to the central perceptual problem with 'seeing' the nature of sound vibrations. Although the event which caused it was a slippery dynamic phenomenon which unfolded through time, the dust figure left behind was a static, spatial pattern, and could be examined at leisure. It could also be reproduced and disseminated on paper through drawings and engravings. Most importantly, the intricate dust diagrams could be apprehended at a glance, providing the viewer with a visual, almost physiognomic recognition that one kind of vibration was different from another, much as the ear could recognize instantly the difference between the same musical pitch played on a violin and trumpet. This was how ephemeral sounds were made to 'draw their own pictures'.[1]

One of the first in Britain to take a careful look at Chladni's sound figures was Charles Wheatstone, who made his ascension from lowly musical instrument-maker to famous natural philosopher in part through his investigation of these dust figures, using them in popular public lectures on acoustics. To Wheatstone's mind, although the elaborate patterns Chladni had revealed were the result of movement, it was a movement structured by stable, fixed forms. The sound vibration drew an image in dust that represented stationary lines, rather than actual movements. They were pictures of an unmoving structure underlying a movement, and as such they called for a rigorous geometrical, spatial analysis. Between 1829 and 1831 Wheatstone painstakingly dem-

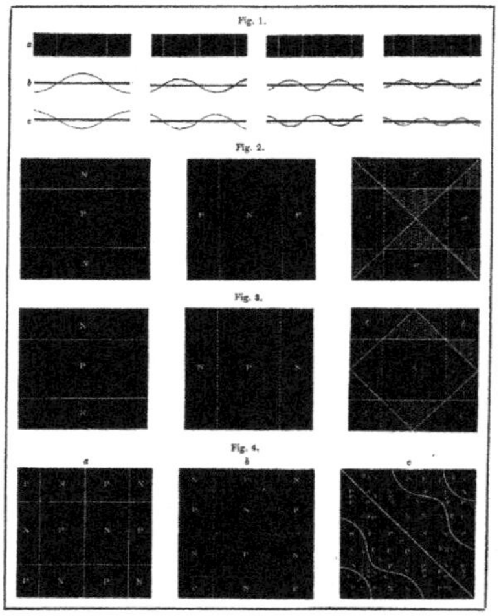

Fig. 1.2 Wheatstone's geometric analysis of acoustic figures in dust (Wheatstone, 1833, 617).

onstrated that even the most complex of the nodal lines traced in sand could be geometrically constructed by superimposing the simplest patterns (fig. 1.2). This implied that every mode of vibration of the plate could likewise be built up by superposing simpler modes of vibration onto one another (Wheatstone, 1833a).

Wheatstone's investigation of the dust figures treated them exclusively as spatial pattern, but it was left to his close friend Michael Faraday to take up the question of their temporal structure. Through his own experiments observing electrical phenomena, Faraday had begun to suspect that events that seemed to the eye to begin and end at the same moment might actually take some imperceptible but very real amount of time. The dust might make the underlying static structure of the sound vibration visible, but it would take further analysis to uncover their hidden temporal structure—how did the plate and the dust move? How did the pattern form, through time?

What interested Faraday was that while coarse sand gathered along the nodal lines Chladni had described, finer dust particles formed a distinctly different pattern, gathering instead at the parts of the plate which the theory argued were most violently agitated (fig. 1.3). Most scientists thought that these puzzling inverted patterns marked the stationary lines of less powerful, inaudible secondary vibrations. In other words, like the original dust patterns, these too were diagrams of a stable, static structure behind a complex movement.

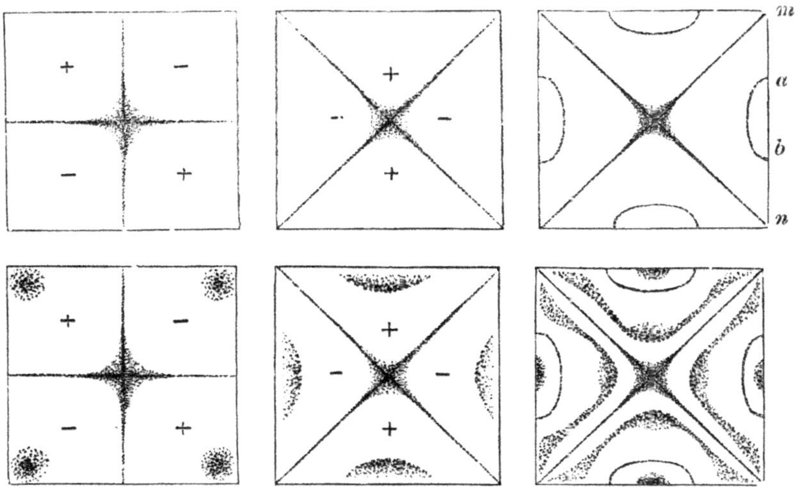

Fig. 1.3 Acoustic figures in coarse sand (top row) and a mixture of coarse sand and fine dust (bottom row). The coarse sand gathers in crisp nodal lines; the fine dust gathers in rounded patterns between the lines and on the plate's edges (Tyndall, 1867, 141, 150). Reproduced by kind permission of the Syndics of Cambridge University Library (Shelfmark IV.30.45).

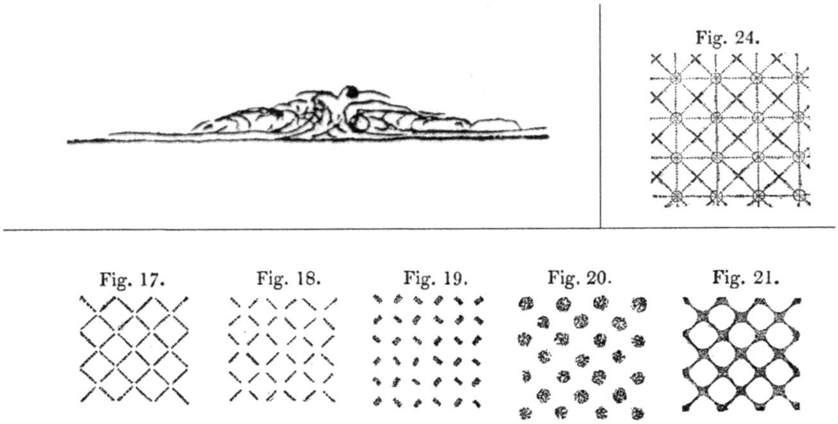

Fig. 1.4 Top left: Faraday's drawing of smoke currents over a vibrating plate (Faraday, 1932, 331).

Top right: Alternating dust heaps; the crosses and the circles indicate two alternating groups of heaps, never existing at the same time but seen by the eye simultaneously (Faraday, 1831, 329).

Bottom: Dust figures on vibrating liquid surface (Faraday, 1831, 326).

Faraday disagreed. He suspected that the patterns were not diagrams of immobility but of an even more complex movement—not of the plate itself but of the air surrounding it. The dust, he proposed, was actually moved by tiny currents of air above the plate, set in motion by its vibration. Moreover, he thought that while the patterns appeared stationary—as though the dust fell into the patterns immediately and then remained there throughout the course of the vibration—this was an optical illusion. These organized heaps of fine dust were actually continually created and destroyed in a cycle that occurred at such a rapid speed that the eye could not distinguish any movement. While the plate vibrated the dust was never still, always moving, and only appeared to be gathering in permanent heaps because of the limitations of the human eye.

To unmask these hidden air currents moving over the surface of the plate, Faraday showed how the dust figures could be deformed into new shapes by deflecting the air currents with pieces of paper near or on the plate, and by showing that these secondary patterns never appeared if the dust-covered plate vibrated in a vacuum. The ephemeral currents themselves could be rendered perceptible by surrounding the vibrating plate with smoke, which was then agitated by the vibrating plate into delicate eddies and whirls (fig. 1.4, top left). If the plate were covered by a layer of water or oil instead, and the dust scattered on the liquid surface, the water itself took on visible currents that generated heaps and patterns of dust on its surface (fig. 1.4, bottom).

Faraday's real aim was to give a convincing spatio-temporal account of how these transient currents would produce the observed patterns through time. Combining his observations of the whirls and eddies in smoke above the plate and the deflections and deformations of dust patterns, he composed a narrative description of the dynamic state of the heaps of dust themselves during the course of a vibration, which he offered in place of the static appearance presented to the eye:

> The aggregation and motion of these heaps [is caused by] the joint action of the vibrating surface and the surrounding medium... When, in the course of a vibration, the part of a plate under a heap rises, it communicates a propelling force upwards to that heap... upon receding from the heap...in performing the other half of its vibration, it forms a partial vacuum, into which the air round the heap enters...and as it enters, carries in the powder at the bottom edge of the heap with it. This action is repeated at every vibration, and as they occur in such rapid succession that the eye cannot distinguish them, the centre part of the heap is continually progressing upwards; and as the powder thus accumulates above, whilst the base is continually lessened by what is swept in underneath, the particles necessarily fall over and roll down on every side (Faraday, 1831a, 316-317).

Sometimes, he noted, different sets of heaps of dust on the surface of the water actually alternated, never existing at the same time—but the eye saw them all at once (fig. 1.4, top right): 'By the rapidity of their recurrence', he observed, these transient alternating heaps '[give] the appearance of simultaneous and even permanent existence (328-329).' The problem was that the sluggish human eye prevented the uninitiated observer from seeing the motion and constant change in the dust patterns at all. The eye flattened these shifting movements into static forms. To demonstrate plausibly that the heaps of dust on the surface of the water were continually changing and moving despite the testimony of the eye, Faraday simulated their movement. He had a silver plate punched with a pattern of bumps about the size of the heaps of dust, and set it in vibration. While at certain angles the bumps' movements were visible, at other angles they appeared to be completely still.

Where Wheatstone had reduced the study of acoustic figures to the spatial analysis of pattern, Faraday instead wanted to unmask these spatial patterns as dynamic events occurring through time. Wheatstone was content to analyze the patterns formed when dust was allowed to gather and amass the cumulative effect of movement over time into a single composite image; what mattered to him was what remained after the plate was exposed to the vibration over a long period of time. But Faraday wanted something else: to animate the dust figures, by taking into account the idiosyncrasies of the human visual experience of time. There was a constant tension between Faraday's mode of representation and its referent. His papers were accompanied by static images of the patterns, but his goal was to show that these images of seemingly enduring static structure actually marked a dynamic and complex movement, with a repeating temporal microstructure. To do the kind of physics he wanted to do—to bring the dust figures to life—Faraday had to take these stilled images of movement and re-animate them in his laboratory through analogy, simulation, and narrative.

Retinal Traces

As Faraday's exploration of acoustic figures demonstrates, observing events that took place over tiny intervals of time brought with it serious perceptual challenges. He and Wheatstone became increasingly interested in a well-known optical illusion known as 'the duration of visual impressions', which governed how the eye sees rapid movement. It had been known since antiquity that the eye often continued to see the presence of an object in a particular position for some time after it had passed, in a phenomenon called 'the duration of visual impressions'. The canonical example was Isaac Newton's famous 'circle of fire', in which a burning coal whirled swiftly in a circle appeared to trace a continuous brilliant circle of light. Newton had explained this as a result of the enduring 'impressions' left on the Sensorium by the moving coal (Newton, 1718, 123, 322). Writers on vision in the 1820s and 1830s tended to attribute this to the sluggishness of the retinal surface itself, which was understood to retain the visual impression of the glowing point in each of its positions as it raced around its circular path. Under certain conditions these impressions could fuse into a single, composite impression, which lingered for some minute but sensible period of time after the initial exposure. This was what made it possible to see an incandescent circle impressed in the air, when presented with what was actually a single glowing point in circular motion.

Though well-known and frequently mentioned briefly in treatises on the eye, this illusion rarely attracted much attention until Wheatstone and Faraday began en-

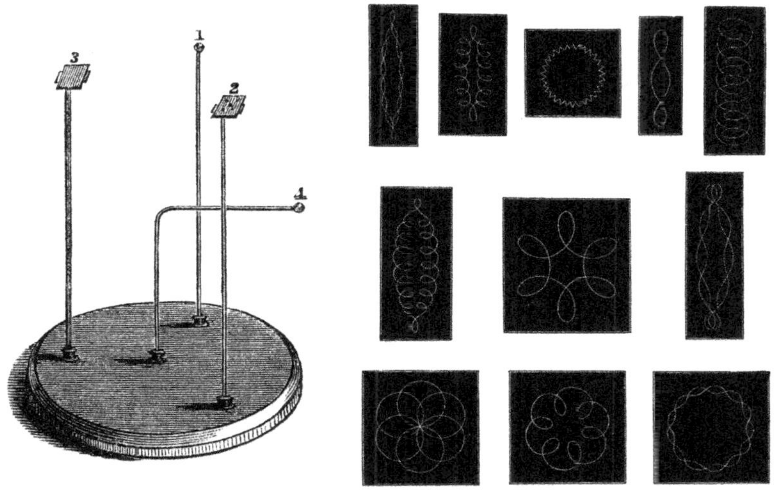

Fig. 1.5 Kaleidophone and figures (Wheatstone, 1827, 22, 26). © The British Library Board (Shelfmark Ac.3019/3).

countering it repeatedly as an obstacle to their observations of transient movements in the laboratory, embarking upon the first systematic investigation of this visual oddity and its effects. In order to see transience in action—to observe sound vibrations, electric sparks, and magnetic movements—the two men learned how to master and manipulate the human visual experience of time. They explored not just how the eye could be deceived, but also how the very mechanism of deception could be exploited to create new kinds of images of invisibly rapid movements.

Staring at sound vibrations in his music shop, Wheatstone frequently observed what he called 'the apparent duration in the same places of visible images after the objects which excite them have changed their position (Wheatstone, 1827, 28).' He began to suspect that under certain conditions the duration of these images could allow the retina to serve a similar purpose to the layer of dust in acoustic figures: a sensitive surface, holding and retaining images of periodic movements, just as the dust on a Chladni plate might retain traces of vibrations.

Between 1825 and 1833, he designed a series of instruments exploiting this peculiarity of human vision to turn invisible acoustic movements into visible and analyzable ocular images. The first of these, the 'kaleidophone', involved illuminating a glass bead at the end of a rod with bright light. When a violin bow was drawn across the rod, causing it to vibrate and emit a musical sound, it traced beautiful curved figures before the eye (fig. 1.5). As with the dust figures, one could extract precise information about the movements of these oscillating rods by analyzing

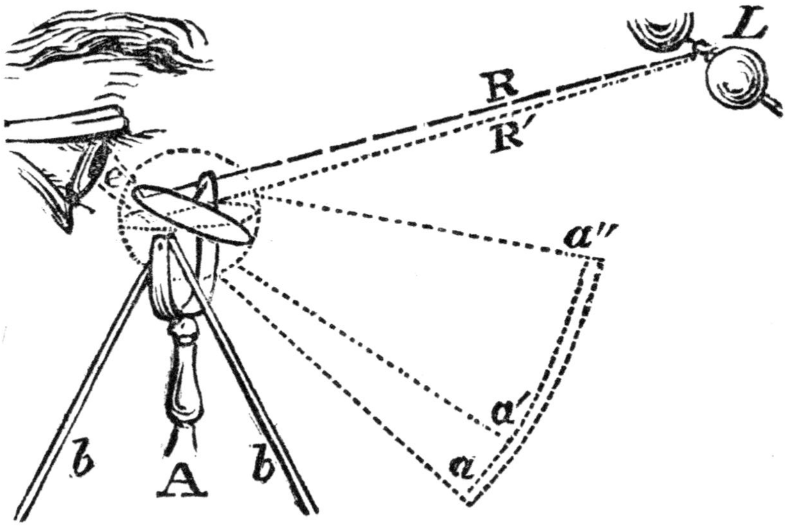

Fig. 1.6 Observing electric sparks in Wheatstone's rotating mirror (Tomlinson, 1853, 149). Reproduced by kind permission of the Syndics of Cambridge University Library (Shelfmark 1859.7.399).

the seemingly static image it presented to the slow-acting retina. The glass bead's movement through time was stretched out into a static spatial pattern, a trajectory that revealed every position through which the bead moved. 'The figures', he marveled, 'do not seem as if formed by successive motion, but appear to exist entire, at the same instant (Wheatstone, 1830, 378-379).'

Wheatstone's next instrument, the 'rotating mirror', took the spatialization of time by visual impressions one step further. Instead of observing a luminous moving object directly, Wheatstone viewed its reflected image in a mirror rotating at a rapid but known velocity (fig. 1.6). As the mirror spun about, images reflected in it were distorted, the successive phases of the movement spread out in a single incandescent figure. Through the regular, mechanized movement of the mirror, temporal intervals were converted into measurable spatial intervals in these reflected diagrams of movement. This was, he declared, a 'new optical means of measuring rapid motions, minute intervals of time, and feeble intensities of light (Wheatstone, 1833b, 205).' Although he had designed it to observe the flickering of flames in vibrating columns of air, he soon applied his new optical instrument to observing all sorts of transient phenomena: the vibrations in a piano wire, shooting stars and projectiles, lightning and other transient atmospheric effects, and the involuntary movements of the eye. By bringing these new subjects under observation and precision measurement—by making their trajectories visible as distorted precision images of movement—he hoped to expand the scope of the new discipline of physics:

> It is possible by the means I have indicated to reduce to actual measurement some of the most transient phenomena even those which occupy but the most evanescent portions of time; and it is not improbable that [this] may assist the progress of physical philosophy in as great a degree as the Microscope and the Telescope have already. The former instrument shows us spaces and the latter distances invisible to the unassisted eye; while the Chronoscope will render the evanescent portions of duration visible (Wheatstone, 1834b).

Wheatstone's rotating mirror met its match, however, when faced with the paradigmatic visual experience of transience: the electric spark, too small, too fast and too bright to be observed fully with the unaided eye. He hoped to draw out its image before the eye with his rotating mirror, to determine how fast and in what direction it moved. But even at the mirror's quickest speeds, the spark's image remained nothing but a small, bright flash with no discernible structure. His sparks were far more ephemeral than the intervals of time measurable by his mirror apparatus—lasting less than a millionth of a second, effectively instantaneous (Wheatstone, 1834a, 591). But sitting in a pitch-black laboratory watching hundreds of electric sparks pierce the gloom, Wheatstone found himself experiencing his first accidental taste of instantaneous vision. Because of its immeasurably short duration, he found that the light of the spark could allow him to 'observ[e] rapidly changing phenomena during a single instant of their continued action (ibid.).' He cited a few examples of these spark-lit images:

> A rapidly moving wheel, or a revolving disc on which any object is painted, seems perfectly stationary...Insects on the wing appear, by the same means, fixed in the air. Vibrating strings are seen at rest in their deflected positions. A rapid succession of drops of water, appearing to the eye a continuous stream, is seen to be what it really is, not what it ordinarily appears to be (ibid.).

While Wheatstone played with sparks, illuminating things 'as they really were', Faraday had also become fascinated by the duration of visual impressions. Now he focused on what happened when the eye confronted rapidly spinning wheels (fig. 1.7). He was inspired, he wrote, by the strange illusions he had seen in spinning carriage wheels and coordinated factory cogwheels. (Faraday, 1831b).[2] But the bulk of his research was conducted on a rotating mechanism he constructed in his basement laboratory to reproduce these illusions. Spinning differently shaped and decorated pairs of cardboard wheels at precisely determined relative speeds, Faraday viewed them from different angles and under different conditions of illumination. When two identical cogwheels were made to rotate rapidly at equal but opposite velocities, and then viewed from one end so that one was superimposed over the other, a phantom wheel appeared, standing perfectly still, with twice the number of cogs. If the cogwheels had slightly different speeds, then the ghostly wheel would slowly rotate in the direction of the faster one. By manipulating the shape of the wheels and their velocities, or even by visually superimposing a wheel with its own shadow or reflection in a mirror, he could produce a bewildering variety of what he called 'spectral appearances', in which image of the phantom wheel might spin slowly, sprout additional cogs, or distort its spokes until they curved in curious symmetric patterns. Each of these strange apparitions could be explained by the eye's power to fuse separate images of one wheel's position over time, as it was occluded and revealed repeatedly by the other.

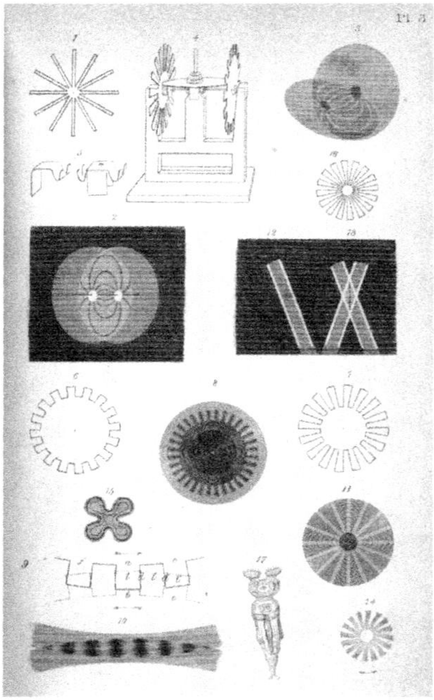

Fig. 1.7 Faraday's wheel illusions (Faraday, 1831b). © The British Library Board (Shelfmark Ac.3024/7).

Faraday's wheel illusions were the direct inspiration for the phenakistiscope, a popular optical toy invented on the continent that took London by storm in 1833 (Chanan, 1996; Mannoni, 2000). This was a spinning disc with regularly placed slits, decorated on one side with a series of sequential images. When the reflection of the images was viewed in a mirror, through the slits, the eye saw a circle of enchanting animated images. The succession of images seen through the slits were fused by the eye into a visual experience of movement. Faraday, like his contemporaries, was captivated by this new device. But he was not simply interested in the retina's power to fuse sequential images into a composite image or an illusion of movement. He was also fascinated by how certain mechanisms could overcome the essential 'durational' quality of the retinal surface in order to decompose movements into sequential or isolated images. Viewing a transient event through a simplified phenakistiscope—a spinning disc with a single slit—or through the edge of one of his cogwheels, one could sometimes see separate stages of movement isolated at multiple discrete instants.

Faraday incorporated these illusions into his experiments as he continued to investigate fleeting events. Between 1836 and 1838, for example, he carried out a lengthy investigation of the electrostatic discharge. He was now attuned to the way that the duration of impressions might not only cause deceptive appearances, but could also be made to reveal the hidden dynamic events behind them. With deft movements of his eye, he found that he could decompose the brush discharge, which lasted longer than the sparks that Wheatstone had studied in 1834, into its temporal stages. Although the brush seemed a continuous emanation of light, it actually consisted of a rapid and discontinuous series of discharges. Simply by moving his eye rapidly but regularly across the brush so that its image passed quickly across the retina, he could see an array of elongated lines, each indicating the existence of a separate eruption (Faraday, 1838). By transforming a sequential series of events into a spatial array, the duration of impressions was a crucial tool in Faraday's project to make time visible in the laboratory.

During the 1830s, Faraday and Wheatstone exploited the duration of visual impressions in order to produce a variety of new visual experiences of transience which could reveal spatial and temporal information that was otherwise inaccessible to the eye. First, the sluggishness of the retina allowed it to gather and accumulate traces of movement over time into composite figures, what we might call 'durational' images: Wheatstone's kaleidophone and rotating mirror images. Second, the visual experience of movement could be mechanically decomposed into images that showed the spatial disposition of moving objects frozen at a single instant, what we might call 'instantaneous' images, like Wheatstone's spark-lit visions. Third, the durational quality of the retina could be combined with a mechanism for instantaneous exposure, producing images that visually superimposed impressions of multiple instants—what might now be called 'stroboscopic' images, like Faraday's wheel illusions. Their visual manipulations of time in the physics laboratory emerged from the interplay between two things: the durational quality of the retina, which tended to aggregate, accumulate, and fuse; and the mechanical control of exposure (whether by the use of spark illumination, slotted discs, or other shutter-like devices) which tended to slice, isolate, and separate.

Photography

We can understand photography as emerging from a similar rhetorical, technical, and aesthetic interplay between duration and instantaneity.[3] The earliest photographic surfaces—whether Talbot's chemically treated paper or Daguerre's silvered plates—required lengthy exposure times, and until the late 1840s the resulting images were essentially durational in quality. Single instants were buried in the aggregation of impressions over time; what appeared in early photographs was that which was stable and endured. Photographs of bustling cities like Paris and London exhibited deserted streets, devoid of pedestrians, carriages, and the whole tumult of urban life (fig. 1.8).

The language of capturing the ephemeral instant still permeated early writings on photography, but it always carried with it the signs of its own elusiveness. Talbot himself marveled in his first official description of his own invention that 'the most transitory of things, a shadow, the proverbial emblem of all that is fleeting and momentary, may be fettered by the spells of our "natural magic", and may be fixed for ever in the position which it seemed only destined for a single instant to occupy (Talbot, 1839).' Even this confident declaration suggested profound temporal challenges to overcome: the temporal limitations on possible photographic

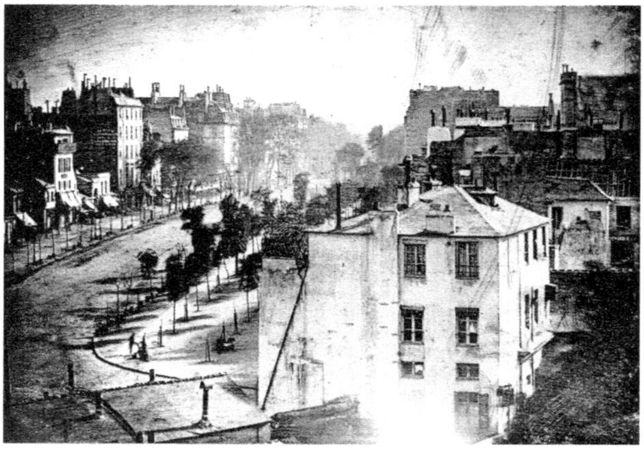

Fig. 1.8 Louis-Jacques-Mandé Daguerre, *Boulevard du Temple, Paris, IIIe arrondissement*, 1839.

subjects, the time required to form the image, and the temporal disintegration of the image over time. These were precisely the experimental problems with which Talbot grappled in the years between 1834 and 1836, his first and most fervent years of secret photochemical research (Schaaf, 1992, 39-44). Such fantasies rarely called for a photographic breach of the temporal limits of vision itself. Instead, when early photographers grasped at 'fleeting' subjects or spoke of instantaneity, their efforts usually reflected a much more modest struggle: how to wrest the spontaneity and vitality of human expression—a shy smile or a natural, easy posture—from the slowness of photographic materials.[4]

It was Talbot who first proposed a radical escape from the durational quality of the photographic surface, and in doing so he drew quite explicitly on his knowledge of the physicists' science of fixing transience. Photogenic drawing, it turns out, was not the only imaging practice Talbot found poised precariously between duration and instantaneity. Numerous proposals for the use of rotating mirrors and rotating disks as optical devices, exploiting the duration of impressions, appeared in his private notes throughout the 1820s, as did comments on acoustic dust figures. After becoming aware of Wheatstone and Faraday's work at a series of lectures they gave at the Royal Institution in March 1833, Talbot resolved immediately to make public his own ideas on manipulating the ocular experience of light, movement, and time by exploiting the duration of visual impressions. The next few months he spent predominantly in London in a whirlwind of scientific activity, racing to develop and publish his own proposals for durational and instantaneous vision, before departing for a long honeymoon voyage to the continent with his new wife.

The first was Talbot's disc photometer, an instrument for quantifying the intensity of light sources and color mixtures (fig. 1.9).[5] A disc with sectors cut out of it was rotated rapidly in front of a light source. At high speeds, the duration of impres-

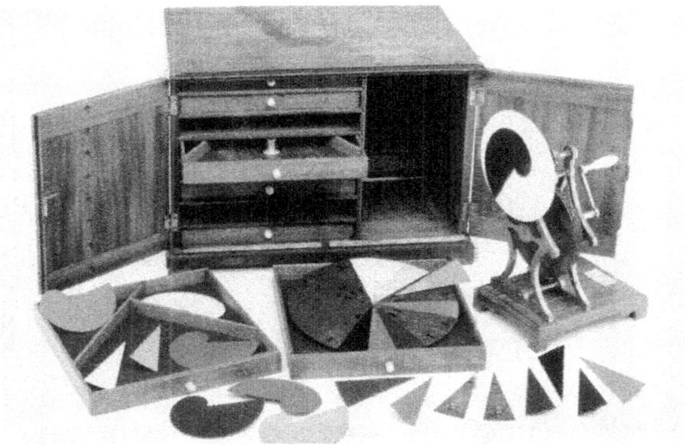

Fig. 1.9 Optical photometer for the measurement of the intensity of light and color, to the design of William Henry Fox Talbot, constructed by W. & S. Jones, London, c. 1835. © Trustees of the National Museums Scotland.

sions would prevent the observer from seeing the periodic interruptions in the light beam. Instead, the light would appear continuous but slightly dimmer than when viewed directly, the intensity diminished by a factor that could be calculated from the number of cut sectors. Colored sectors and spiral shapes could also be mounted on the wheel. The disc photometer used the duration of impressions to produce aggregate images before the eye which could then be used as an objective, linear scale for color or light (Talbot, 1834a; Simpson, 1996).

Talbot also played with instantaneous vision in his proposal for how to see 'A Body in rapid Motion, yet apparently at rest (Talbot, 1834b, 113).' Here he described how a periodic repeating movement like a rotating object or a vibrating rod could be seen frozen in place in an otherwise unseeable position, when viewed under a bright light source made intermittent through reflection in a rotating mirror. Individual, isolated images of single instants were fused by the duration of impressions into a single enduring image (Talbot, 1834b). Privately, he experimented with what he called 'optically fixing moving bodies': viewing a succession of static, frozen images of moving objects by observing them under intermittent light produced by hiding a constant light source behind a spinning slotted disc. The images he described viewing under these conditions echoed Wheatstone's spark-illuminated visions:

> 'The immovable drop' or 'selfsuspended liquid'...The 'motionless tetotum'. A swinging pendulum which would have the appearance of 2, 4, or more distinct pendulums. The motionless wheel which nevertheless will not allow anything to be passed between its spokes (Talbot, 1834-1835, 98).[6]

In June 1833, three months after reawakening his long-dormant interest in durational and instantaneous vision, Talbot had left for the continent with his wife and sister. He later recalled that it was on the shores of Italy's Lake Como, frustrated at his own poor draughtsmanship, that he first fantasized about the possibility of fixing the images of the camera obscura on paper (Talbot, 1844). Returning to Britain in early 1834, he immediately threw himself keenly into photochemical research (Schaaf, 1992, 39). But as Talbot slowly mastered the art of capturing images traced in light on light-sensitive papers, he also continued to play with the retina's own power to produce instantaneous and durational images. His notes on the instantaneous visions seen through a slotted disc, for example, are dated 7 March 1835, right in the middle of his most productive period of photographic research.[7] It seems possible and even likely that he would have imagined capturing these frozen images of movement in photographs, but no documentary record of such speculation exists. It was probably the frustrating weakness of existing photochemistry that prevented him from planning such an experiment for over a decade after photography was made public.

In 1851, Talbot took the first crisp photograph of a rapidly moving object frozen in its position at a single instant. This decisive experiment, carried out in Michael Faraday's basement laboratory at the Royal Institution, was the new medium's first excursion into the elusive realm of high-speed movement. Talbot began by fastening a piece of paper printed with text onto a disc attached to a rotating mechanism. Setting the disc in motion, he increased the speed until the disc looked like a mere grey blur. He then installed a camera containing one of his new, highly sensitive Amphitype plates in a suitable position for capturing its image. He closed the shutters of the room, plunging the room into absolute darkness, opened the camera, and discharged a carefully placed Leyden jar. The brilliant spark briefly illuminated the rotating paper on the disc. The next day he triumphantly informed Faraday that the image of the printed letters thus obtained was 'just as sharp as if the disk had been motionless (Talbot, 1851a).'

His success convinced him that it was time to redefine the very notion of photographic instantaneity. Previous photographs might be called instantaneous, he wrote to a French colleague, 'but that has only been a figure of speech. Strictly speaking they are far from being so, for the objects which move with great speed have escaped photographic representation until the present time (Talbot, 1851b).' Now, he declared triumphantly, there would be a new kind of photography, one which for the first time could present 'distinct images of bodies moving swiftly across the field of view...we shall be able to arrest and embody the most fugitive phenomena which present themselves to the eye (Talbot, 1851c).'

The image itself has not survived, and perhaps it is not hard to imagine why. Unlike the famous later photographic interventions into radical instantaneity (fig. 1.10), Talbot's photograph would not have shocked viewers with unimagined, awkward poses. In fact, as he had proudly proclaimed, it looked just as it might have had the disc been perfectly motionless and the experiment conducted in full daylight. Moreover, it did not portray a view of the spinning disc that no eye could ever see—in fact, the structure of the experiment mimicked the ocular experience of instantaneity that Faraday, Wheatstone and Talbot had already mastered. Any

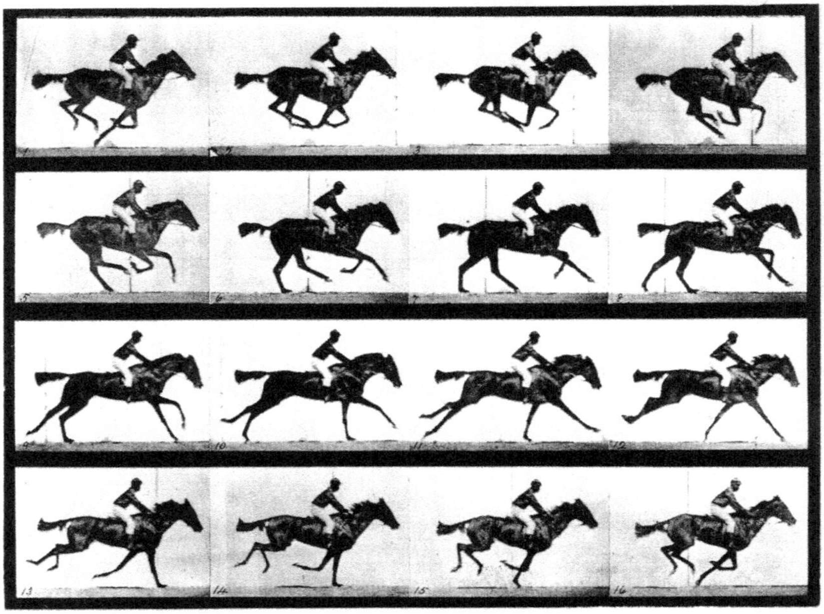

Fig. 1.10 Eadweard Muybridge, Plate from *Animal Locomotion*, 1872-1885. © National Media Museum/SSPL.

observer sitting with Talbot in the dark laboratory would also have witnessed the frozen wheel flashing into view when the spark appeared. But this very analogy to the eye was precisely what made this missing disc photograph so radical. The experiment overcame the sluggishness of light-sensitive chemical emulsions by the same visual-instrumental system of spinning disc, darkness, and sudden illumination that Faraday, Wheatstone, and Talbot himself had previously used to overcome the sluggishness of visual impressions. The notion of a photographic instantaneity that could mechanically slice invisible instants from the continuous flow of time, overcoming the essential durational quality of the photographic surface, was predicated on the analogy to the eye, and on the scientists' techniques of fixing transience.[8]

Conclusion: Images of Time

I have discussed three methods of fixing transience: sound-figures inscribed in dust, light-figures traced on the retina, and light-pictures etched on photosensitive paper. There were, of course, stark differences among them. Unlike dust figures and photographs, Wheatstone's kaleidophone figures and Faraday's wheel-visions were phantoms, floating or flashing before the eye and vanishing when the ingenious devices generating them were stilled. Dust figures were synesthetic transformations of one sense into another, visual records of fundamentally non-visual information; retinal traces and photographs, on the other hand were drawn by light itself, the foundation of the visual sense. And many (but not all) photographs, unlike the other experimental imaging practices described here, offered not just visual records but pictures that offered the illusion of direct seeing. Only photography among these imaging practices could produce pictures that might engage, however uncomfortably and ambiguously, with the codes and conventions of western representational art.

But here I have chosen instead to emphasize the real continuities among Wheatstone, Faraday, and Talbot's image-making and transience-fixing techniques. All three involved the direct, indexical inscription of a visible record on a sensitive surface; they converted the spatio-temporal complexity of a dynamic event into a static, spatial, two-dimensional representation; and they allowed the viewer the enticing fantasy that in looking at an image one could, somehow, 'see' features of transient events otherwise inaccessible to the eye. They could all be understood as epistemic practices: ways of producing knowledge about the (moving and ephemeral) world through (static and stable) image-making. With attention to these connections, we can see that what might seem like uniquely photographic approaches to time have actually had important analogues and predecessors in other kinds of images and visual experiences. The slow durational gathering of traces, the mechanical decomposition of experience into time-slices of the single instant—neither of these is uniquely photographic. Duration and instantaneity, stroboscopic composites and blurry long exposures: these were all central interpretive features of many kinds of images understood to be inscribed by nature rather than by any hand.

In fact, any image drawn by nature is always drawn through time—whether a sensible interval or one that passes in the blink of an eye. The oft-repeated analogies of the fingerprint and the shadow obscure this irreducible temporality of the indexical trace, as does the assumption that the photographic surface is itself inherently instantaneous. There is a vast and phenomenologically complex field of inscription practices existing throughout experimental science, in which a two-dimensional pattern or image is produced through time as a direct physical consequence of the event that causes it. We must, as Talbot enthusiastically did, take a closer look at these, if we are to understand how photography is used not simply to capture objects located in space, but to fix events occurring through time.

Acknowledgements

Research for this article was funded by the U.S. National Science Foundation and the Mellon Foundation/ACLS. Material from the Talbot Collection in the British Library is quoted by courtesy of the British Library Board and Mrs. Petronella Burnett-Brown; material from the Wheatstone Collection at the King's College Archives is quoted by courtesy of King's College London.

Notes

[1] Note the parallels to the discourse around graphical recording devices and the graphic method in physics and physiology in the 19th century (see Brain, 2002, 2008; Brain & Wise, 1999; de Chadarevian, 1993).

[2] Peter Mark Roget carried out a mathematical analysis of one of these illusions some years earlier (Roget, 1825). The mechanically spinning wheel was a frequent object of study for physicists interested in the temporal limits of visual perception (Ramalingam, 2008).

[3] See also de Duve's discussion of the time-exposure and the snapshot as two ways of engaging with photographs (de Duve, 1978), although my interpretation differs considerably from his.

[4] Other 'instantaneous' subjects pursued by photographers in the 1840s and 1850s included street scenes and seascapes (see Prodger, 2003; Gunthert, 1999).

[5] This device was described in (Talbot, 1834a), and the one in fig. 1.8 was sold soon afterwards by a London instrument maker, but it is not known whether others were made (Simpson, 1996).

[6] It is not clear from this notebook entry whether Talbot actually carried out this experiment and saw these visions himself, or merely proposed it and imagined them.

[7] A few pages (and one week) earlier in the same notebook, for example, is the first record of Talbot's original idea of using a negative image to make multiple positive prints (Talbot, 1834-1835, 90). For a thorough account of Talbot's photographic research in this period (see Schaaf, 1992, 39-44).

[8] By the end of the 19th century spark-illuminated photography had became widely used by scientists interested in observing rapid and transient phenomena (Braun, 1992, 1997; Galison & Daston, 2007; Geimer, 2004; Schaffer, 2004, 177-187).

Bibliography

¬ Robert Brain, 'Representation on the Line: The Graphic Method and the Instruments of Scientific Modernism', in Bruce Clark and Linda Dalrymple Henderson (eds) *From Energy to Information: Representation in Science, Art, and Literature* (Stanford: Stanford University Press, 2002), 155-178.

¬ Robert Brain, 'The pulse of modernism: experimental physiology and aesthetic avant-gardes circa 1900,' *Studies In History and Philosophy of Science*, 39, 3 (September, 2008): 393-417.

¬ Robert Brain and M. Norton Wise, 'Muscles and Engines: Indicator Diagrams and Helmholtz's Graphical Method', in Mario Biagioli (ed.) *The Science Studies Reader* (New York: Routledge, 1999), 51-66.

¬ Marta Braun, *Picturing Time: The Work Of Etienne-Jules Marey (1830-1904)* (Chicago: University of Chicago Press, 1992).

¬ Marta Braun, 'The Expanded Present: the Photography of Movement', in Ann Thomas (ed.) *Beauty of Another Order: Photography in Science* (New Haven: Yale University Press, 1997), 150-184.

¬ François Brunet, 'Visual Semiotics versus Pragmaticism: Peirce and Photography', in Vincent Michael Colapietro and Thomas M. Olshewsky (eds) *Peirce's Doctrine of Signs: Theory, Applications and Connections* (Berlin: de Gruyter, 1996), 295-313.

¬ Soraya de Chadarevian, 'Graphical method and discipline: self-recording instruments in nineteenth-century physiology', *Studies in History and Philosophy of Science*, 24, 2 (1993): 267-91.

¬ Michael Chanan, *The Dream That Kicks: The Prehistory and Early Years of Cinema in Britain*, 2nd edition (London: Routledge, 1996).

¬ Ernst Florens Friedrich Chladni, *Die Akustik* (Leipzig: Breitkopf und Härtel, 1802).

¬ Thierry de Duve, 'Time Exposure and Snapshot: The Photograph as Paradox', *October*, 5 (1978): 113-125.

¬ Michael Faraday, 'On a Peculiar Class of Acoustical Figures; and on Certain Forms Assumed by Groups of Particles upon Vibrating Elastic Surfaces', *Philosophical Transactions of the Royal Society of London*, 121 (1831a): 299-340.

¬ Michael Faraday, 'On a peculiar class of optical deceptions', *Journal of the Royal Institution*, 1 (1831b): 205-223.

¬ Michael Faraday, 'Experimental Researches in Electricity. Twelfth Series', *Philosophical Transactions of the Royal Society of London*, 128 (1838): 83-123.

¬ Peter Galison and Lorraine Daston, *Objectivity* (Boston: Zone Books, 2007).

¬ Peter Geimer, 'Picturing the Black Box: On Blanks in Nineteenth Century Paintings and Photographs', *Science in Context*, 17, 4 (December 2004): 467-501.

¬ André Gunthert, 'La Conquête de l'instantané: Archéologie de l'imaginaire photographique en France, 1841-1895', Ph.D Thesis, Ecole des Hautes Etudes en Sciences Sociales, 1999.

¬ Laurent Mannoni, *The Great Art of Light and Shadow: Archaeology of the Cinema*, trans. Richard Crangle, (Exeter: University of Exeter Press, 2000).

¬ Patrick Maynard, *The Engine of Visualization: Thinking Through Photography* (Ithaca, N.Y: Cornell University Press, 1997).

¬ Isaac Newton, *Opticks: or, a Treatise of the Reflections, Refractions, Inflections and Colours of Light*, 2nd edition (London: Innys, 1718).

¬ Phillip Prodger, *Time Stands Still: Muybridge and the Instantaneous Photography Movement* (Oxford: Oxford University Press, 2003).

¬ Chitra Ramalingam, 'Stopping time: Henry Fox Talbot and the origins of freeze-frame photography', *Endeavour*, 32, 3 (September 2008): 86-93.

¬ Peter Mark Roget, 'Explanation of an Optical Deception in the Appearance of the Spokes of a Wheel Seen through Vertical Apertures', *Philosophical Transactions of the Royal Society of London*, 115 (1825): 131-140.

¬ Larry J.Schaaf, *Out of the Shadows: Herschel, Talbot & the Invention of Photography* (New Haven: Yale University Press, 1992).

¬ Simon Schaffer, 'A Science Whose Business is Bursting: Soap Bubbles as Commodities in Classical Physics', in Lorraine Daston (ed.) *Things That Talk: Object Lessons from Art and Science* (New York: Zone Books, 2004).

¬ A.D.C. Simpson, 'Talbot's photometer, or developments before photography', *Studies in Photography* (1996): 8-10.

¬ William Henry Fox Talbot, 'Experiments on light', *Philosophical Magazine*, 5, 29 (November 1834a): 321-334.

¬ William Henry Fox Talbot, 'Facts relating to Optical Science, No. 1.' *Philosophical Magazine*, 4, 20 (February 1834b): 112-114.

¬ William Henry Fox Talbot, 'Scientific Notebook M' (1834-1835), Talbot Collection, British Library, London.

¬ William Henry Fox Talbot, 'Some account of the Art of Photogenic drawing, or the process by which natural objects may be made to delineate themselves without the aid of the artist's pencil', *Philosophical Magazine*, 14 (1839): 196-208.

¬ William Henry Fox Talbot, *The Pencil of Nature* (London: Longman, Brown, Green, & Longmans, 1844-1846).

¬ William Henry Fox Talbot, Letter to Michael Faraday (16 June 1851a). Document 6432 in The Correspondence of William Henry Fox Talbot Project (hereafter 'Talbot Correspondence') http://foxtalbot.dmu.uk (Original: Faraday F1M n.137, Royal Institution, London).

¬ William Henry Fox Talbot, Letter to Jean-Baptiste Biot (16 June 1851b). Document 06429 in Talbot Correspondence, (Original: LA51-023, Talbot Collection, British Library, London).

¬ William Henry Fox Talbot, 'Important Experiment at the Royal Institution', *Athenaeum* (June 28, 1851c): 688.

¬ Jennifer Tucker, *Nature Exposed: Photography As Eyewitness in Victorian Science* (Baltimore: Johns Hopkins University Press, 2005).

¬ Charles Wheatstone, 'Description of the kaleidophone, or phonic kaleidoscope; A new philosophical toy, for the illustration of several interesting and amusing acoustical and optical phenomena', *Quarterly Journal of Science, Literature and Art*, 23 (1827): 344-351.

¬ Charles Wheatstone, 'Lecture at the Royal Institution', *Athenaeum* (June 19, 1830): 378-379.

¬ Charles Wheatstone, 'On the Figures Obtained by Strewing Sand on Vibrating Surfaces, Commonly Called Acoustic Figures', *Philosophical Transactions of the Royal Society of London* 123 (1833a): 593-633.

¬ Charles Wheatstone, 'Remarks on one of Mr. Talbot's proposed Philosophical Experiments', *Philosophical Magazine*, 3, 15 (September 1833b): 204-205.

¬ Charles Wheatstone, 'An Account of Some Experiments to Measure the Velocity of Electricity and the Duration of Electric Light', *Philosophical Transactions of the Royal Society of London*, 124 (1834a): 583-591.

¬ Charles Wheatstone, 'Visual Duration of the Impressions of Light', Folder 4/1 (1834b). Papers of Charles Wheatstone, Archives of King's College London.

2 Spooked Time: The Temporal Dimensions of Spirit Photography

Louis Kaplan

An Untimely Introduction

If our subject is the relationship between time and photography, then these speculations on spirit photography and the suspect practice of William Mumler must be considered rather *untimely* (fig. 2.1). Whether anachronistic or posthumous, the untimely refers to something that surely takes place, but where the timing is off. When dealing with such an improper, inexpedient time, one has the suspicion that something comes too early (prematurely) or too late (belatedly). When it comes to the ghosts conjured by spirit photography, it is important to acknowledge the rushed or forestalled entrance of the untimely which produces that strange

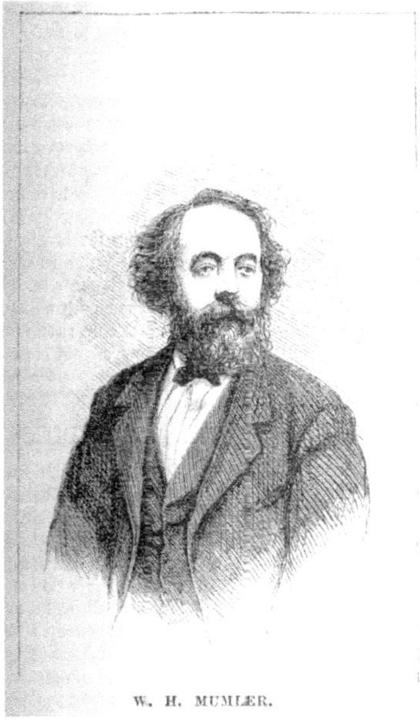

Fig. 2.1 'W. H. Mumler', *Harper's Weekly*, 8 May 1869, cover, wood engraving after photograph.

feeling of a being-haunted. If one wants to debunk spirit photography as nothing more than a parlor trick or an unseemly game of duplicitious double exposure, then this untimeliness would be located in the spatio-temporal disjunctions of the elements involved in double printing or montage operations. This leads to thinking the spirit photograph in terms of visual anachronism. On the other hand, if one believes in the 'beautiful truths' communicated by spirit photography, then such untimely and uncanny effects are derived from the wondrous intervention of the afterlife onto the plane of conventional photographic reality.

In 'To Scan A Ghost—The Ontology of Mediated Vision', Tom Gunning takes up the discourse of spirit photography as 'phantasmatic' and he situates ghostliness next to untimeliness. 'The ghostly represents a fundamental untimeliness, a return of the past not in the form of memory or history but in a contradictory experience of presence, contained, as Derrida has shown us, in the term *haunting* (Gunning, 2007, 117).' I will elucidate further the late Jacques Derrida's logic of haunting (*hauntology*) or that which brings a ghostly aspect to ontology and which structures the temporal dimensions of spirit photography and photography in general. But if we are going to consider the haunted temporality of spirit photography, we ought to think very seriously about referring to this subject as 'Untimeliness and Photography'. For the practice of spirit photography is implicated in questions of untimeliness, mourning, and loss through its haunting of the present and by promising Gunning's 'return of the past' through the return of the dead in the photographic image. Nevertheless, the Spiritualist believer in spirit photography for whom this miraculous phenomenon bears witness to a leap out of time would offer another title—'The Timeless and Photography'. For spirit photography has been conceived by Spiritualists as the means by which to offer the visual proofs of immortality and the existence of the afterlife. For the Spiritualist, the faces of the 'living dead' who appear in spirit photography attest to the fact that photography has somehow opened up a virtual window into a realm freed from the constraints of time entirely. This is the dream of those who invest in these phantasmatic figures as immortal and on par with the heavenly hosts (fig. 2.2).

In order to investigate the temporal dimensions of spirit photography and the 'spooked time' it inhabits and haunts, I draw upon concepts derived from deconstruction and psychoanalysis. These spooked theories offer hospitality to the ghost and haunting in their critique of the metaphysics of presence and ontology. Therefore I will explore the relationship of spirit photography to the uncanny

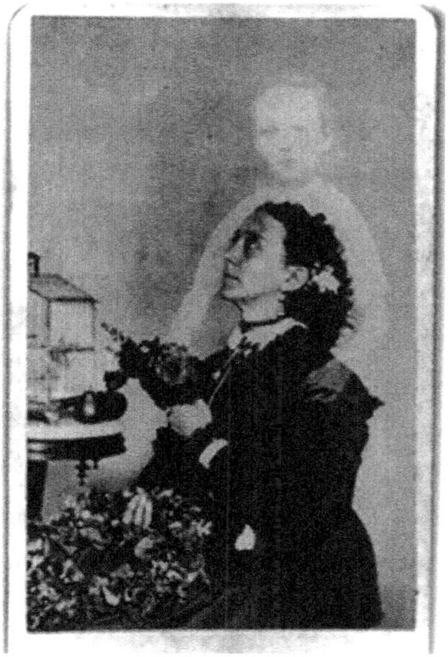

Fig. 2.2 William H. Mumler, 'Fanny Conant with the spirit of an unidentified child', 1862-1875. Reproduced by kind permission of the College of Psychic Studies, London.

via Sigmund Freud's haunted concept of the *unheimlich*, the psychoanalytic discourses of mourning and bereavement, and haunting and *hauntology* as first articulated by Derrida in *Specters of Marx* (1994). These constructs bear upon spirit photography's spooked time reminding us that the discourse of spirit photography offers 'an intense familiarity with the ineluctable originarity of the specter (Derrida, 2005, 53).' This paradoxical idea of the specter at the origin induces the 'double takes' of spiritual photographic inspection and helps us to better understand what Gunning means by the 'contradictory experience of presence contained in the term haunting.' However, it is not my intention to leave these spectral constructs and untimely effects 'up in the air' without attaching them to an exemplary spiritual photographic practice. Therefore, I examine the invention of spirit photography and the career of William Mumler in the historical context of the religious doctrines of Spiritualism (specifically the belief in communication with the dead) and against the mournful backdrop of the American Civil War in the 1860s.

This also means a quick review of Mumler's moment of international notoriety. In 1869, Mumler's spirit photographic practice was the subject of a sensational court case in New York that put Spiritualism itself on trial. While skeptics (including master of the humbug, P.T. Barnum) argued that these photographs were darkroom tricks produced by purely mechanical means, Mumler's defenders (including respected Spiritualist Judge Edmonds) believed that these images were produced by supernatural means. In this way, Mumler's trial became a flash point for larger debates pitting skeptics against the religious faithful regarding Spiritualist beliefs. While accused of perpetrating fraud and larceny by the 'mechanical illusionists' who focused on the manipulability of the photographic medium and its ability to fool around with real time, Mumler was found not guilty. However, this judgment had nothing to do with 'supernatural realism' or the view that these images provided important evidence for the existence of spirits. According to Jennifer Mnookin, Mumler managed to stay out of jail because of the triumph of the 'anti-evidentialist position'. This view held 'that the photographs themselves could not provide definitive evidence about their mode of manufacture; for this, it was necessary to look not at the product but at the process (Mnookin, 1998, 40).' That means that despite nine purported methods of deceit enumerated in the proceedings, the prosecution could not figure out how Mumler actually committed the deed and therefore he was found not guilty.

Mumler's story and the emergence of spirit photography as a commercially viable practice in New York and Boston in the 1860s could not have happened without the intellectual and spiritual support and patronage of the religious movement known as Spiritualism. This mid-19th century American phenomenon allied itself to progressive reforms and the championing of women's rights. It sought to reconcile science with religion, extolled the cosmic virtues of harmony and sympathy, and attracted followers seeking to make spiritual connections in order to counteract the encroachments and threats posed by industrial and technological modernization and secularization (see Braude, 2001). It is important to frame a few aspects of Spiritualist belief that made it especially conducive to the rise and flourishing of Mumler's spirit photographic practice. To understand how Spiritualist religious doctrine could have fostered the strange case of William Mumler, one recalls the credo of the New England Spiritualists' Association: 'Our creed is simple, Spirits do communicate with man (1854, 14).' If the essence of Spiritualist faith could be reduced to the communication of spirits with mankind, then Spiritualist practice manifested the various means (or media) through which spirit communication could and did happen. According to this credo, the faithful who believed and felt passionately about the truth of Spiritualism and spirit manifestations were invested in a system of thought designed to prove the existence of the afterlife and the immortality of the soul. Spiritualists were driven by an otherworldly desire to deny death and to abolish the limits of human finitude and they looked to old and new communication technologies to achieve these ends. On the other hand, NESA's credo and its granting of agency to the spirits opened itself up to skeptical attack and a demystifying inversion of the above statement to argue that only human beings have the power to communicate with spirits that they have themselves invented.

In *Haunted Media*, Jeffrey Sconce begins with a remarkable analysis of the birth of Spiritualism and the phenomena of the Fox Sisters in upstate New York in 1848 and frames these ghostly developments in terms of their purported invention of the *spiritual telegraph*. The conjuring of the ghosts of the dead through the mediumistic powers of Katie and Margaret Fox was viewed as a popular religious response to Samuel F.B. Morse's invention of the telegraph in 1844 as a wondrous or magical medium. Sconce reviews the spooked theory guiding spiritual telegraphy as an occult technology and pedagogy preaching an agenda of social reform. 'Through séances conducted under gifted "mediums", they believed the material world could receive transmissions from the dead through what they called the "spiritual telegraph". More than a metaphor, the spiritual telegraph was for many an actual technology of the afterlife, one invented by scientific geniuses in the world of the dead for the explicit purpose of instructing the land of the living in the principles of utopian reform (Sconce, 2000, 12).' If the new communications medium of the telegraph had it within its power to defeat space and time, then Spiritualists believed that its own haunted medium 'could defeat the seemingly unassailable temporal and spatial void of death itself (ibid.) ' In light of this analysis, it was not too great a leap from the hopes and dreams of spiritual telegraphy to the so-called *spiritual photography* of William Mumler in the early 1860s. Since photography had already conquered space and time to reveal the microscopic and the telescopic, why not consider this new extension of the medium? Here was the possibility of a visual 'technology of the afterlife' to bridge the living and the dead (or visible and invisible) via photographic images to complement the aural rapping and table turning of the séance room.

Uncanny

One crucial way in which psychoanalytic thinking comes to bear on the temporal dimensions of spirit photography and the specters of Mumler is through the concept of the uncanny—that incomplete translation of the German term, *unheimlich*. Sigmund Freud first published his essay on this haunting and untimely subject in 1919 or exactly fifty years after Mumler's trial. Freud's essay and the theoretical literature that it has stimulated in recent years attest to the relevance of the concept of the uncanny for understanding the issues involved in Mumler's case and the phenomenon of spirit photography. The concept of the uncanny

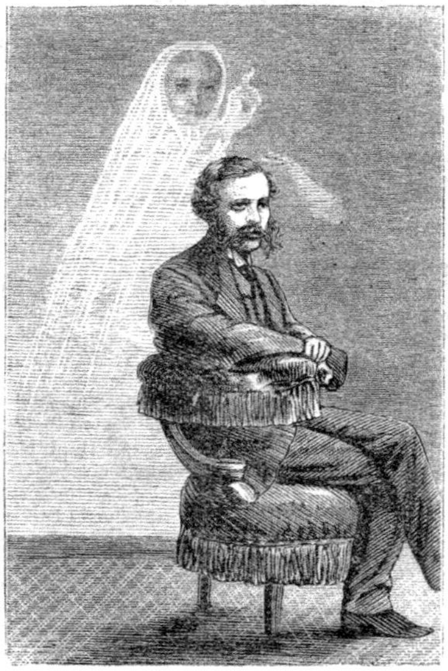

Fig. 2.3 William H. Mumler, 'Charles Livermore with the spirit of his wife', *Harper's Weekly*, 8 May 1869, cover, wood engraving after spirit photograph.

is literally the 'un-homely' site where psychoanalysis and deconstruction converge to open up a space for the ghosts and for the discourse of spirit photography as it haunts and disturbs the sleep of reason.[1]

Freud believed that the uncanny was associated with a terrible feeling of anxiety and dread—one caused by putting oneself in confrontation with death or its return, with something that would make one feel as if he or she had seen a ghost or were being haunted. If such is the case, then spirit photographic practice offers the living (dead) proofs that engage this psychoanalytic concept in summoning the ghostly return of the dearly departed (fig. 2.3). Let me cite this morbid passage in 'The Uncanny' where Freud outlines this set of connections or 'hanging together' of the uncanny with death and the haunting of the creatures of the night.

> The uncanny/*unheimlich* appears to many people in the highest degree as that which hangs together with death, with corpses, with the return of the dead, with spirits and ghosts. We have indeed heard that many modern languages cannot translate our expression '*ein unheimliches Haus*' ('a haunted house') other than through the reinscription—a house, in which 'it spooks' (*es spukt*). We might have properly begun our investigation with this perhaps strongest example of uncanniness / *Unheimlichkeit*, but we did not do it because in this case the *Unheimliche* is too much mingled with the gruesome and partly covered over by it (Freud, 1919/1959, 395; translation modified by the author).

This intriguing passage links the uncanny with the horrible, terrifying, and gruesome. It suggests that people find in the terrifying and gruesome that which takes them outside of their comfort zones and safety nets in the house of being and that renders them 'not at home' with themselves. From a Freudian perspective, the commercial practice of spirit photography dealing 'with the return of the dead, with spirits and ghosts' is not just the making of a pretty picture. (One recalls how Mumler resorts to terms of beauty to describe spirit photography in an aestheticized manner to cover over this fact.) It is rather engaged in the gruesome task of summoning the dead to return and haunt us. Spirit photographs are *unheimlich* because they expose familial photography to the estranging and defamiliarizing forces that haunt the house of being. If the uncanny is un-homely for psychoanalysis, this is because it reminds the subject that this strange return represses something mortally close that will not go away and that shatters domestic order and tranquility.[2] From a psychoanalytic perspective, Mumler's ghostly developments—by 'disseminating this beautiful truth of spirit-communion'—can be viewed as a cosmetic means of comforting and reuniting families that have been ripped apart (Mumler, 1875, 3). In other words, a contemporary theoretical reading no longer guided by Spiritualist beliefs situates the uncanny spirit photograph as that which enables consumers to forget their losses by restoring the domestic scene, familiarity, and community in the face of the gruesome and inconvenient fact of mortality always lurking just beneath the surface of Mumler's spooked images.

Meanwhile, Tom Gunning's 'Phantom Images and Modern Manifestations: Spirit Photography, Magic Theater, Trick Films, and Photography's Uncanny' takes up the Freudian concept of the uncanny as a means to understand spirit photography. Gunning's analysis returns to another aspect of Freud's (and Otto Rank's) thinking about what makes something appear uncanny and untimely—repetition and doubling. While psychoanalysis does not single out photography, its relation to the following Freudian list of what one might dub 'double troublemakers' is quite obvious. Freud writes: 'The theme of the "double" has been very thoroughly treated by Otto Rank. He has gone into the connections the "double" has with reflections in mirrors, with shadows, guardian spirits, with the belief in the soul and the fear of death (Freud, 1919/1959, 387).' Gunning summarizes his own position as follows: 'In spirit photography, we find an extraordinary conjunction of uncanny themes, the visual double, the "constant recurrence of the same thing", and the fascination with death and its overcoming through the technical device of mechanical reproduction (Gunning, 1995, 68).' This encounter with the visual double offers another way to characterize the spooked time of spirit photography or when time goes out of joint.

While Freud views 'the invention of doubling as a preservation against extinction' in a former age of animism and magical thinking, he believes that the func-

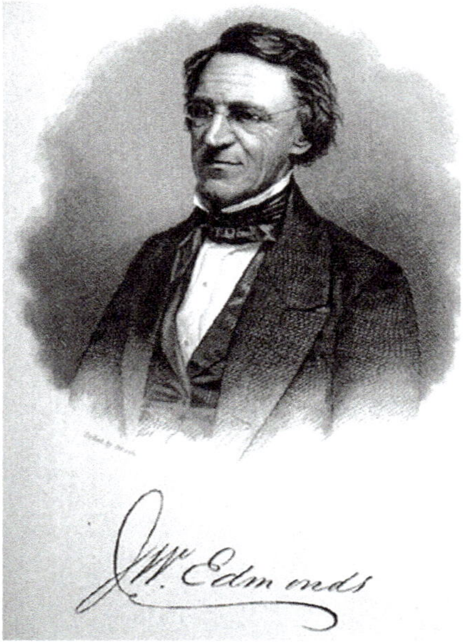

Fig. 2.4 Anonymous engraver, 'Judge John Edmonds', before 1869. Engraving from Emma Hardinge Britten, *Modern American Spiritualism* (New York: W. Britten, 1869).

tion of the double has been altered in his own 'post-Enlightenment' times. 'From having been an assurance of immortality, he becomes the ghastly harbinger of death (Freud, 1919/1959, 387).' From this perspective, the uncanny aspect of spirit photography which involves the appearance of the visual double no longer affirms the Spiritualist belief in immortality. Instead, it serves as a reminder of this more ghastly aspect. Playing at rationalist and evolutionary scientist, Freud also argues that we get a feeling of the uncanny when something happens in the world that would appear to support those animistic beliefs that should have been discarded as superstitions. It is the spooked time of the anachronism locating spirit photography as one such animistic return of the repressed. Freud offers the following statement that has a Spiritualist ring to it and sounds as if it could have been uttered by one of Mumler's satisfied spirit photographic customers. 'Then the dead do continue to live and appear before our eyes on the scene of their former activities! (402).' In this way, the ambivalent rhetoric of spirit photography offers the promise of a future life and the overcoming of death to those who invest in it while serving as a 'ghastly harbinger' and an untimely reminder of the death of the physical body and the survival of the spectral image for non-believers. Lurking beneath its more benevolent aspect, the vision of the spirit photographic double confronts the self with and as another to spook the beholder with what Freud calls 'morbid anxiety' (394).

Freud also believed that the uncanny is revealed in the breakdown of the distinction between reality and imagination. 'An uncanny effect is often and easily produced by effacing the distinction between imagination and reality, such as when something that we have hitherto regarded as imaginary appears before us in reality (398).' This speaks directly to the testimony of a key defense witness in Mumler's trial. Should Judge John Edmonds' 'evidence' be regarded as uncanny strange (where something hitherto regarded as imaginary appeared before him in reality) or simply delusional? Edmonds testified both that he had received a Mumler spirit photograph that he positively identified and that he had close encounters with a ghost in the courtroom that helped him to solve a case (fig. 2.4). On April 22, 1869, *The Tribune* reported his remarkable testimony:

> I believe that the camera can take a photograph of a spirit, and I believe also that spirits have materiality...for I have seen them. Only a few days since I was in a court in Brooklyn, when a suit against a life assurance company for the amount claimed to be due on a certain policy was being heard. Looking toward that part of the court-room occupied by the jury, I saw the spirit of the man whose death was the basis of the suit. The spirit told me the circumstances connected with the death; said that the suit was groundless, and that he had committed suicide. I drew a diagram of the place at which his death occurred, and on showing it to the counsel, was told that it was exact in every particular.[3]

The return of the suicide victim as witness at his own case testifying against the claimant that he did not die a life-assuring death illustrates yet again the gruesome appearance of the specter in the realm of the uncanny. Armed with this 'insider information', Edmonds proceeds to solve the mystery. Meanwhile, the prosecuting attorney Elbridge T. Gerry would have none of this Spiritualist supernaturalism and tried to steer such testimony away from the spooked and uncanny perception and toward the cracked hallucination and mental delusion. He refers to both Judge Edmonds and Paul Bremond's testimony in his closing argument as follows: 'Their extraordinary testimony, as to what they saw and heard, can be accounted for only as statements of hallucinations; in other words, that what each described was "a false creation, proceeding from an oppressed brain". [Now] I do not assert that they are insane. They are not the only men of intelligence who have been afflicted in this way with mental delusions (Gerry, 1869, 30).'

But according to Derrida, the debate between Gerry (the scoffing skeptic) and Edmonds (the visionary believer) will never be decided or resolved on account of the elusive properties of the *es spukt* ('it spooks') at the heart of the uncanny and its inability to be determined or fixed. Both the photographic specters of Mumler and the courtroom specters of Edmonds have the terrifying look and feel of the 'living-dead' where 'one cannot decide between hallucination and perception'. To recite his *Specters of Marx*:

> Everything is concentrated then in the German expression *es spukt*, which translations are obliged to circumvent. One would have to say: it haunts, it ghosts, it specters, there is some phantom there, it has the feel of the living-dead. The subject that haunts is not identifiable, one cannot see, localize, fix any form, one cannot decide between hallucination and perception (Derrida, 1994, 135-136).

Mourning

What would spirit photography be without mourning and loss, without the ritual practices and coping strategies that accompany bereavement? The socio-cultural circumstances in which spirit photography arose in the 1860s were not only permeated by the doctrines of Spiritualism but also part of a culture of mourning linked to high infant mortality rates and the Civil War. P.T. Barnum's unmasking of Mumler reviewed how Senator Colorado Jewett attempted to employ Mumler to summon the ghosts of dead Presidents and elder statesmen to provide sage counsel and heal the breach in the war-torn nation. This anecdote points to how the specters of Mumler thrived in the context of such a grieving American body politic (Barnum, 1866, 114-119). But rather than reviewing the social-cultural frameworks for such practices of mourning, I want to focus on how it provided another major theoretical basis for understanding the success of Mumler's spirit photography. In this context, one should remember that Freud once wrote that 'man's first theoretical achievement' was 'the creation of spirits (Freud, 1950, 93).' He believed that theory itself begins in the animistic era with the positing and projecting of spirits (or that which spooks). If such is the case, then spirit photography is linked to mankind's primordial theoretical activity in fixing the spirits of the dead onto film. According to psychoanalysis, this 'projective creation of souls and spirits' (ibid.) is prompted by the work of mourning as survivors seek to find a way to deal with the loss of their ancestors and to carry on without them.

In his creative revamping of Freud's thinking via what he calls *Aberrations of Mourning*, Larry Rickels recalls the importance of projection for a psychoanalytic theory of spirit photography. 'In *Totem and Taboo* Freud saw the origin of phantoms and ghosts as lying in projection...The very first projection of ghosts was conceived, then, as disposal of the dead without proper burial (Rickels, 1988, 147).' Rickels underlines this point elsewhere: '[P] hotography and film project and animate those phantoms which... haunt those who are unable to grant the dead proper burial (297).' This idea has major implications for spirit photography and its relationship to mourning. Rather than signaling a final laying to rest of the dead and thereby marking an end to the work of mourning, these haunting images may be viewed paradoxically as symptomatic signs of the *improper* burial of the dead who cannot yet be laid to rest (fig. 2.5). Meanwhile, the transcendentally inclined Spiritualist with a fervent desire to step out of time would refute Rickels' reading of improper burial seeing the image as a clear indicator of immortality where the 'undying' spirit has been captured. The satisfied customer Mr. Hambleton suggests as much to Mumler: 'Thus is added another of those incontrovertible evidences that our friends can return from the "other shore," bringing us the knowledge of their heavenly home and of their undying sympathy for the children of mortality (Mumler, 1875, 53).' In contrast to psychoanalysis, the otherworldly Spiritualists who achieve 'knowledge of their heavenly home' view such spirit photographs as the very antithesis of the 'unhomely' (*unheimlich*).

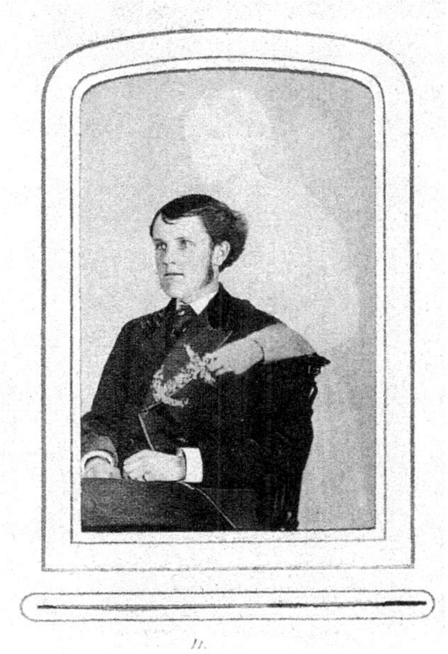

Fig. 2.5 William H. Mumler, 'Herbert Wilson with the spirit of a young lady to whom he had once been engaged', 1870-1875. Reproduced by kind permission of the College of Psychic Studies, London.

There is only one passage in Rickels' psycho-analysis where he refers to spirit photography directly. He calls it 'transcendental photography' and therefore a direct corollary to transcendental philosophy. Rickels points out how psychoanalysis deals with the conjuring of phantom images on film but that Freud limited the relationship of technology with the occult to the technique of 'transference' rather than affirming a full-blown belief in spirit photography. 'While "transcendental photography" offered testimony that the camera could conceive images of the otherwise indiscernible phantoms conjured in séances, Freud responded by linking and limiting the occult effects and analogues of the technical media to the workings of transference (Rickels, 1988, 358).' Such transference occurs for instance when the survivor projects evil and paranoid thoughts about the dead ancestor onto the conjured spirit who then comes back to haunt him as a demon. But one gets the sense that the atheist Freud (who saw religion as the 'future of an illusion') would not have been very generous to those who believed that they were in the presence of their dead ancestors when they beheld Mumler's photographs. Instead Freud would see this investment as a clear-cut aberration of mourning. In 'Mourning and Melancholia', Freud writes how 'this struggle [to wean oneself away from the loved object] may be so intense that a turning away from reality ensues, the object being clung to through the medium of a hallucinatory wish-psychosis (Freud, 1917/1959, 154).' In other words, spooked communication with the dead at the séance table or the visualization of the dead in spirit photographs help survivors cling to an object of loss and function as the mediated staging of 'a hallucinatory wish-psychosis'.

Freud also believed that 'mourning has a quite specific psychical task to perform: its function is to detach the survivor's memories and hopes from the dead (Freud, 1950, 65).' In this light, the specters of Mumler may be viewed as 'transitional objects' detaching the survivor's memories and hopes from the dead and displacing them unto these photographic keepsakes. Thus, Mumler relates the satisfaction of Hugo Leibing who traveled from Berlin to Boston for a sitting with the renowned spirit-artist shortly after the tragic death of his son. Leibing's loss of his son on earth is recompensed by becoming connected to him in the spirit world through Mumler's tele-technology. Mumler recounts: 'Who can describe the joy that filled this father's heart when he discovered that his son was not dead? That in passing through the change he had become more closely allied! He felt that the doom that surrounded him had been dissipated, and looked forward with pleasure to the time when they should meet on the evergreen shore (Mumler, 1875, 63).' The reader empathizes with the therapeutic consolation that this image affords the grieving father. Mumler's phrasing 'that the doom that surrounded him had been dissipated' resonates with the Freudian view that the survivor seeks a psychic detachment from the dead and from death in the work of mourning.

Reviewing the testimony of the spiritual photographic consumers in Mumler's memoirs makes it clear that these images helped them to cope with the loss of their loved ones and assisted in the bereavement process. This again points to the therapeutic function of spirit photography and helps to explain why Hannah Mumler—a faith healer and sympathetic medium herself—worked hand in hand with her husband. This was certainly the case at the session that yielded Mumler's most celebrated photograph of Mary Todd with the spirit of her beloved husband Abraham Lincoln and their son Thaddeus in 1872 (fig. 2.6). Mumler's account indicates that Mrs. Mumler communicated with the dead spirits while he secured this ghostly development. Even though it was already seven years after the assassination of the President, Mrs. Lincoln appeared dressed in black veil and mourning garb. One notes the emotional catharsis that Mrs. Lincoln experienced through this verbal and visual communication with her loved ones in the spirit land. Mumler recalls, 'When my wife resumed her normal condition, she found Mrs. L. weeping tears of joy that she had again found her loved ones, and apparently anxious to learn, if possible, how long before she could join them in their spirit home. But this information of course could not be given (Mumler, 1875, 30).' Even though the spirit photographic mediums claimed to open up communication with the dead and offer proofs of the immortality of the soul, neither could solve the mystery of mortality or when Mrs. L. would pass over to the other shore.

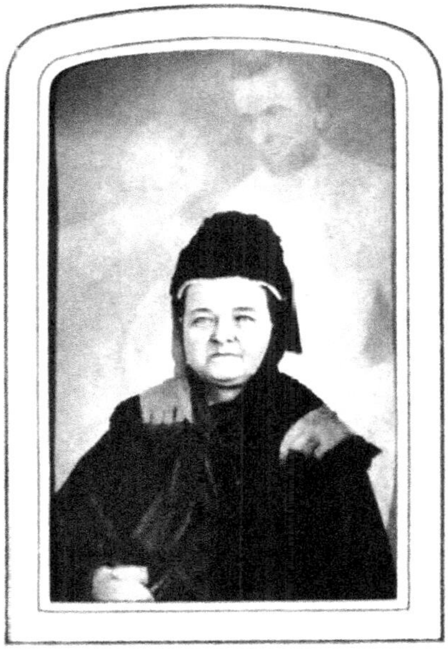

Fig. 2.6 William H. Mumler, 'Mary Todd Lincoln with the spirit of her husband President Abraham Lincoln and son Thaddeus', 1872. Reproduced by kind permission of the College of Psychic Studies, London.

But from another perspective, spirit photographs and Spiritualism offered a way of disavowing the painful work of mourning by detaching or displacing it onto the promise of immortality. Here, one recalls Mumler's claim that his images offered 'evidences of a future existence (Mumler, 1875, 3).' This disavowal is supported by Jacques Lacan's interpretation of *Hamlet* that ghosts arise when there has been no satisfactory mourning ritual to mediate these mortal matters. 'This explains the belief we find in folklore in the very close association of the lack, skipping, or refusal of something in the satisfaction of the dead, with the appearance of ghosts

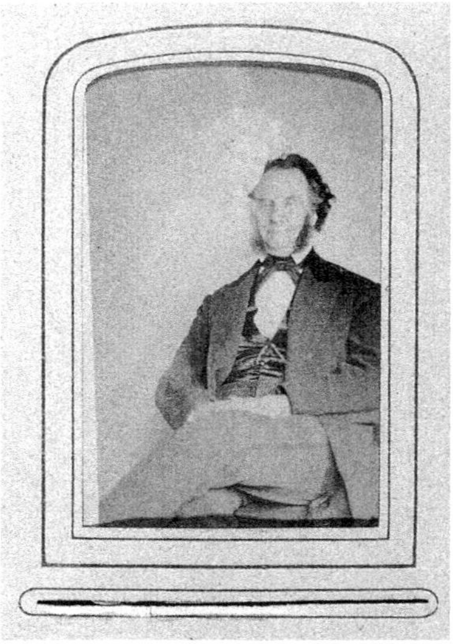

Fig. 2.7 William H. Mumler, 'Moses A. Dow and the spirit of Mabel Warren', 1871. Reproduced by kind permission of the College of Psychic Studies, London.

and specters in the gap left by the omission of the significant rite (Lacan, 1977, 39).' The ghosts of spirit photography illustrate then what returns in the repression of proper mourning rituals—'timeless' images that offer Spiritualist believers a glimpse of a future life that nullifies the concept of death. This disavowal is embodied in the rhetoric of the spirit of Mabel Warren in communication with the editor of the *Waverly Magazine*, Moses Dow, at the séance before the photo shoot that would produce another famous image (fig. 2.7). 'Promise me that you will not use the word death when you speak of me, for I am not dead, but alive, and am always with you (Mumler, 1875, 37).'

Mabel's therapeutic words not only provide consolation to the grieving Moses Dow but also help him to better cope with his own mortal fears. In *Radical Spirits*, Ann Braude confirms this general pattern. 'Spiritualism's denial of death offered a unique kind of consolation to the bereaved. Messages frequently focused on the spirit's happiness after death and continued concern for surviving family members (Braude, 2001, 52).' Braude quotes Andrew Jackson Davis regarding the desire to replace mourning rituals with the celebration of the soul and its passage to a higher life. 'If, as Davis claimed, "*Death* is but a *Birth* of the Spirit from a lower into a higher state", then it did not justify mourning (54).'[4] Returning to Dow's vision of Mabel, he has no choice but to conclude that spirit photography offers the living proofs of immortality. 'It also proves the immortality of the soul of man, and that immortality is a blissful one. Freed from that body, it is a spirit-form, and is free to act itself; and that it will advance in brightness and glory during the endless ages of eternity (Mumler, 1875, 40).' For Dow, the spirit-form revealed in this image attests to the abolition of time. It is extraordinary to think of the power invested in the photographic medium by Dow's spooked theory when Mumler's image of Mabel Warren was said to hold the key to the mystery of eternal life.

Haunting

In his memoirs, *The Personal Experiences of William H. Mumler in Spirit Photography*, Mumler looks back at his practice in a way that always already looks forward. His curious prose partakes of a temporality marked by the 'future anterior' tense emblematic of the haunting and resurrection promised by spirit photography in its production of the *revenant*. Here, Mumler relinquishes his authorial agency in order to become a spiritual instrument who turns himself over to impersonal higher powers and who gains knowledge 'of a future existence' through the proofs of spirit photography and spirit communion. For Mumler, the beautiful truth of Spiritualism and its visual adjunct spirit photography offer nothing less than the casting off of this mortal coil—transmuting morbid anxiety into the promise of eternal life. 'As I look back upon my experience, I feel that I have been the gainer, personally, for all the sacrifices I have made, and all the troubles I may have endured in the knowledge I have gained of a future existence, and in the soul satisfaction of being a humble instrument in the hands of the invisible host that surrounds us for disseminating this beautiful truth of spirit communion (Mumler, 1875, 3-4).'

With the apparitional appearance of Mumler's ghosts and the delivery of some 'soul' satisfaction, ontology—that which belongs to a thinking of being—gives way to *hauntology*—that which insists upon being as being-haunted and that offers hospitality to the stranger in the house, to the stranger always already in the house and haunting the philosophical house of being. Hauntology evades the metaphysics of presence and introduces haunting into every concept to the extent that ontology becomes the forever failed attempt to exorcise the ghosts from the concept. As Derrida writes, 'To haunt does not mean to be present, and it is necessary to introduce haunting into the very construction of a concept. Of every concept, beginning with the concept of being and time. That is what we would be calling here a hauntology. Ontology opposes it only as a movement of exorcism (Derrida, 1994, 161).' This point would serve as a model for the relations between photography and spirit photography as well. Photography opposes spirit photography only as the movement that attempts to exorcise the spirits that haunt it. In this way, the (haunted) photographic image challenges the distinction between what is present and what is not, between what is living and what is not. Interestingly enough, Derrida introduces hauntology—the 'logic of haunting' that guides our thinking about photography as a ghostly enterprise—in *Specters of Marx* amid a discussion of the specters of Hamlet haunting Marx's *The Communist Manifesto* (which begins with the specter of Communism haunting mid-19th century Europe). Given that Marx's writings are contemporaneous with the rise of Spiritualism, they can be viewed as historical materialist attempts to exorcise this craze.

From the perspective of hauntology, the strange case of William Mumler and the conjuring of his ghosts represent a spirit photographic haunting of the house of being that is wondrous strange. Spirit photography functions as a technological practice that offers the ghosts a place to haunt, and, on the flip side, that offers skeptics a place from which to chase them and hunt them down. Therefore *hauntology* acknowledges that there are more things in heaven and earth that are dreamt of either in the philosophy of the skeptics seeking to debunk Spiritualism and the specters conjured by the spirit photography of William Mumler *or* the believers who would seek to turn Spiritualism and 'spiritual photography' into something more substantial and substantive thereby removing its strangeness and relationship to the uncanny (or that which haunts). This latter point is something which Mumler himself can be accused of doing throughout *The Personal Experiences*. Again and again, the defensive defendant seeks to assert spirit photographs as a 'positive proof' (Mumler, 1875, 19), as 'spiritual truths' (4), or as a 'correct likeness' (50) to establish his practice on the firm ground of empiricism and as a discourse of photographic truth. In seeking to identify these haunting subjects (that would evade identification by definition), he seeks in effect to exorcise his own spirit photography.[5] But this venture is doomed to self-destruct because in playing into the hands of natural science and in making his appeal to empirical reason, Mumler overlooks the resources and the powers of the 'invisible host' upon which his photo-hauntological practice necessarily rests (Mumler, 1875, 4). These hauntological forces manage to return no matter how hard Mumler may try to repress them. In this way, the 'virtual space of spectrality' is summoned as the necessary condition of both materialist *and* spiritual photography.

All in all, hauntology represents the spooked theory and temporality that guides any speculations on spirit photography and illustrates how William Mumler's spirit photographs—these uncanny, untimely, and mournful images—serve as an emblem for all photography as a generator of ghosts. One recalls Roland Barthes' famous formulation of photographic exposure—of being posed in exteriority and becoming a specter when sitting for a photograph. 'I then experience a micro-version of death (of parenthesis). I am truly becoming specter (Barthes, 1981, 14).' In this way, spirit photography's being in the world—which can only be formulated as a being-haunted—reminds us that a ghostly production marks all photographic reproduction.

Acknowledgements

This chapter is reprinted from Louis Kaplan, *The Strange Case of William Mumler, Spirit Photographer*, Minneapolis: Minnesota University Press, 2008 (copyright 2008 by the Regents of the University of Minnesota).

Notes

[1] For a review of how the uncanny and the supernatural enter into recent literary discourse with the help of psychoanalysis and deconstruction see Nicholas Royle, *The Uncanny* (Manchester: Manchester University Press, 2003).

[2] Peter Buse and Andrew Stott write, 'It is entirely appropriate, then, that Freud likened the repressed idea to an unwelcome house-guest (1999, 9).'

[3] The article was reprinted in *The Spiritual Magazine* n.s. 4, no. 7 (July 1869): 244-245.

[4] Braude cites Andrew Jackson Davis, *The Great Harmonia; being a philosophical revelation of the natural, spiritual, and celestial universe* (Boston: B.B. Mussey, 1850), vol. 1, 171.

[5] Derrida remarks upon the idea that 'the subject that haunts is not identifiable' in his discussion of Karl Marx and Max Stirner (see Derrida, 1994, 136).

Bibliography

¬ P.T. Barnum, *Humbugs of the World* (New York: Carleton Publishers, 1866).

¬ Roland Barthes, *Camera Lucida*, trans. Richard Howard (New York: Hill and Wang, 1981).

¬ Ann Braude, *Radical Spirits: Spiritualism and Women's Rights in Nineteenth Century America*, 2nd ed. (Bloomington: Indiana University Press, 2001).

¬ Peter Buse and Andrew Stott (eds), *Ghosts: Deconstruction, Psychoanalysis, History* (London: Macmillian, 1999).

¬ Jacques Derrida, *Specters of Marx: The State of the Debt, the Work of Mourning, & the New International*, trans. Peggy Kamuf (New York: Routledge, 1994).

¬ Jacques Derrida, '*Shibboleth*: For Paul Celan', trans. Joshua Wilner and Thomas Dutoit, in Derrida, *Sovereignties in Question: The Poetics of Paul Celan* (New York: Fordham University Press, 2005), 1-64.

¬ Sigmund Freud, 'Mourning and Melancholia' (1917) in *Collected Papers*, vol. 4, trans. Joan Riviere (New York: Basic Books, 1959), 152-170.

¬ Sigmund Freud, 'The Uncanny' (1919) in *Collected Papers*, vol. 4, trans. Joan Riviere (New York: Basic Books, 1959), 368-407.

¬ Sigmund Freud, *Totem and Taboo*, trans. James Strachey (New York: Norton, 1950).

¬ Elbridge T. Gerry, *The Mumler 'Spirit' Photography Case* (New York: Baker, Voorhis & Co., 1869).

¬ Tom Gunning, 'Phantom Images and Modern Manifestations: Spirit Photography, Magic Theater, Trick Films, and Photography's Uncanny', in Patrice Petro (ed.) *Fugitive Images: From Photography to Video* (Madison, Wisconsin: University of Wisconsin Press, 1995), 42-71.

¬ Tom Gunning, 'To Scan a Ghost: The Ontology of Mediated Vision', *Grey Room*, 26, (Winter, 2007): 94-127.

¬ Jacques Lacan, 'Desire and Interpretation of Desire in *Hamlet*', *Yale French Studies*, 55/56 (1977): 11-52.

¬ Jennifer Mnookin, 'The Image of Truth: Photographic Evidence and the Power of Analogy', *Yale Journal of Law and the Humanities*, 10, no. 1 (1998): 1-74.

¬ William Mumler, *The Personal Experiences of William H. Mumler in Spirit-Photography* (Boston: Colby & Rich, 1875).

¬ New England Spiritualists' Association, *Constitution and By-Laws, List of Officers and Address to the Public* (Boston: George K. Snow, 1854).

¬ Laurence A. Rickels, *Aberrations of Mourning: Writing on German Crypts* (Detroit, Michigan: Wayne State University Press, 1988).

¬ Nicholas Royle, *The Uncanny* (Manchester: Manchester University Press, 2003).

¬ Jeffrey Sconce, *Haunted Media: Electronic Presence from Telegraphy to Television* (Durham and London: Duke University Press, 2000).

¬ *The Spiritual Magazine* n.s. 4, no. 7 (July 1869): 244-245.

3 Modern Time: Revisiting the Tableau

Joanna Lowry

Technology, Medium and the Event

The debates about photography's relationship to time involve complex negotiations of the relationship between two very different ways of thinking about photography. On the one hand photography can be considered as a 'technology', one that has certain characteristics that produce very distinctive types of signs and which seems to be intrinsically related to the stopping of time through the operation of the shutter mechanism and the chemistry of the darkroom. On the other hand photography can be considered as a 'medium', a historical and cultural formation of the photographic that is engaged with the production of photographs as aesthetic or otherwise meaningful objects and which may have the function of 'representing' time, or at least producing a visual language which would render the concept of temporality in a meaningful way. Obviously the boundary between these two ways of understanding photography is an ambiguous one and the distinction between the two discourses is not always clear. How can we think the one without the other? In what sense is it useful to think about the semiotics of the photograph as bound by its origins in a technical process rather than by its representational function? Conversely, how can it be possible to discuss the cultural, representational and aesthetic discourses with which photographs are engaging without also recognizing the distinctive origins of the photographic sign in a process of technological production? Moreover surely, indeed, the peculiarities of the photographic sign have been embraced by the discourses of representation—they have themselves become coded, and therefore part of the meta-discourse through which we understand the photographic image.

One of the most well-known examples of this peculiarity of the photographic sign was offered by Walter Benjamin in 'A Little History of Photography', when he talked about the way in which the long exposures that sitters had to endure in the early years of photography seemed to inscribe an experience of duration and presence into the image so that we could now read the haunting presence of those sitters in a distinctive way. He described a photograph of a Newhaven fishwife by Hill and Adamson in which, he suggested, the imposition of the technology of photography upon the subject, its demand for an extended pose, inadvertently exposed a deep subjective relationship to time and duration that in the course of history the technology was itself to play a part in eventually destroying. In drawing our attention to this phenomenon he was situating his argument at just this ambiguous interface between the ideas of technology and medium (Benjamin, 2008). The question of the technology itself seemed, in his text, to produce a representational discourse about photography that was dependent upon it and yet also had its own autonomy. Similarly Raymond Bellour has pointed out how a blurred or out of focus image comes to operate not only as a sign produced *by* the effect of movement or the lens, but has also come to be read as a sign *of* movement, indeed as a sign that represents the 'photographic' within the photograph (Bellour, 1990).

Yet I would suggest that whilst this ambiguity that persists at the heart of much of the theoretical debate about photography has undoubtedly been productive and is, one might argue, the very source of our fascination with the image, it is also worth occasionally unpicking this knot and recognizing that the very moment of indeterminacy between two different ways of figuring the photographic may indeed be a fundamental 'undecidable', a fissure point between two irreconcilable discourses. And where such undecidables exist we find ourselves, as we look at the image, motivated as much by desire as by logic. Our encounter with the image is possessed by the need for a kind of resolution of the problem, a problem that we sometimes only begin to intuit, and the photograph itself becomes the site of an overdetermined metaphysics of time, one that might indeed become the vehicle for more pervasive cultural desires.

A similar ambiguity to the one that I have described here has been noted by Jacques Derrida in a conversation with Hubertus von Amelunxen and Michael Wetzel. He describes two different modalities of the photographic. Firstly the *techné* of photography, a term that, drawing on Heidegger, he uses in a way that correlates with what I have described as the 'medium' above. He refers to the cultural productivity of the photographic image that is able to produce heterogeneous temporalities, where even a simple still image

> presupposes a duration that postpones and differentiates...and within that time subevents can form, differentiations, micrological modifications, providing the occasion of possible compositions, dissociations and recompositions, 'tricktakes' if you will that make a definite break with the presupposed phenomenological naturalism which saw in photography the miracle of a technology that obliterates itself so as to give us the natural purity, time itself. Once one considers the calculability of time in perception as a photographic take, once one does not see time as a sequence of irreducible and atomistic moments but as a more or less calculable differential duration, a duration that is correlative to a technology, then the issue of reference, and subsequently the question of art, of photography as techné becomes complicated (Derrida, 1993; Campany, 2003, 220).

This 'calculable differential duration' has to be seen against its remainder which is photography's dumb referentiality, the focus of a more Barthesian analysis:

> A point at which it registers passively...It seizes a reality that is there, that was there, in an indissoluble now...a basically uncontrollable experience, that which takes place only once. Under these circumstances one would be passive and exposed, the gaze itself would be exposed to the exposed thing in the time-without-density of zero time, in an exposure time reduced to the point of the momentary (ibid.).

It is interesting that Derrida situates this aspect of photography's engagement with the reality of the 'thing itself', a reading of the photographic that can be aligned with what I have called above the 'technological', as an almost impossible hypothetical state of being. This is what the complexity of the discourse of duration is pitted against. And this moment of pure openness to the world is figured not by the 'single take' of the photographic snapshot but by an absolute zero-time, in the 'momentary' that is, in effect, pure reference. The pure referentiality of photography-as-technology, the point at which the object gazes back, stands, from this perspective, outside time.

Derrida's comments suggest, then, a way of confronting this set of entangled discourses by situating temporality in the field of art rather than death; by situating it in culture, as something that moves away from the concerns of ontology, whilst also always recognizing that the 'moment' of pure reference, is always potentially there as an irruptive force within the image. Whereas Roland Barthes saw 'time' as the punctum that potentially sears the image with its intimation of the real, Derrida's position seems to suggest that it might be 'non-time' that is the irruptive force. Temporality is, from this perspective, a complex cultural construction, one that may utilize a meta-discourse about the origins of the photographic sign in its elaborations, but which is in no sense determined by those origins.

This 'moment' of pure reference that Derrida comments upon also bears some relationship to the way in which Mary Ann Doane describes the 'event'—as a 'deictic marker of time'. 'As such' she says 'it is pure indication, deprived of meaning...The event somehow persists, in a semiotic limbo, as a kernel of the real that awaits only a second event whose collision with the first generates readability. In a sense any event is by its nature that which is unassimilable, that which resists meaning, that which, like the index, serves primarily as an assurance of the real—"something is happening" (Doane, 2002, 140).'

The 'event' then, from Doane's perspective, can be seen as representing a moment of pure reference that stands outside time, but that also, paradoxically, can only be grasped through the way in which it is differentiated within the visual from the process of the representation of time. It is also, in its unassimilability necessarily linked back to the unassimilable real of Lacanian theory, to that traumatic real that always threatens to pierce the surface of the simulacral mirror (see Iversen, 2002).

Mary Ann Doane, in formulating this point, was writing about cinema and the moving image and considering the way in which early cinema became developed as a machinery for producing a modern sense of the event. On the one hand the very first documentary films at the end of the 19th century seemed to be unequivocally tethered to the real through their absolute indexicality; on the other hand they seemed necessarily to be the agents of production of an alternative temporality outside the point of their own origin. These early films were forced to produce a calibration of the event, as that which might be filmed, to define a temporal ontology for the event which effectively suppressed the contingency of its actual temporal origins. Doane argues that this tension between structure and event was central to the experience of modernity at the end of the 19th century. Drawing on Derrida's essay 'Structure Sign and Event' and taking as her examples the struggles experienced by Baudelaire and Freud in wrestling with the dangerous yet simultaneously desirable notion of contingency, she suggests that through the invention of cinema the idea of the event emerges as an overdetermined space within which the culture can be seen to be dealing with anxieties around the taming of chance and contingency.

> The last half of the nineteenth century witnesses the growth of the perception of contingency as both threat and lure. And both could be said to be linked to its tenuous and unstable relation to meaning. The cinema emerges in this context as a technology that appears to be capable of representing the contingent, of providing the ephemeral with a durable record. This capability is the source of both fascination and anxiety. For the idea of representation without meaning involves the forfeiture of limits, and hence of semiotic control. The cinema is forced to confront the episteme wherein structure and event both oppose and tantalize each other (Doane, 2002, 167).

What emerges from this discussion is a recognition that the calibration of the temporal implied by photographic technologies is always necessarily in tension with the implied indexicality of those technologies. Like cinema the photographic sign is trapped within a recurring opposition and play between structure and event. The event is always on the side of the referent—as an implied presence that might rupture any sense of a secure coupling between the Saussurean signifier and its signified. The temporality encoded in the photograph as image is implicitly put into question by the events surrounding its production, by that moment when the object looks back.

Technology and the Tableau

It is perhaps the tableau photograph that most obviously bears the traces of this tension between the technology of the event and the medium of representation. The genre of the photographic tableau establishes photography's lineage back into the world of theater and the amateur dramatic pastimes of the 19th century. Such tableaux, images that were based upon their own problematic stilling of the bodies of the actors in the scene, were often based as much upon painting as on theater, the actors arranging themselves so as to reconstruct the pictorial spaces of painting. Framed by the borders of the picture itself and situated within an Albertian perspectival space, the action inevitably complied with the aesthetics of compositional form in history painting. Any event that was represented had, necessarily, to be constructed as a narrative device, as a posed moment around which the multiple temporalities of the image could be embellished. The coherence of the scene was always thus threatened by the disruptive presence of the real bodies of the actors, discomfortingly exposed by the process of the taking of the picture.

Something of the complexity of the way in which photographic technologies calibrated the temporal can be grasped by looking back at some of the earliest forms of production of photographic tableaux: at the elaborate combination prints of photographers like O.G. Rejlander and Henry Peach Robinson, works that were testament to the immense photographic labor that was necessary in order to tame the real. These photographers created elaborate narrative scenes in the tradition of history or genre painting through combining a number of different photographs to create the effect of a single composition. By fragmenting the desired image into a multitude of separate photographic fragments, and then recombining these to produce the desired 'artistic' composition, it seemed as though the referentiality of the photograph, a kind of obscene reminder of its brute origins in the mundanity of the world, could be held at bay. In the process of post-production therefore the temporality of the photograph itself became subsumed by the more dominant discourse of temporal narrativity inherited from the history of painting. Such works were focused upon the attempted construction by entirely artificial means of an idealized moment of narrative time that could be traced back to Lessing's formulation of the 'pregnant moment'. The resultant image had a strangely discontinuous hallucinatory quality that made it both compelling but also oddly dissatisfactory. The complex and uneasy effects of this clash between technology and medium, between the temporality of the index and the elaborated cultural coding of the temporality of the tableau, were not lost on the 19th century public, and the response to this form of photographic artistry was decidedly lukewarm. It quickly fell out of fashion, consigning its proponents to a place in the backwaters of photographic history for a century or more.

The constructed stillness of the tableau, with the demands it made on the spectator to see the image as a unity—to experience a unitary time of the image almost in the face of and despite the conditions of its production—provided then one scenario for the development of photographic arts. But the preoccupation with photography's representation of this kind of pictorial time, was soon to be displaced by a fascination with its capturing of the event. In the 1880s, a new form of photographic dry plate process was developed in France by Lumière that transformed photography's relationship to time and the spectator. This process allowed for greatly reduced exposure times and enabled the photographer to capture the moving object in full flight. This technique rapidly spread throughout the amateur photography world and offered a completely new way for the spectator to think about the photographic image. Now photography could be seen as a revelatory practice, revealing the world as a place of comic and unexpected oddities, strange poses, people in flight: a world of events that had been hitherto hidden from the human eye. This was spectacularity of a different order from that represented by the carefully composed and constructed scene of the tableau, this was a spectacularity of the strange and uncanny, a quality that was revealed as being potentially present in the most banal and ordinary of settings and events.

In 1887 Auguste Lumière was photographed leaping over a kitchen chair in his courtyard. Objects and bodies in flight—the way in which photography could create the illusion of levitation—became a popular theme in amateur photographic journals of the time. Tom Gunning has suggested how this new technology offered a completely new discourse of the body in its relationship to space and time, and argues that, apart from their innate absurdity, such images 'guarantee the frozen moment of the photograph (Gunning, 2001, 89).' He argues that these images of instantaneity, literal precursors of the cinematograph, also prefigure a profound shift in the visual discourses of the body away from the disciplined, posed bodies represented in the photographic studio towards the more casual, everyday body represented in play and leisure that would become the chosen object of fascination for cinema. 'Such images' he argues, 'created a new modern self image, a casual self presentation diametrically opposed to the formal, almost allegorical poses of studio portraiture (90).'

But there were more profound implications of this new form of photo-imaging. Instantaneous photography was also implicated in the emergence of the notion of 'the event' as a key problematic in modern vision. Almost because of its peculiar isolation from the flow of time the ball suspended in motion operates as an index of the fact that something happened. As a kind of visual aporia between the ball being thrown and caught the image is situated on the very cusp of time. In these photographs the event—that deictic marker that seems to point to the moment of non-time that Derrida saw as being fundamental to our understanding of photography—emerges as the still point around which the image is organized. This is the point at which the object looks back. A point of pure technological production of time becomes the centre of the composition, replacing the discursive narrative temporality that was at the centre of the traditional tableau.

While the photographic tableau and the instantaneous image may appear in some ways to be directly opposed to each other—the one a careful construction of pictorial time based upon the historical conventions of the tableau, and the other a piece of pure referentiality made visible only by the apparatus itself, a function of the rapid shutter release, they are both nevertheless, in their different ways forms of picture making that are locked into their origins in the technological restrictions of the apparatus. And there is a sense in which each of them is slightly inadequate in relationship to the picture that we, as spectators, hope to see. Photography seems to offer us a set of disruptive temporal effects that disturb the visual contract with the spectator. The constructed pictorialism of the tableau is always internally fissured by the effects of the demands of the long exposure on the participants or alternatively by the fractured technology of the combination print. On the other hand the instantaneous snapshot image is in itself also a kind of fissuring of the visual field. What we see arising out of these different practices is the play of relationships between the constraints of the technology and our aesthetic assumptions about how we engage with the image, with the complexity of our desire for the possibility of representation itself. But if instantaneous images signaled for Gunning a shift towards a modern sense of the self they also indicate a shift towards a reflexive response to the technology itself—in a sense the emergence of a modernist construction of the notion of photography as a medium:

> Instantaneous photography stands not only as an emblem of modernity, with its new technological ability to transform time and representation, but also relates in a profound sense to aesthetic modernism...Instantaneous photography's self-reflexive imaging of its own conditions of representation places it in line with the aspirations of the avant-garde (Gunning, 2001, 97).

Modernity and the Tableau: Catastrophe and Utopia

The aesthetic modernism to which Gunning refers, whilst it might indeed relate to a certain reflexivity in relationship to the issue of medium, is also premised upon a certain atemporality in relationship to the visual field. The security of photography's place as a modernist art form in recent years has been premised upon the promotion of a formalist, objective aesthetic that positions the spectator outside any personal or historical engagement with the image: high art photography is dominated by a spatialized aesthetic of presentness in relation to the image. Meticulous in their technique and awe-inspiring in the way in which they situate us at a critical distance from the surface of the print, these photographs also, in a sense, present us with photography as an idealized form: as a form of picturing that places us outside the historicity of the image: in 'modernist' space. Nevertheless the spectator of the image is always ultimately placed in a complex temporal relationship to the image by the peculiar specificity of the technology itself and it is this hiatus between the photograph as technology and its aesthetic status as medium, this moment that I have referred to above as an undecidable, that has provided the opportunity for a number of artists to open up again the possibility of revisiting the tableau as a form of photographic picture making that might be able to interrogate something about our very modern relationship to time. In each of the works I shall discuss here the instantaneous snapshot image provides the central focus of the tableau, the imponderable moment of indexical referentiality that fissures composure of the picture, the still moment of the non-temporal that paradoxically provides that point of predication around which the temporal narrative of the picture can be organized. I have argued above that such moments of undecidability in the image may become the focus of an unfulfilled desire on the

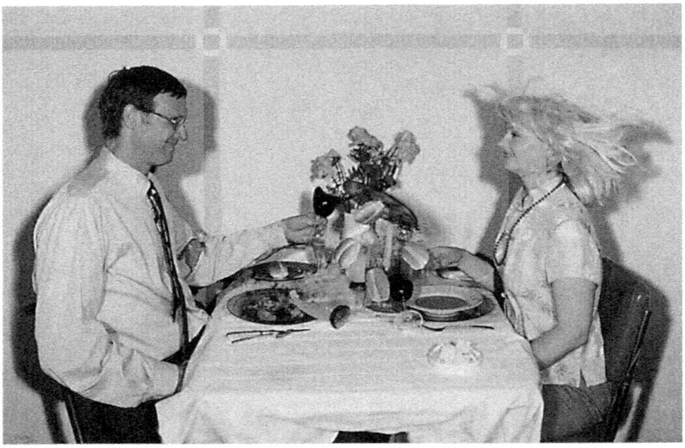

Fig. 3.1 Michael Snow, *Flash! 20:49, 15/6/2001* (2001). Laminated color photograph on aluminum, 122x183 cm. Courtesy of the artist.

part of the spectator, a desire which may itself tell us something about the fragility of modernity's relationship to time.

In my first example, Michael Snow's photograph *Flash! 20:49, 15/6/2001* (2001) (fig. 3.1), this desire is focused upon a moment of catastrophe. The title of the work—*Flash*—ambivalently descriptive and imperative—operates almost performatively in relationship to the technology, jolting the image into existence, and placing it in a very particular relationship to the temporal. The meticulous noting of time and date in the title provides a further calibration of the moment that the picture was taken. The photograph itself takes the form of a traditional tableau, showing a man and a woman seated opposite each other at a table in a café in perfect symmetry. The scene has the appearance of a cheap advertisement, or perhaps an image from a technical handbook on amateur photography. There is a compelling banality to the props, and the actors, and the slightly old fashioned quality of the color print. A gust of wind blows through the scene toppling a plate of bread rolls and wine glasses in the air between the two diners. The photograph captures this moment of temporary anarchic disorder as the rolls tumble, the plate falls, the wine spills. The couple are frozen and unable to respond to or prevent this disastrous irruption of the real at the dinner table. The visual tangle at the centre of the image has a peculiarly flattened quality. Snow has declared an interest in the potential that the photograph has to flatten things and reduce them from three dimensions to two. The rectangular grid on the walls behind the two diners reinforces this quality in the image as does the presence of the sharp shadows behind the actors' profiles, rendering them curiously similar to cut-outs in a *découpage*.

Snow makes a connection between on the one hand the flash of light that produces the image as an event within representation and on the other hand, the gust of wind that produces the central event within the narrative of the image—a toppling melee of bread rolls, crockery and spilt wine. The spectator becomes uncannily positioned in a problematic visual relationship to the scene as tableau, whilst this unassimilable kernel of the real, the place where it all falls apart, is positioned as the temporal hinge around which the visual field of the photograph must orient itself. This is 'event' defined as an accident, a disordering of the formally ordered space of the picture: nature taking its malicious revenge on culture.

Jeff Wall's *A Sudden Gust of Wind (After Hokusai)*(1993) (fig. 3.2) famously takes the same motif—the wind that blows all the land surveyor's papers and his hat up into the air—a spiraling moment of chaos, loss, and disorder frozen into the stilled durational field of the tableau. This photograph was made in the tradition of Rejlander's combination print and involved the combining of several different images into one seamless whole. What is also clear is the way in which Wall uses this carefully constructed composition to play with the relationship between the flattened staging of the tableau of figures in the foreground and the receding landscape of modernity that is always the true subject of Wall's pictures, that lies behind them. Our own gaze, in this moment of non-time, follows that of the central figure up to the lost hat sailing overhead, the clarity of whose reproduction belies the naturalism of the photograph as a whole.

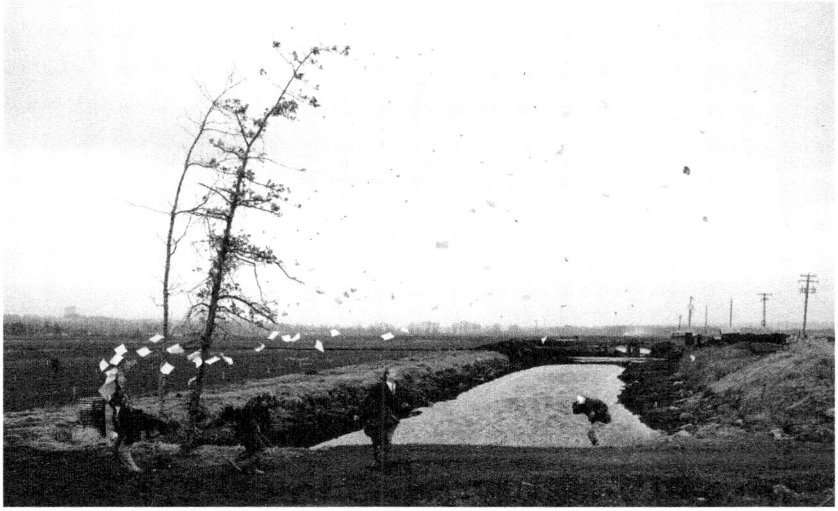

Fig. 3.2 Jeff Wall, *A Sudden Gust of Wind (after Hokusai)* 1993. Transparency in lightbox, 229 x 377 cm. Courtesy of the artist and the Centre for Contemporary Canadian Art.

The tableau as a pictorial form is always traditionally organized around a key moment—the peripateia, or what Gotthold Lessing (1766) called 'the pregnant moment'. The task of the artist is to represent, through the arrangement of figures within the frame, a visual compression of both the temporal and the spatial, so that its significance can be grasped in a moment. This is a moment that situates the spectator, then, outside time; it implies an atemporal position from which the complexity of temporality can be observed. Both of the photographs described here use the flying, disordered object, as an index of fundamental disorder within the picture: a moment of loss that can only be revealed through photography. The structure of the tableau directs our gaze towards this unassimilable event, this gesture of pointing to the real, by showing what cannot otherwise be seen. In each case the artist is making us aware of the contrivance of the photograph as a device for the taming of this event. The space of the photograph can be seen as a fantasmic staging of desire around this fundamental moment of loss.

Both of these works are, in effect, comments upon the peculiar productivity of the photographic in relationship to time. In a self-reflexive gesture that is only possible within the photograph they reveal a convergence between two very different constructions of time. They bring these two photographic discourses together, exposing their technological origins, and engaging our gaze as one that cannot sit in a disinterestedly aesthetic relationship to the image, but that is also bound into a number of different temporal contracts with the photographic apparatus. The first is associated with the historically embedded concept of the tableau—and with the careful construction of a staged moment, a construction that is dependent upon the identification of a key moment from which the past and the future may be seen to unfold, an organization of the figures within a scene that has a duration and which places the spectator in a position of reflection and judgment in relationship to the scene. The other is associated with the revelation of an event by photography, a 'flash' that disrupts our position as spectator, that takes us by surprise, a reminder of the index, of our potential relationship to the real.

These images then are very particular examples of images that reflect upon the relationship between time and technology, the complex manner of their production both producing and offering a cultural commentary upon the nature of modern time. They are, each in their own way, as compelling as Benjamin's Newhaven fishwife in their indication of a particular spatialization of the temporal that has been produced by the emergence and development of these technologies. And, just as the fishwife seemed to Benjamin to characterize a particular moment of early 19th century sensibility, one which was soon to pass into history, so perhaps we can see these complex articulations of composite photographic time, these ambiguously fissured tableaux, as also having a certain eloquence in relationship to our own moment in history, their poised ambivalence in relationship to the event seeming to indicate a powerful sense of our contemporary anxieties about the relationship between technology, reality and time.

At the beginning of this essay I suggested that images like these, images that were constructed around an internal reflexivity and that offered a little window onto that 'undecidable' complexity in the relationship between technology and medium, between time as an effect of technical production and time as part of a history of cultural representations, were also potentially, almost because of this indeterminacy, powerful vehicles for the representation of much more profound and pervasive concerns about time and modernity. Something of this is explored in the third piece of work that I would like to discuss here, David Claerbout's *Sections of a Happy Moment* (2007) (fig.3.3). This is a work that is not so much a photographic tableau as an exercise in both the dismantling and the expansion of the very concept of the tableau. Premised upon the existence of one brief and transitory 'happy moment', a scene in which a family play with a ball in the courtyard of an estate of tower block apartments, Claerbout offers us a series of extended still images, each taken from a different point of view of the scene. The series is presented as a slow sequence of still projected photographs accompanied by gentle music.

In the 'happy moment' that Claerbout chooses to represent the group of adults and children gaze upward at a ball that has been thrown in the air—that classic signifier of instantaneity, of the event. The group appear to be from the Far East, and this casting points to the way in which the figure of a new—non-specific oriental figure has taken on a certain allegorical force in contemporary art as the 'global citizen': the oriental or perhaps 'pacific rim body' articulating a complex future of late modernity—a utopian future, severed from western imperialism, set in a new globalised economy, but haunted, for the European spectator, by other issues such as the domination of capital, totalitarianism, migration, inequality. This happy moment can be seen in this context then as an allegory of utopianism in modernity: a transient event held in a kind of suspension around which all the forces of modern history revolve.

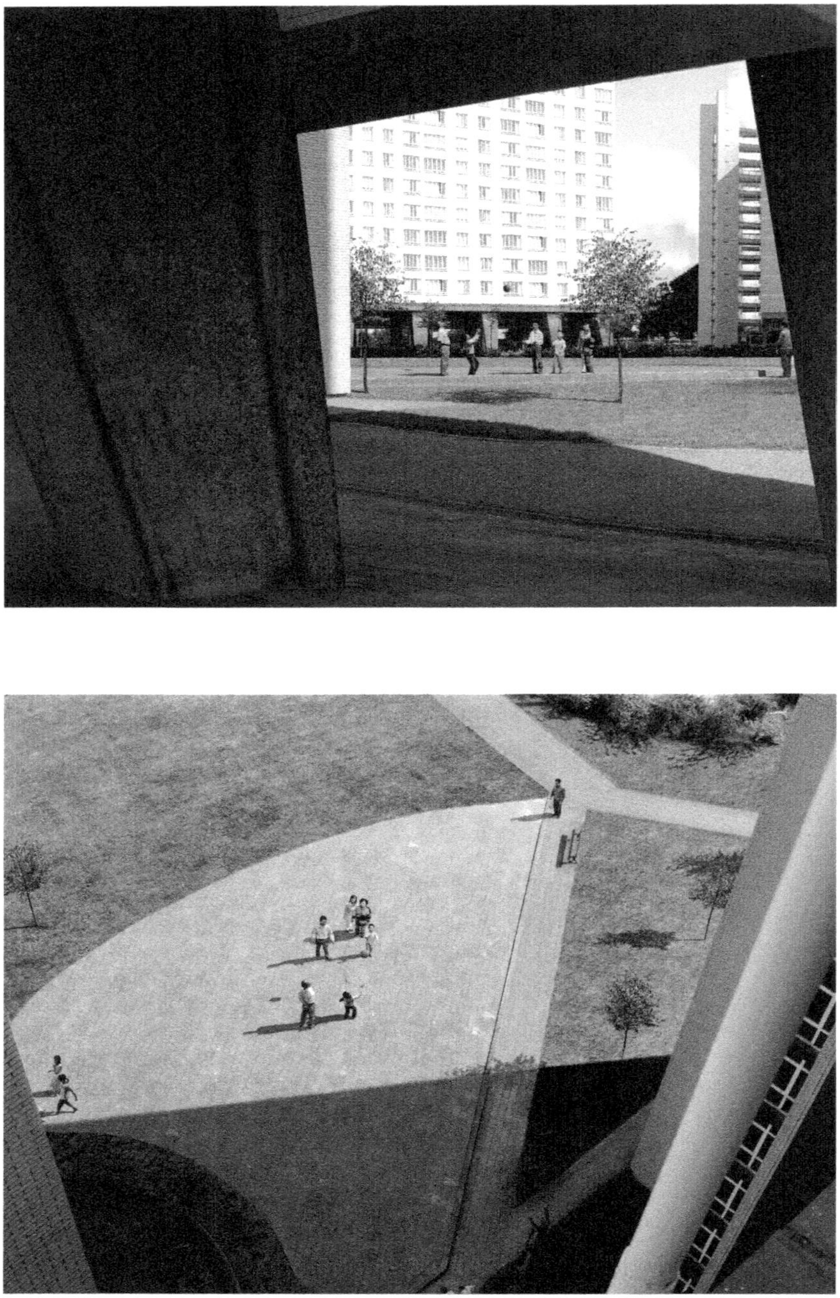

Fig. 3.3 David Claerbout, stills from *Sections of a Happy Moment* (2007). Video projection. Courtesy of the artist and galleries Hauser and Wirth, Zurich, London, and Yvon Lambert, Paris, New York.

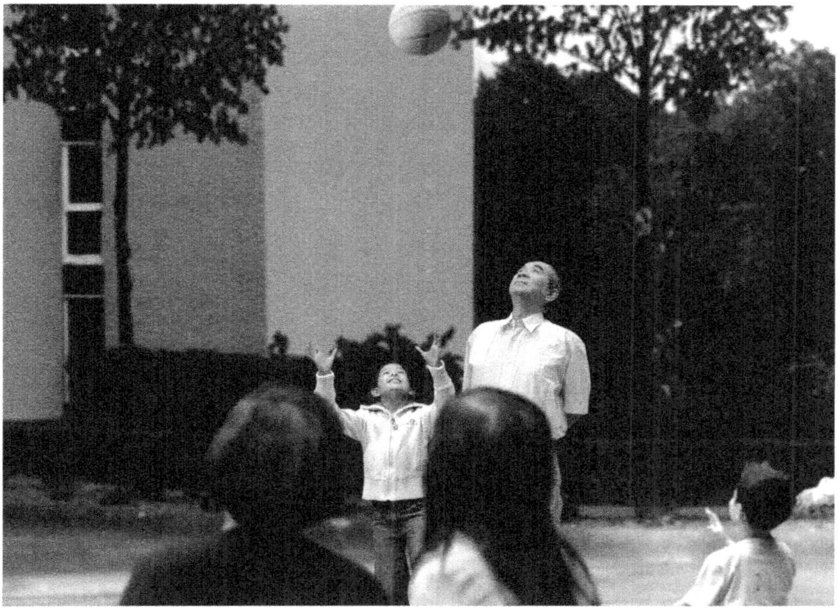

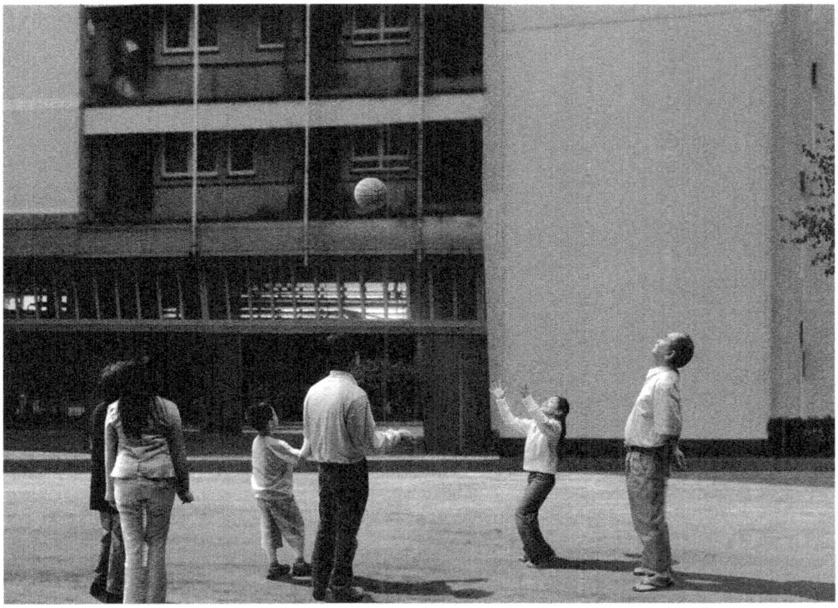

The family group gaze at the ball as other figures walk by or watch from afar. All the figures in the picture are linked by their relationship to this one over-determined object. They each play their role in one spatialized narrative structure, their attention focused upon this one moment when the ball is poised between one state and another, at that moment of undecidability before gravity claims it and it falls into history.

In this case, however, in reality there never was such a moment. The image is an elaborate construction, assembled in a studio. The site was identified and photographed from a number of different perspectives, but the actors in the scene performed their roles in the artist's studio, their images taken from different viewpoints by a number of simultaneous cameras, so that they could be deftly and meticulously inserted into the scene and bestowed there with a virtual solidity in the space that is entirely imaginary. A 21st century elaboration of the 19th century composite photograph, this technique is equal to its forebears in its demonstration of technical virtuosity and the many long hours of labor necessary for its production. It also bears some similarities to those early composites in the vaguely hallucinatory quality of the figures in their occupation of the pictorial space. Through presenting us with a scene that is viewed simultaneously from multiple viewpoints Claerbout offers us a vision of time and space folded in layers around the central event. The decisive moment at the centre of the tableau is thus extended into a space that is uneasily dispersed across multiple viewpoints.

By presenting us with a tableau in three dimensions rather than two Claerbout also fragments any sense of spectatorial unity that the tableau convention might normally suggest. If the tableau normally demands of us that we as spectators occupy the point of unification, the space of aesthetic contemplation that holds the composition together and stops it falling apart, then here that unitary place of spectatorship is denied. The happy moment is seen from everywhere—not in a filmic narrative sense as viewed by a series of characters in time—but in the sense of a dispersed perspectivalism implicit in the architecture of modernity itself: this is a more metaphysical construction of the concept of surveillance as a pervasive distribution of the gaze.

Claerbout's images are often self-consciously modernist in their careful and considered framing of the subject-matter. This piece of work uses time as a device to disrupt the security of that aesthetic. Here he recognizes the 'event' as a potential point of fracture in the photographic image and he also recognizes the demands it makes upon us as spectators, using it as a device to pose far-reaching questions about what it is that the idea of the photograph is seeking to hold together. In a previous essay about uses of the imagery of the panorama by contemporary artists I have discussed the way in which modern technologies of time, through the challenges they present to our ideas about representational space, constantly put pressure upon the security of the representation of the subject within history. The work that I have described here, despite the sedative effect of the changing slides and the soft music accompanying it, occupies the same space of anxiety. Claerbout presents us with a timed sequence of photographs in which time itself appears to have stopped. But in the very artificial construction of that singular moment around which they revolve he also seems to suggest that this 'happy moment' is only a utopian fantasy, and that the space that we occupy in the world is merely one rather insecure function of those many complex apparatuses, among them photography, through which our experience of time is produced.

Bibliography

¬ Roland Barthes, *Camera Lucida* (New York: Hill and Wang, 1981).

¬ Walter Benjamin, 'A Little History of Photography', in W. Benjamin, *The Work of Art in the Age of Its Technological Reproducibility, and Other Writings on Media* (Cambridge, Mass. and London: The Belknap Press of Harvard University Press, 2008).

¬ Raymond Bellour 'The Film Stilled', *Camera Obscura*, no.24 (September, 1990): 98-123.

¬ Jonathan Crary, *Techniques of the Observer: on Vision and Modernity in the Nineteenth Century* (Cambridge, Massachussets: October Books, 1992).

¬ Jacques Derrida, 'The Photograph as Copy, Archive and Signature' in conversation with Hubertus Amelunxen and Michael Wetzel (1993). Excerpt published in David Campany, *Art and Photography* (London: Phaidon, 2003), 220. The English translation is based on the German translation by Michael Wetzel published in *European Photography*, 20, no.66 17 (Fall 1999/Winter 2000).

¬ Mary Ann Doane, *The Emergence of Cinematic Time: Modernity, Contingency, the Archive* (Cambridge, Massachussetts: Harvard University Press, 2002).

¬ Tom Gunning, 'New Thresholds of vision: instantaneous photography and the early cinema of Lumiere', in Terry Smith (ed.) *Impossible Presence, surface and screen in the photographic era* (Chicago: University of Chicago Press, 2001), 71-101.

¬ Margaret Iversen, *Beyond Pleasure, Freud, Lacan, Barthes* (Philadelphia , Pennsylvania State University Press, 2007).

¬ Gotthold Ephraim Lessing, 'Laokoon', 1766. 'Laocoon' trans. William A Steel, in Lessing: *Laocoon, Nathan the Wise, Minna von Barnhelm* (London: J.M. Dent & Sons, Everyman's Library 1930), 2-110.

part 2

Returning Time / Memory / Order

4 Time and Memory in William Henry Fox Talbot's Calotypes of Oxford and David Octavius Hill and Robert Adamson's of St Andrews

Graham Smith

> Can one narrate time as such, in and of itself? Most certainly not, what a foolish undertaking that would be.
>
> Thomas Mann, *The Magic Mountain*

> But at least, if strength were granted to me for long enough to accomplish my work, I should not fail...to describe men first and foremost as occupying a place, a very considerable place compared with the restricted one which is allotted to them in space, a place on the contrary prolonged past measure—for simultaneously, like giants plunged into the years, they touch epochs that are immensely far apart, separated by the slow accretion of many, many days—in the dimension of Time.
>
> Marcel Proust, *Remembrance of Things Past*

'For me the noise of Time is not sad,' confided Roland Barthes in *Camera Lucida* (Barthes, 1981, 15). 'I love bells, clocks, watches', he continued, 'and I recall that at first photographic implements were related to techniques of cabinetmaking and

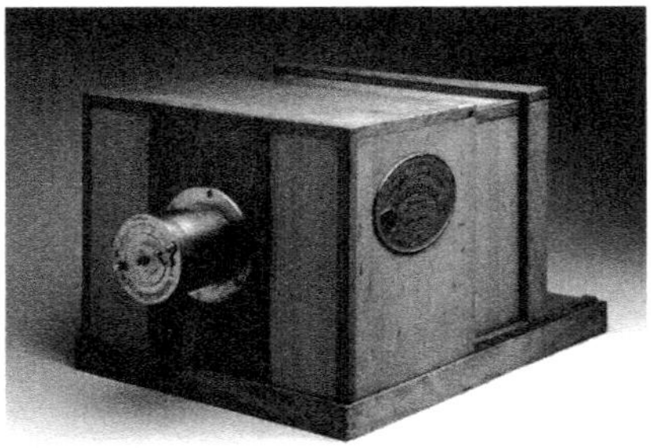

Fig. 4.1 Alphonse Giroux in partnership with Louis-Jacques-Mandé Daguerre, *Daguerreotype Camera*, 1839. The National Media Museum, Bradford. Photograph © Science & Society Picture Library, London.

the machinery of precision: cameras, in short, were clocks for seeing, and perhaps in me someone very old still hears in the photographic mechanism the living sound of the wood.' When he composed this passage, Barthes may have had in mind the cameras made in 1839 by Alphonse Giroux in partnership with Louis-Jacques-Mandé Daguerre (fig. 4.1), or he may have been thinking of the elaborate daguerreotype outfits that were manufactured in Paris a few years later by Pierre Ambroise Richebourg (Spira, 2001, 27). In contrast to those elegant French apparatuses, the earliest cameras associated with William Henry Fox Talbot appear to have been made by a journeyman carpenter on the Lacock Abbey estate in Wiltshire (fig. 4.2). Called 'mouse traps' by Talbot's wife in a letter of 7 September 1835 (Schaaf, 2000, 38), these primitive cameras would not have looked out of place beside the *muscipula diaboli* (the Devil's mousetrap) and the carpenter's tools that Robert Campin painted in the 1420s in the Joseph wing of the Mérode Altarpiece (The Cloisters Collection, The Metropolitan Museum of Art, New York; Schapiro, 1945). Notwithstanding their rough carpentry and simple design, Talbot's rustic cameras are also precursors of Barthes' 'clocks for seeing'.

In the autumn of 1840 Talbot came to realize that the relatively brief units of time measured by clocks and watches were critical to the viability of his invention of photography. This is evident from the manuscript list of negatives that he compiled at Lacock Abbey between November 1839 and October 1840.[1] On 29 September 1840, for instance, Talbot recorded photographing a terracotta sculpture of Diogenes, the ancient Athenian philosopher, in the entrance hall of Lacock Abbey, jotting down the entry 'Diogenes small with g[allic acid] 1' 20".' A week later, he recorded having photographed this sculpture once more, entering 'Diogenes, without sun,

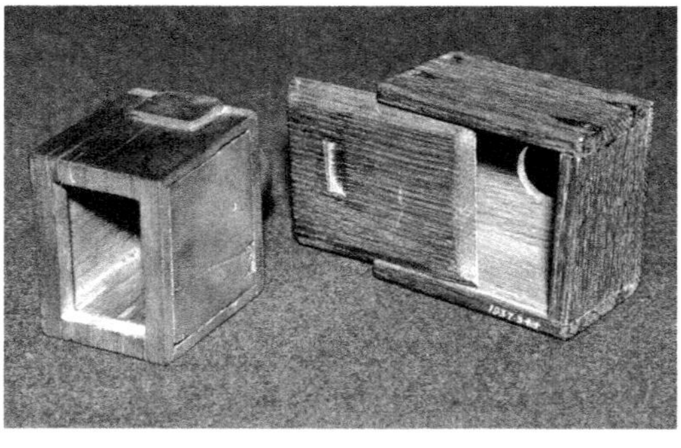

Fig. 4.2 Unidentified Craftsman, *Two of William Henry Fox Talbot Experimental 'mouse trap' Cameras*, ca 1835. The National Media Museum, Bradford. Photograph © Science & Society Picture Library, London.

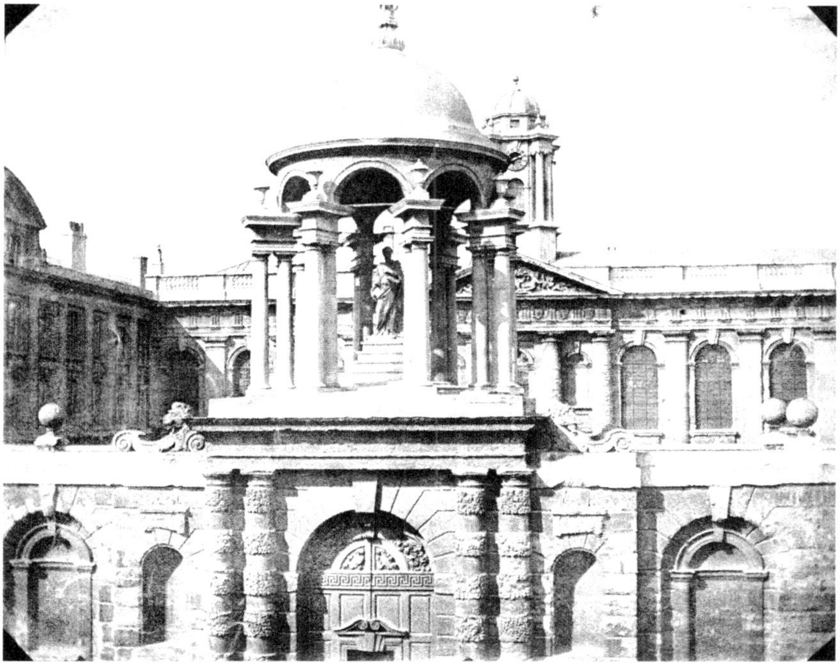

Fig. 4.3 William Henry Fox Talbot, *Queen's College, Entrance Gateway, Oxford*, 9 April 1843. The National Media Museum, Bradford. Photograph © Science & Society Picture Library, London.

17', small.' A pivotal entry, made four days afterwards, on 10 October 1840, records 'C[onstance]'s portrait 30" blue glass,' indicating that Talbot had succeeded in reducing exposure times to a point where it had become practicable to capture live subjects with his mousetraps.

But occasionally time was embedded literally and visually in Talbot's pictures. This is the case, for instance, with a view of Queen's College, Oxford (fig. 4.3), that Talbot made in 1843 and published in 1845 in the third fascicle of *The Pencil of Nature*. In his commentary accompanying this plate Talbot observed:

> In examining photographic pictures of a certain degree of perfection, the use of a large lens is recommended, such as elderly persons frequently employ in reading...It frequently happens, moreover—and this is one of the charms of photography—that the operator himself discovers on examination, perhaps long afterwards, that he has depicted many things he had no notion of at the time. Sometimes inscriptions and dates are found upon the buildings, or printed placards most irrelevant, are discovered upon their walls:

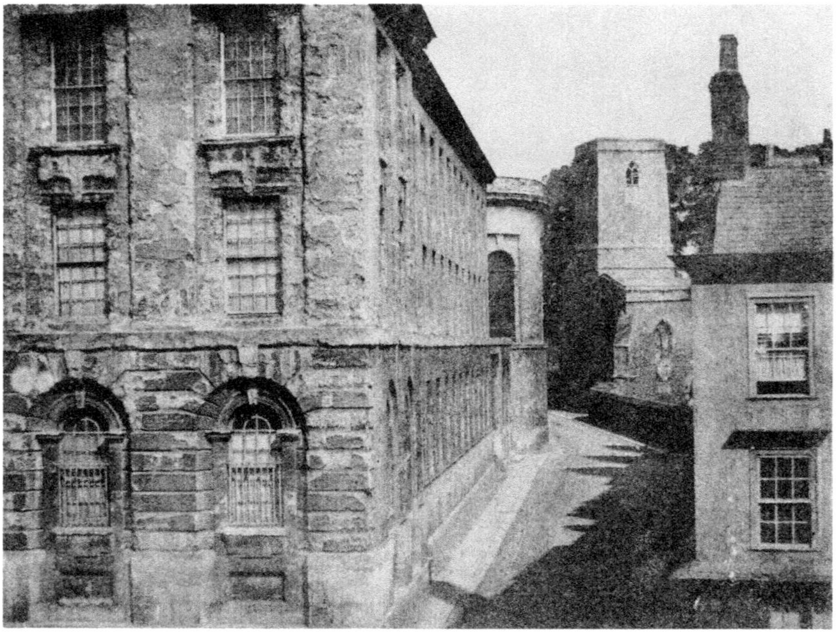

Fig. 4.4 William Henry Fox Talbot, *Part of Queen's College, Oxford*. 4 September 1843. The National Media Museum, Bradford. Photograph © Science & Society Picture Library, London.

> sometimes a distant dial-plate is seen, and upon it—unconsciously recorded—the hour of the day at which the view was taken.

In fact, a magnifying glass is hardly necessary to discover the 'distant dial-plate' in Talbot's view of Queen's College and to see that it records to the minute the time when the negative was taken (soon after two in the afternoon).

Elsewhere in *The Pencil of Nature* Talbot focused upon other ways in which time manifested itself in his photographs. Consider, for instance, his observations concerning the first plate in *The Pencil of Nature*, entitled *Part of Queen's College, Oxford* (fig. 4.4):

> This building presents on its surface the most evident marks of the injuries of time and weather, in the abraded state of the stone, which probably was of a bad quality originally. The view is taken from the other side of the High Street looking North. The Time is morning. In the distance is seen at the end of a narrow street the Church of St Peter's in the East, said to be the most ancient church in Oxford, and built during the Saxon era.

Talbot mentions time at three points in this brief paragraph. In the first sentence the passage of historical time is suggested by the abraded nature of the stone on the 18th century exterior of Queen's College, and in the final sentence the existence of a still more remote time is implicit in the reference to the 12th century church of St Peter's in the East, described by Talbot as 'the most ancient church in Oxford'. In between there is a reference to the 'present' time of the photograph, indicated by Talbot's statement that the photograph was taken in the morning.

Because of the long and complex history of the buildings of Oxford, it might be suggested that the very fabric of time is embedded in Talbot's photograph. In other words, Talbot's picture functions metonymically to allude to various periods in time through the physical structures of Queen's College and St Peter's in the East and by means of the indications of the particular time at which the photograph was taken. Notwithstanding Thomas Mann's conviction concerning the futility of attempting to narrate 'time as such, in and of itself', as he expressed it in *The Magic Mountain* (1924) (Mann, 2005, 641), it may be posited that this photograph provides a readily legible narrative of time. Indeed, it might be suggested that it offers a form of visual grammar or syntax for time: first there is the immediate past, the time when the picture was taken; next there is the 'perfect' tense of the 18th century, which is encapsulated in the view of the exterior of Queen's College; and, finally, the 'pluperfect' is embodied by the church of St Peter's in the East.

Talbot's commentary on the plate entitled *Gate of Christchurch*, which he published in June 1845 in the fourth fascicle of *The Pencil of Nature*, is also infused with the vocabulary of time, suggesting that Christchurch and Oxford are, in many respects, the very embodiment of Time:

> Those who have visited Oxford and Cambridge in vacation time in the summer must have been struck with the silence and tranquillity which pervade those venerable abodes of learning. Those ancient courts and quadrangles and cloisters look so beautiful so tranquil and so solemn at the close of a summer's evening, that the spectator almost thinks he gazes upon a city of former ages, deserted but not in ruins; abandoned by man but not by Time. No other towns in Great Britain awake feelings at all similar. In other towns you hear at all times the busy hum of passing crowds, intent on traffic or on pleasure—but Oxford in the summer season seems the dwelling of the genius of Repose.

Instead of contradicting Talbot's assertion that Oxford during the summer recess appears 'abandoned by man but not by Time', two ghostly gentlemen conversing in the shadows of Pembroke College, on the right side of the composition, and a third figure standing at the end of the wall, on the left side, seem to make visible this sense of abandonment. Conversely, Time, in the form of a prominent clock face on Tom Tower, presides visibly over the entire scene.

Talbot's preoccupation with the ways in which his photographs reveal time is not limited to these three images of the buildings of Oxford but is also apparent from observations prompted by photographs of Lacock Abbey, his own home in the country. In fact, Talbot was clearly enchanted by photography's capacity to make accurate and detailed records of historic monuments—preserving them in time, so to speak—and by its ability to provide the viewer with an authentic window into the past, in part by capturing the arbitrary marks that gave such buildings the patina of time. It is also clear that Talbot relished the opportunities that photographs offered to connect emotionally and visually with the events and personalities of the past. In this regard, he appears to have shared Samuel Johnson's view, articulated in 1775 in *A Journey to the Western Islands of Scotland*, that humankind's contemplation of the past was an activity that was intrinsically elevating. 'Whatever withdraws us from the power of our senses; whatever makes the past, the distant, or the future predominate over the present', affirmed Johnson on arriving at Iona, 'advances us in the dignity of thinking beings (Johnson, 1817, 230).'

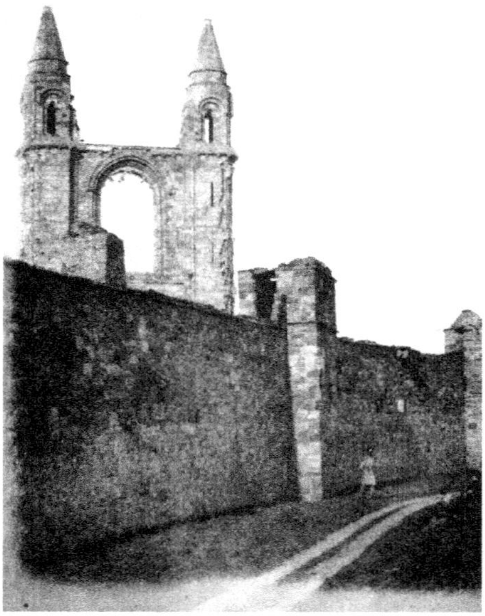

Fig. 4.5 David Octavius Hill and Robert Adamson, *The East Gable of the Cathedral and the Priory Wall from the Northeast*, salt print from a calotype negative, ca 1845. University Library, St Andrews / Hay Fleming Trustees. Photograph courtesy Special Collections, University Library, St Andrews.

Talbot's claims concerning the unique character of Oxford as 'the dwelling of the genius of Repose' are somewhat exaggerated, for very similar observations were made almost precisely contemporaneously about the ancient Scottish burgh of St Andrews, another 'venerable abode of learning.' Writing in April 1844, after having spent a weekend in St Andrews, Henry Cockburn, a prominent Edinburgh jurist, reformer, and author, observed:

> It is an asylum of repose—a city of refuge for those who cannot live in the country, but wish for as little town as possible. And all this in unison with the ruins, the still surviving edifices, the academical institutions, and the past history of the place. On the whole, it is the best Pompeii in Scotland (Cockburn, 1975, 145).

The accuracy of Lord Cockburn's characterization of St Andrews is apparent from a body of photographs taken in and around the town in 1844 or 1845, and published, in large part, in *A Series of Calotype Views of St Andrews*, a photographically illustrated book issued in Edinburgh in 1846 by David Octavius Hill and Robert Adamson.[2] This volume, and other photographic incunabula of St Andrews, came about as a result of Talbot's friendship with the eminent Scottish natural philosopher, Sir David Brewster, who, in 1838, had been appointed Principal of the United College of St Salvator and St Leonard at St Andrews.[3] In the remainder of the present essay I will focus upon three views of St Andrews Cathedral that Hill and Adamson included in the *Series of Calotype Views of St Andrews*, examining them within the framework provided by Talbot's commentaries in *The Pencil of Nature* and considering them similarly as representations or embodiments of time.

The first of these images shows the upper portion of the east gable of the cathedral, with its great east window and twin towers, as seen from the northeast from outside the priory wall (fig. 4.5). 'The time is morning', as Talbot wrote of the first plate in *The Pencil of Nature*, for the masonry is evenly lit by the morning sun, and this is confirmed by the shadow cast by the gentleman standing at the base of the square tower. The great window is empty, except for some precarious fragments of tracery that cling to the masonry and remind us of the arbitrary nature of Time. In addition to establishing scale, the presence of a human figure in this predominantly architectural scene points to the coexistence in this picture of two widely separate historical epochs: on the one hand there are the grandiloquent, ominous, but fragmentary remains of Scotland's medieval past, a past that, in a period of reform in the 1840s, which saw the establishment of the Free Church of Scotland, must have been viewed with some ambivalence; on the other is the narrative 'present,' represented by this figure and by his companions seated on a grassy hillock on the right side of the composition. In a sense, the figure contemplating the remains of St Andrews Cathedral might be one of those 'giants plunged into the

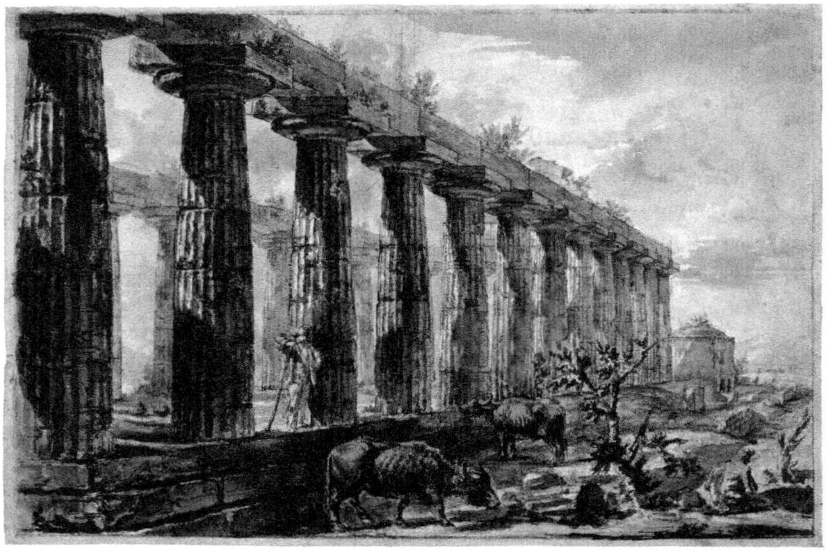

Fig. 4.6 Giovanni Battista Piranesi, *The Temple of Juno at Paestum*, ca 1770/1778, pen and ink and brown wash over chalk on paper, 465 x 765 mm. Rijksmuseum, Amsterdam.

years' that Marcel Proust in the complex final sentence of *Remembrance of Things Past*, described as 'touch[ing] epochs that are immensely far apart, separated by the slow accretions of many, many days (Proust, 1982, III, 1107).'

Hill and Adamson's photograph is linked visually and thematically to a long tradition of images of ruins with figures, a tradition that is exemplified by a drawing of the 1770s by Giovanni Battista Piranesi depicting the Temple of Juno at Paestum (fig. 4.6), in which a herdsman leans against one of the temple's great Doric columns while his animals graze around the building. This tradition was discussed at length in 1953 by Rose Macaulay in her *Pleasure of Ruins* (reprinted 1966), a book of which the declared aim was 'to explore the various kinds of pleasure given to various people at various epochs by the spectacle of ruined buildings (Macaulay, 1966, xv).' Asserting that 'delight in decayed or wrecked buildings' began very early, in her introduction Macaulay laid out some of the principal forms of pleasure that travelers had derived from ruins:

> Since down the ages men have meditated before ruins, rhapsodized before them, mourned pleasurably over their ruination, it is interesting to speculate on the various strands in this complex enjoyment, on how much of it is admiration for the ruin as it was in its prime... how much aesthetic pleasure in its present appearance...how much

> is association, historical or literary, what part is played by morbid pleasure in decay, by righteous pleasure in retribution...by mystical pleasure in the destruction of all things mortal and the eternity of God...by egotistical satisfaction in surviving...by masochistic joy in a common destruction, and by a dozen other entwined threads of pleasurable and melancholy emotion, of which the main strand is, one imagines, the romantic and conscious swimming down the hurrying river of time, whose mysterious reaches, stretching limitlessly behind, glimmer suddenly into view with those wracks washed on to the silted shores (Macaulay, 1966, xv-xvi).

Piranesi's drawing might have been conceived to illustrate the Latin adage '*Sic transit gloria mundi*' (thus passes away the glory of the world), for the Temple of Juno appears to be in the process of returning to nature. The fact that this great structure now serves as a grazing area for cattle and their herdsmen prompts viewers to contemplate its melancholy decline, while also transporting them into the remote period in the history of ancient Italy that brought the building into being. In other words, the drawing juxtaposes past and present in such a way as to stimulate viewers to ponder the dramatic contrast between ancient greatness and contemporary rusticity. At the same time, Piranesi's precise rendering of the architectural perspective of the Doric colonnade gives the viewer an accurate and compelling sense of how impressive the structure had been 'in its prime'. It is noteworthy that the site also prompted travelers to contemplate their own mortality, not only in the sense of viewing the ruinous nature of the building as a metaphor for their own futures, but also because of the real danger to which they had exposed themselves by visiting a site that was surrounded by a pestilential swamp which put travelers at risk of contracting malarial fever.

Hill and Adamson's photograph of the precinct wall and east gable of St Andrews Cathedral offers many of the same forms of ruin-pleasure, but it also has the additional dimension of depicting Roman Catholic remains in post-Reformation Scotland. As such, it attests to what Samuel Johnson, writing about Elgin Cathedral in his *Journey to the Western Islands of Scotland*, defined as 'proof of the waste of reformation (Johnson, 1817, 30).' In fact, Jeffrey Hart has argued that the principal theme running throughout Johnson's book is the tragedy of 'the destruction of pre-Reformation Christian Culture (Hart, 1960, 45).' Earlier in the book, when he visited the 'ruins of ancient magnificence' at St Andrews, Johnson observed with profound sadness the 'poor remains' of the cathedral, which had been 'demolished, as is well known, in the tumult and violence of Knox's reformation (Hart, 1960, 3).' For Johnson, such fragmentary ruins also functioned as metaphors for the wide-ranging decay in culture and society that he discerned in contemporary Scotland.

What Johnson termed the 'mournful memorials' of pre-Reformation St Andrews may have inspired in some visitors a 'morbid pleasure in decay' or a 'righteous pleasure in retribution' (Macaulay), but in most educated travelers they had more likely generated feelings of melancholy, which had been intensified by the modern town's 'silence and solitude of inactive indigence and gloomy depopulation'. In addition, any lingering religious antipathy felt towards the pre-Reformation Christian ruins must have been offset for most viewers by the general admiration for the Gothic style that prevailed in the 18th and 19th centuries and by the fact that such fragments came to be perceived by many as 'national antiquities' (Choay, 2001, 47). The Gothic was certainly adopted in Britain during the 19th century as the only appropriate style for church building, and it is noteworthy in the present context that in 1846 even the headquarters of the new Free Church of Scotland in Edinburgh were executed in this style.

In the end, however, whether the gentleman in Hill and Adamson's photograph was relishing or regretting the ruinous state of St Andrews Cathedral is immaterial, for the important point is that his meditation had led him to conjure up the structure's pre-Reformation magnificence and, as Macaulay put it, '[to swim] down the hurrying river of time.' In other words, what Macaulay termed the 'broken beauty' (Macaulay, 1966, xvii) of such ruins must have caused writers like Johnson and artists such as Hill to project themselves into the distant past (and perhaps also to ponder with agreeable pessimism the uncertainties of the immediate future). And, finally, the very act of Hill and Adamson's photographing the cathedral and other pre-Reformation ruins in St Andrews affirmed the status of the fragments, for the photograph itself was a new form of monument, at once constituting a 'certificate of presence' and, implicitly, authenticating and authorizing the subject (Choay, 2001, 10).

The second photograph I have chosen to discuss was taken from a vantage point adjacent to the south transept of the cathedral and shows the first level of the east gable wall of the sanctuary, the area that once contained the shrine of St Andrew (fig. 4.7). The time is early afternoon, for the sun is now in the southwest. The range of three 12th century windows provides the primary interest in the picture, but the photograph also records where the walls of the sanctuary connected to the gable and includes a fragment of the east wall of the south aisle chapel. As was the case with the previous photograph, the architecture is complemented by a figure wearing a top hat. In this case, however, he is absorbed into the remains of the masonry that formed the angle of the south wall of the sanctuary and the east end of the aisle chapel, seeming almost to fuse with it. Like his counterpart in the first picture, this individual provides a human yardstick for the immense structure, but he is also a reflective, even poetic character, who appears to be deep in a personal meditation upon the remains of the past. Moreover, he appears to wish to be assimilated bodily into their fabric, as if he wanted literally to be embraced by or entombed within the architectural remains. It is noteworthy, perhaps, that he turns his back on the very part of the fabric that was most redolent with association, the area of the choir that once housed the relics of St Andrew.

For some, this photograph may bring to mind a famous drawing of about 1780 by the Swiss artist, Johann Heinrich Füssli, the study known as *The Artist Overwhelmed by the Magnitude of the Fragments of Antiquity* (Zürich, Kunsthaus, Graphische Sammlung). Like the artist in Füssli's study, the Victorian gentleman in Hill and Adamson's photograph transforms what might have been a straightfor-

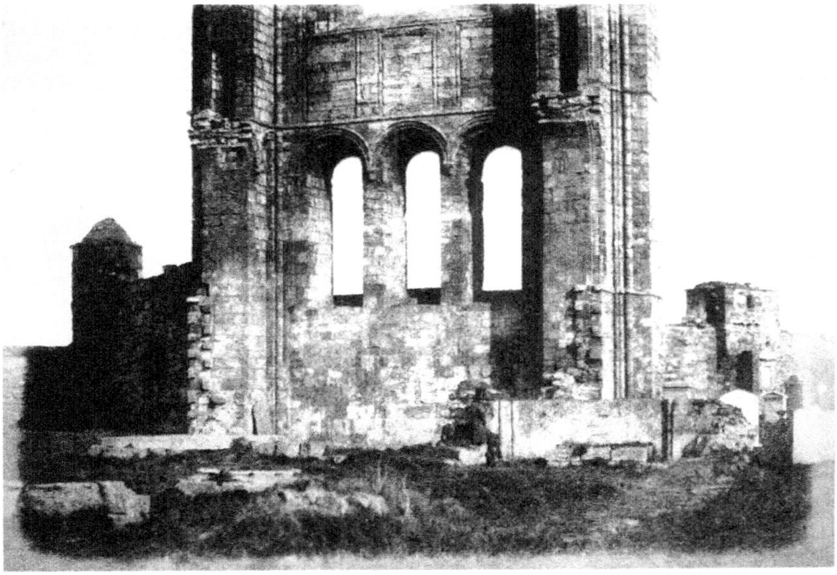

Fig. 4.7 David Octavius Hill and Robert Adamson, *Near View of the East Gable of the Cathedral from the Southwest*, salt print from a calotype negative, ca 1845. University Library, St Andrews / Hay Fleming Trustees. Photograph courtesy Special Collections, University Library, St Andrews.

ward documentary image into a meditation on time and mortality, articulating a visual soliloquy on the scale of the achievements of the past, while also drawing attention to the impermanence of even the most grandiose of humankind's religious creations—'*hic transit gloria monasteriorum*,' as Macaulay put it (Macaulay, 1966, 345). It is also reasonable to think that the picture is a meditation upon mortality, for the figure sits in close proximity to a the ancient burial ground for the parish of St Andrews.

The desire to connect with the past and to commune with the dead was a common theme in England and in Scotland during the 18th and 19th centuries, one that was expressed famously by Thomas Gray in 1751 in his 'Elegy Written in a Country Churchyard'. One verse in particular provides a fitting caption to Hill and Adamson's picture:

> Perhaps in this neglected spot is laid
> Some heart once pregnant with celestial fire;
> Hands, that the rod of empire might have swayed,
> Or waked to ecstasy the living lyre.

Gray's 'Epitaph,' at the end of this poem, might also be read prophetically as a memorial to Robert Adamson, who, on 18 January1848, less than two years after the publication of the *Series of Calotype Views of St Andrews*, would be buried in the family grave, a few yards from the spot where the gentleman is seated in Hill and Adamson's photograph:

> Here rests his head upon the lap of earth
> A youth to fortune and to fame unknown.
> Fair Science frowned not on his humble birth,
> And Melancholy marked him for her own.

Hill attended his friend's burial in St Andrews, as is indicated by a moving letter that he wrote later the same day to his friend and future brother-in-law, the painter Joseph Nöel Paton. 'I have today assisted in consigning to the cold earth all that was earthly of my amiable true & affectionate Robert Adamson', Hill recorded. 'He died in the full hope of a blessed resurrection. His truehearted family is mourning sadly, especially his brother the Doctor—who has watched [over] him as a child during his long illness. I have seldom seen such a deep & manly sorrow (Stevenson, 2002, 18).'

My third photograph offers a distant view of the cathedral complex, looking west from the harbor to the priory walls, which enclose the 12th century tower of St Regulus in addition to the east gable and west front of the cathedral (fig. 4.8). (According to legend, it was St Regulus who brought the bones of St Andrew to Scotland in the 4th century). The time is early afternoon. Marooned in the harbor itself, in the near foreground, are two sea-going vessels, whose tall masts are canted at awkward angles. Beyond, partly concealing the priory walls, can be seen the vernacular buildings of the fisher community. Among the masts, spires and towers there is also a chimney stack, an intrusion from the 19th century, which provides a counterbalance to the west tower of the cathedral. Seated in the immediate foreground is a young boy who may be dreaming of a life at sea. For many viewers, however, Hill and Adamson's photograph may bring to mind Francis Bacon's vivid metaphor, in *The Advancement of Learning* (1605), characterizing 'antiquities' as 'remnants of history which have casually escaped the shipwreck of time (Bacon, 1605, Second Book, II, 1).' In the plural, the phrase 'shipwrecks of time' perfectly describes the nature of the ruins of the cathedral and the church of St Regulus as they appear in Hill and Adamson's photograph. It is also relevant in this context that the idea that a ship may signify the church is, of course, as old as Christianity itself. Images that come to mind range from Giotto's mosaic *Navicella*

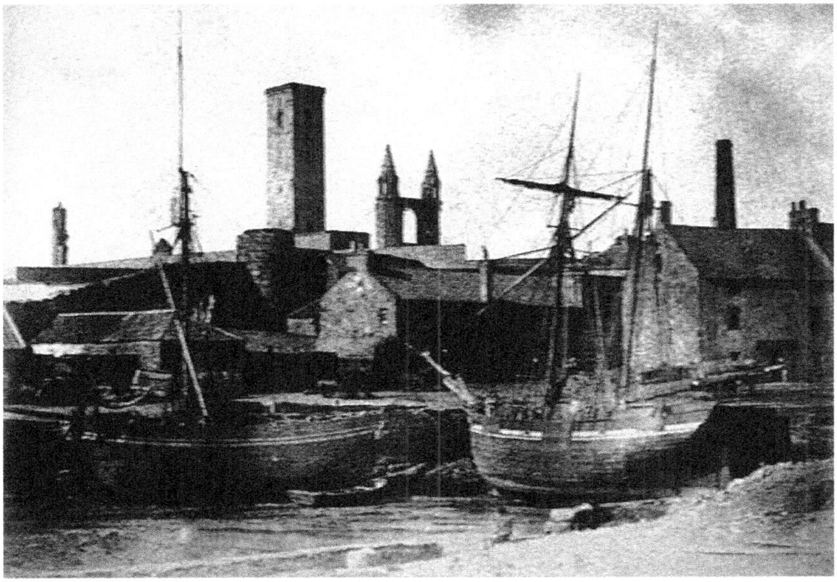

Fig. 4.8 David Octavius Hill and Robert Adamson, *St Andrews Harbor with the Cathedral Precinct Wall, St Rule's Tower and the Cathedral from the Southeast*, salt print from a calotype negative, ca 1845, University Library, St Andrews. Photograph courtesy Special Collections, University Library, St Andrews.

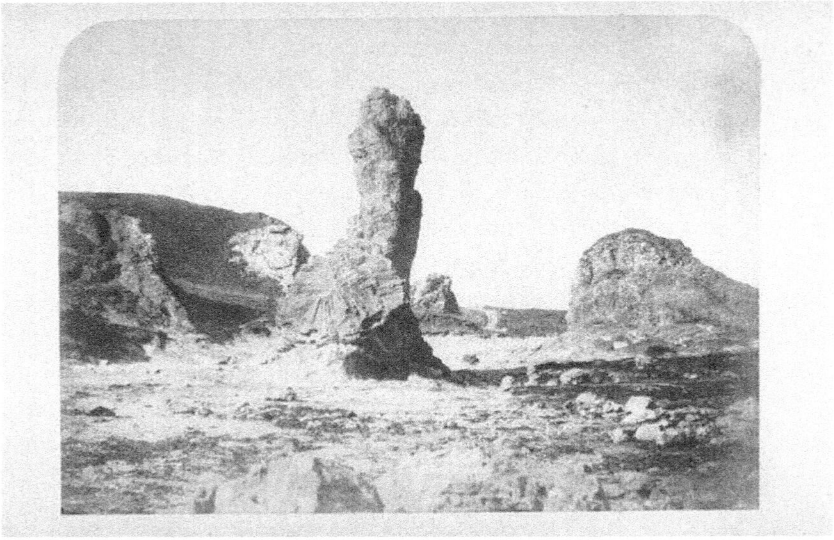

Fig. 4.9 David Octavius Hill and Robert Adamson, *The Rock and Spindle by St Andrews*, salt print from a calotype negative, ca 1845, University Library, St Andrews. Photograph courtesy Special Collections, University Library, St Andrews.

on the narthex of Old St Peter's in Rome and Gianlorenzo Bernini's *Barcaccia* in the Piazza di Spagna to the model ships that still hang today over the crossings of medieval Scandinavian churches.

In keeping with Talbot's comments on his photograph of the gate of Christchurch, the spectator viewing this photograph might think that he too 'gazes upon a deserted city of former ages...abandoned by man but not by Time.' Not only is there no 'busy hum of passing crowds', there is no town whatsoever. The impression that time has stopped is in keeping with Lord Cockburn's description of St Andrews as 'an asylum of repose—a city of refuge for those who cannot live in the country, but wish for as little town as possible (Cockburn, 1975, 228).' But Hill and Adamson's picture may also be thought of as a tapestry in which the principal theme is Time. By interweaving past eras by means of the masts and towers silhouetted against the bleached sky, the photograph provides a synoptic panorama of a segment of history that extends from the early 12th century to the mid-19th. In this respect, it is similar to Talbot's first plate in *The Pencil of Nature, Part of Queen's College, Oxford*, in the manner in which it 'narrates' time.

I want to end by introducing one other photograph from Hill and Adamson's *Series of Calotype Views of St Andrews*. This is a view of the so-called Rock and Spindle (fig. 4.9), a geological curiosity and natural monument that is situated in a sheltered cove two miles along the coast, to the east of St Andrews. The vertical rock (or distaff) is the plug of a long-extinct volcano that has been exposed over the ages by the relentless ebb and flow of the ocean, whereas the spindle is the circular form, about twelve feet in diameter, made up of pyramids of basalt which give the overall mass a star-like appearance. In the 1840s a favorite Sunday excursion from St Andrews was to walk along the cliffs to picnic by the Rock and Spindle. Once there, excursionists could wonder at what Sir Archibald Geikie, Professor of Geology at the University of Edinburgh from 1871 to 1882, once termed 'the inner architecture of volcanoes' (Knight, 1903, 4) and attempt to connect with a time that was so distant as to be beyond normal human comprehension. A prolonged meditation upon time may also have been prompted by the popular name given to this curiosity, for the spindle and distaff are themselves ancient symbols of time, referring specifically to life times (or life lines) that would be cut short by Atropos, the oldest of the three Fates. It might be said, then, that the Rock and Spindle constitutes a geological emblem or hieroglyph signifying Time.

When they made their way back to St Andrews along the coastal path, Victorian excursionists may have been infused with tea and Time and naturally predisposed to draw visual and thematic connections between the ancient chimney of the Rock and Spindle and the historic towers and spires that of the cathedral precinct (and the contemporary chimney stack) that drew them back to St Andrews. Fur-

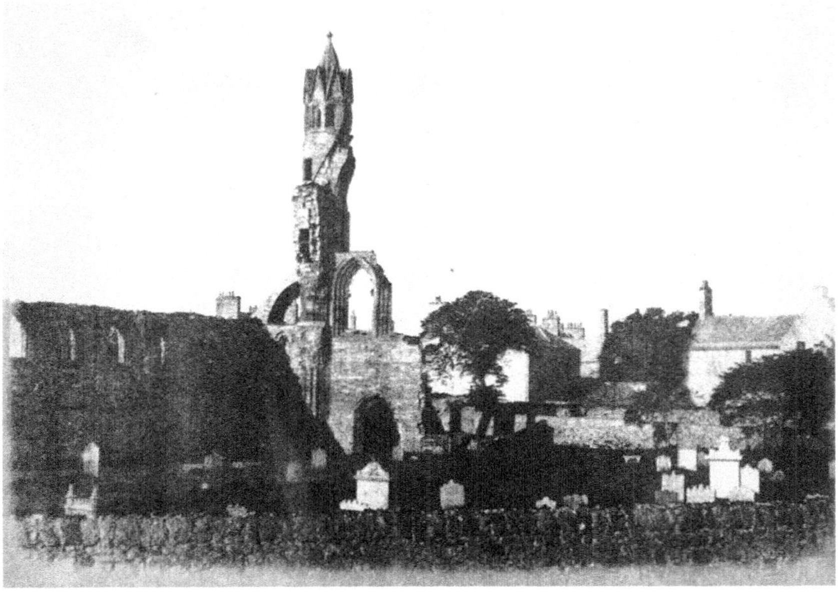

Fig. 4.10 David Octavius Hill and Robert Adamson, *Near view of the West Gable of the Cathedral from the Northeast*, salt print from a calotype negative, ca 1845, University Library, St Andrews. Photograph courtesy Special Collections, University Library, St Andrews.

thermore, as they walked along the path by the north segment of the priory wall, their recollected image of the Rock and Spindle may have fused with the near view of the west gable of the cathedral, with its solitary surviving tower (fig. 4.10). Some romantics may also have been inspired by these visual analogies to ruminate upon and wonder at the seamlessness of the vast tapestry that is Time.

Acknowledgements

I would like to thank Jan Baetens, Alex Streitberger, and Hilde Van Gelder for inviting me to take part in the conference, 'Time and Photography', held at Leuven and Louvain-la-Neuve in March 2008, and I would also like to compliment Rein Deslé and Mieke Bleyen on their roles in the planning and administration of this exceptional event. Cilla Jackson and Norman Reid, friends and former colleagues at the University of St Andrews, were typically helpful in providing me with high resolution scans of photographs by David Octavius Hill and Robert Adamson in Special Collections. Magdalena Mayo was similarly efficient in providing me with excellent scans of the Giroux-Daguerre and Talbot cameras and Talbot photographs from the Science and Society Picture Library Collection in London.

Notes

[1] Four pages from this manuscript are reproduced as the endpapers of Schaaf, 2000.

[2] For earlier studies of this album, see Smith, 2003.

[3] On Brewster's role in the introduction of Talbot's process into St Andrews, see Morrison-Low, 2001.

Bibliography

¬ Francis Bacon, *The Two Books of Francis Bacon, of the Proficience and Advancement of Learning, Divine and Humane* (London: Henrie Tomes, 1605).

¬ Roland Barthes, *Camera Lucida: Reflections on Photography* (New York: Hill and Wang, 1981).

¬ Françoise Choay, *The Invention of the Historic Monument* (Cambridge: Cambridge University Press, 2001).

¬ Henry Cockburn, *Circuit Journeys*, reprint edition (Edinburgh: James Thin Mercat Press, 1975).

¬ Thomas Gray, 'Elegy Written in a Country Churchyard' (London: Dodsley, 1751).

¬ Jeffrey Hart, 'Johnson's *A Journey to the Western Islands*: History as Art', *Essays in Criticism*, 10, 1 (1960): 44-59.

¬ Samuel Johnson, *A Journey to the Western Islands of Scotland* (Glasgow: Stanhope Press, 1817).

¬ William Angus Knight, *Andreanopolis Being Writings in Praise of St Andrews* (Edinburgh: David Douglas, 1903).

¬ Rose Macaulay, *Pleasure of Ruins*, reprint edition (New York: Walker and Company, 1966).

¬ Thomas Mann, *The Magic Mountain* (New York, London, Toronto: Alfred A. Knopf, 2005).

¬ A. D. Morrison-Low, 'Brewster, Talbot and the Adamsons: The Arrival of Photography in St Andrews', *History of Photography*, 28, 3 (Summer, 2001): 130-141.

¬ Marcel Proust, *Remembrance of Things Past* (New York: Vintage Books, 1982).

¬ Larry J. Schaaf, *The Photographic Art of William Henry Fox Talbot* (Princeton and Oxford: Princeton University Press, 2000).

¬ Meyer Schapiro, '"Muscipula Diaboli," The Symbolism of the Mérode Altarpiece', *The Art Bulletin*, 27, 3 (September, 1945): 182-187.

¬ Graham Smith, 'Imagination and the Genius of Antiquity at St Andrews', in *Northern Light: Photographs by David Octavius Hill and Robert Adamson from the University of St Andrews*, exh. cat. (Middletown, Connecticut: Davison Art Center, Wesleyan University, 2003), 29-45.

¬ S. F. Spira with Eaton S. Lothrop, Jr. and Jonathan B. Spira, *The History of Photography as seen through the Spira* Collection (New York: Aperture, 2001).

¬ Sara Stevenson, *The Personal Art of David Octavius Hill* (New Haven: Yale University Press, 2002).

5 Between Present and Past: Photographic Portugal of the 1950s

Susana S. Martins

The image of a place is always formed by a multitude of cultural mediations where photographs play a crucial and unquestionable role. This article aims at investigating how photography, mainly in the temporal dimensions and qualities it evokes, relates with broader phenomena such as national discourses, identities and representations. In order to tackle this particular problem, I will concentrate on a single case study, focusing on photographic travel books on Portugal published during the 1950s and the 1960s. In the first part of this essay, a wide approach on photographic travel books as decisive agents in nation-building processes is outlined, with particular emphasis given to the fact these books are 'time-structured' and 'time-proposing devices'. The second part is devoted to the concrete case of Portugal, where the relevance of time in photographic travel books and in the spreading of national narratives is more thoroughly taken into consideration. Starting from some visual examples, my point is to examine how photographs, by forging temporal environments and pointing to historical landmark moments, contribute to the creation, maintenance or denial of recurrent Portuguese fictions. Moreover, I also demonstrate how ideological frames can be understood and perceived as a matter of time.

Imaging and Imagining

The simple name of a country always implies the instant production of an image. Obviously, this image has multiple dimensions and can assume a wide variety of forms: one can actually imagine the country's shape and its position on a map, remember its most significant and iconic monuments, a particular kind of landscape, a traditional custom, the colors of the flag or the gastronomic specialties. Furthermore, a country can also be related to certain features that characterize it in terms of the experiences one had or can have there: some places are understood as romantic, others as exotic, some are culturally fervent, others wild, almost unknown and adventurous. In any case however, it is plainly understood that it is not necessary to travel to a country to have an idea or an opinion on it. Obviously, the development of a country's image is a process that is hard to define as this image is culturally constructed and historically changeable. But if there is such a thing as an 'image' of a country, this image is predominantly shaped by a multitude of other cultural mediations to which we are primarily exposed. On a further level, this general 'image' of a country is always formed by other types of images, in the sense of W.J.T. Mitchell's 'family of images', whose genealogy includes graphical, optical, perceptual, mental and verbal images (Mitchell, 1984, 505).

Amongst this ample family of images, the role played by photographic mediations is a highly significant one, not only because photographs are ubiquitous but also for their qualities of visuality, resemblance and indexicality. Moreover, even if one can 'imagine' a country in the same light as Benedict Anderson and consider the nation as an 'imagined community' (Anderson, 1983, 6), one cannot neglect the simultaneous existence of a visual body of images where this nation is pictured and recorded. In such images we can actually see the country in some of its aspects, namely by viewing its landscapes, its villages, its people, etc. These pictures are widely accessible for they are material objects integrated in vigorous circulation networks and therefore, they are able to efficiently reach a large number of viewers who, most of the time, are unintentionally confronted with them. All together, photographs enable the inhabitants of a certain place to see each other and to see their own country, at the same time that they provide a representation of that very same country for foreigners. In the end, and despite how different their manifestations and contexts may be, they undoubtedly create and contribute to a common imagery of a defined place.

Guided by Pictures: Freedom and Blindness

It became evident in the study of the particular case of the international image of Portugal during the 1950s to focus on the centrality of photographic images. Photographs are indeed to be found all over, but from the great variety of shapes they can assume (postcards, press reportages, photo-essays, personal photo albums, books, touristic or propagandistic advertisements, to name but a few), I will here draw particular attention to a specific kind of object: travel and touristic photographic books.

The photographic travel books I here propose to analyze are primarily inscribed within a touristic context but it should be noted that they are not so much guides (in the sense of being books that provide all kinds of practical information such as hotels or restaurants) as they are general books on countries, in which the notion of travel is anyway never absent. The task of these books appears to be an introducing and invitational one for they really present a country both geographically and culturally to a traveler with little prior knowledge. The relationship established with questions of nationality and national representation is evident and lies fundamentally in the fact that these books seem to function at first as 'cartes-de-visite' of a country, providing a wide collection of its particularities, of what is 'different and out of the ordinary' (Ramamurthy, 1996), but in the end they turn out to be much more than that.

But what makes the pictures in these travel books so particular? As Allan Sekula pointed out in his seminal text 'On the invention of photographic meaning', 'all photographic communication seems to take place within the conditions of a kind of binary folklore. That is, there is a "symbolist" folk-myth and a "realist" folk-myth (Sekula, 1982, 108),' the first being commonly associated with art photography, metaphors and affective expression while the second is more often related to documentary photography, reportage, witnessing and informative objectivity. Departing from this double mythology, I would say here that one of the distinctive features of travel books' photographs lies in the fact that they perfectly embrace this duality, carrying out a negotiation between a documentary and an artistic tradition. They comprise both these myths simultaneously because on the one hand, they are an analogon of what exists, an inventory of what can be seen and experienced, while on the other hand, they severely embody the symbolic function, given that they represent and stand for a national identity.

Although the notion of national identity is controversial enough, I am inclined to adopt the idea of Anne-Marie Thiesse which says that the concept of the nation does not coincide with the figure of the state or with the geographical limits of the country, for the nation is mainly a principle, a fiction, a narrative. However, she continues, if 'the nation originates from a postulate and an invention...it can only survive by means of a collective adhesion to that very same fiction [*si la nation naît d'un postulat et d'une invention...elle ne vit que par l'adhésion collective à cette fiction*] (Thiesse, 1999, 14).' Accepting that the nation is fundamentally an invention, this invention is something that has to be taught and widely promulgated in order to become a profound and interiorized national feeling. Pictures in guidebooks undoubtedly participate in the consolidation of the national fiction. And they additionally carry a complex, double assignment in the sense that they have to certify what exists and at the same time give the nation principle, which could not be more vague and abstract, a visual expression, an actual representation. They show not only what to see but also, and especially, how it should be read and interpreted. Their involvement in representing nationality is always a dual movement which can be firstly identified as going from reality to fiction (the corpus of existing images creates a common imaginary and participates in the construction of the national image), but it also moves from fiction to reality, in the sense that pictures ought to give an expression to national principles and narratives previously recognizable and already soundly established.

Photographic travel books configure a particular kind of visual and descriptive archive of the country they refer to. Naturally enough, and like any other archive, they hold to an idea of neutrality but in the end they are far from neutral as they are always the result of an interpretative, biased selection and they are helplessly connected to grand structures of power and larger discourses (like tourism or politics, for example) that will necessarily restrain and determine their final appearance. In their alleged transparency, they seem to impartially show the reader what the country is like, while in reality they only shape an extremely selective inventory of what is worth seeing. These guidebooks propose specific circuits to be followed, they highlight certain places and experiences in detriment of others, delineating the topographies of a travel and mapping the diagrams of influence. As expected, what is suggested in them changes from book to book, according to the type of public they want to reach and to the interests of the networks of power they are inscribed in. But independently from their circumstances of production and reception, to a certain extent, they are always supposed to influence and adjust travelers' behaviors and choices, even if this can be attained in a clearly non-imposing style.

It is precisely because of this feature that travel books become very powerful objects: assertive and pointing, in terms of content, and at the same time self-effacing and disguising their guiding responsibility, which is never completely innocent. The supposed transparency we find in most of these books turns them into trustworthy items, objective catalogs where the reader finds herself in the controlling position of choosing. I believe we can apply here William W. Stowe's words, written however in the context of 19th century travel, where he states that it seems that:

> one of the guidebooks' most important functions was to endow the traveller with all the freedom and power of the bourgeois consumer by serving as a catalog of tempting products among which he or she was free to choose and by constructing an implied reader who felt well informed, authoritative, and ultimately superior to other tourists, indigenous peoples, and previous generations (Stowe, 1994, 45).

These photographic travel books follow metonymically a dynamic in which the entire country, by the presentation of some of its aspects, is meant to be thoroughly represented. Also metonymically, the ordinary traveler/reader, in buying, consuming, and possessing the book (always an incomplete portrait of the nation), starts the process of consuming and possessing the country in question. The concept of possession is here twofold: what you can buy and therefore consume and benefit from in that place (travel as commodity), and the possession of knowledge about your destination. There is something very paradoxical about touristic travel for the foremost motivation is usually related to the pursuit of a feeling of novelty (being for the first time in a certain location where one has never been before and where one has everything to discover), but simultaneously, that novelty cannot be too extreme. Travel books crucially mediate in the comfortable process of making the completely unknown sufficiently familiar. The typical tourist of those years, and even the contemporary tourist, looks for new experiences, avoiding nonetheless the danger of total freedom which might lead to an undesirable sense of chaos. There is a necessity to look at the map, to know the shape of the country and its location, and to learn something about the place that should prepare the traveler for what to expect. Without this expectation it is not possible for the traveler to achieve the sought-after fulfillment that the trip experience is supposed to provide. Every travel is motivated by a previous expectation (even if it is the expectation of the totally unexpected) and travel books are, among other devices, powerful agents in reassuring the reader of the safety he or she seeks to find. But strangely enough, as Barthes has already observed in his text on the 'Blue Guide', travel books are, in the end, exactly the opposite of what they promise to be: they are no more than mere instruments of 'blindness' (see text 'Le Guide Bleu' in Barthes, 1957, 138).

Time as Structure

Focusing now more closely on the subject of time, I will outline how present and decisive time is found within illustrated travel guides or books. My point here will be to explore the different time levels that can overlap in these objects in order to understand travel books in terms of their temporal structure.

As one attempts to tackle this problem by paying particular attention to the circumstances of production, it can be observed that photographic travel books integrate *a)* the 'time of the actual travel' carried out by the photographer and the writer (times that may or may not coincide with each other). At this point, pictures function as witnesses of a concrete presence in specific places, and this first level of temporality is mostly attested via photography's indexical character.

On a further level these books also incorporate *b)* the 'condensed time'. In order to make a transposition of the real experience of travel into a book, the pictures are submitted to a tight process of selection, and this choice shall suggest what the country is like and which places are relevant enough to deserve a visit. The time of the real travel, already shortened in the initial amount of photographic records (which can never reproduce every aspect of the trip), is once again summarized into the time of a photographic sequence. It is of course an artificial and interpretative time that is at stake, forged in principle by the editorial team who outlines the final creation of a country's image, as it will be published in the end. For the construction of this condensed time, different travel times of different photographers can be gathered in order to build a single sequence that shall express a very specific image. Even if indirectly, it reflects what is intended to be apprehended.

But if we also scrutinize these photographic travel books by concentrating on their circumstances of reception, from the perspective of the readers or travelers (and I am here simply considering the typical figure of the tourist of those years, going to a foreign location for the first time), we find that other categories of time generally converge in them. First and foremost, like in any other book, we find in these books the *c)* 'time of reading', the actual time involved in the act itself—starting, finishing, choosing only some pages, coming back to certain passages, etc.

By paying more attention to the photographs themselves and to what they expose as subject, one can additionally refer to *d)* a 'represented time', the time of the depicted scene. This is not simply the time that allows a photographic subject matter to be placed as a moment within a concrete timeline, but it can also refer to another temporal dimension. A particular picture can actually be shot in a precise moment of a given day, in a concrete year, but visually allude to another temporal moment or even evoke a certain 'eternal' time, solid and almost surpassing temporality itself.

But if we consider guide books as a kind of compacted travel, we can also detect here *e)* an 'anticipation time' which is clearly a future one. The reader is offered the possibility to see and to travel before the travel itself. He or she can manage an imaginary journey in the sense that it is both mentally produced and supplied by pictures and images. It is a mediated practice that shall result in the formation of a general image of that country, which enables the viewer to anticipate and experience what she has not seen yet. This anticipation becomes also a planning time for the reader will be able to make decisions, through the pictures, about which places she wants to visit in function of the time available for the travel. Touristic books are thus influential agents in anticipating the time of the travel—for the traveler will only choose to go and experience the things she already knows something about.

Then, photographic travel books also embrace *f)* a 'retrospective time'. They make it possible for the traveler to perform an imaginary post-travel by taking active part in the structuring of the memories and in the remembrance of the most impressive experiences. Manifestly different from personal photo-albums, it seems to me that photographic travel books still comprise the possibility of arranging a mental map of the most important aspects to bear in mind.

Finally, not only through the reading, but also during the concrete act of traveling are photographic travel books present as well, in the sense that the classical practice of tourism is very much about seeing in reality what we have already seen in mediations. At this point, and this is what interests me the most, travel turns out to be an act of returning to where we have never in fact been, and travel books configure thus *g)* a 'returning time'. Strangely enough, this practice seems to defy the proof-like character of photographs: if photographs seem to attest at first to the existence of particular features in a specific place (and the traveler displaces herself to an actual destination because she believes the pictures), the journey itself appears to function not as a discovery but as a confirmation that reality matches with what the pictures showed it would be like.

The Barefoot Countess: Time as Subject

After this brief characterization, we can conclude that travel books, namely in their visual component, are time-structured devices. At this point however, it becomes also necessary to observe the question of time in terms of content, regarding how it was represented differently in photographs, according to the visual narratives proposed to the reader. I intend now to analyze the particular role of represented time with the help of a concrete case study. My primary interest to deal with the photographic image of Portugal, as it was internationally perceived during the 1950s and the 1960s, has obviously directed me to a large quantity of travel books which have either been produced by foreign photographers and writers or elaborated in Portuguese context but meant to circulate abroad (the last particularly in contexts of propaganda or of plain national promotion). From all the different types of publications I have come across in my investigation (from reportages to propaganda books or to young-adult literature), travel books appeared to be extraordinarily appealing objects, not only for the specificities of their photographs and texts, but also for their quantity. Taking the symbolic year of 1955 as a starting point (Edward Steichen's exhibition *The Family of Man* and Cartier-Bresson's book *Les Européens*), one can observe the immense popularity of documentary photography during this period, confirmed also by the enormous success picture magazines (and photojournalistic expression) reached in Europe during the post-war period. Along with this post-war logic and in association with a certain idea of the reconstruction of Europe, a sudden increase of publications on countries and national identities is noticeable throughout these years. Among the wide range of typologies, travel books were no exception to this tendency and series such as *Les Albums des Guides Bleus, Les Beaux Pays or L'Atlas des Voyages* are just some examples in a more vast scenario, within which I can locate the example I am about to consider.

In 1957, a book on Portugal was published in Paris by Les Éditions du Seuil (see Villier, 1957), as part of the famous series *Petite Planète*, a series which, between 1954 and 1958, was edited under the coordination of Chris Marker. Straightforwardly, the title was *Portugal*, the author of the text was Franz Villier and the pictures of the book were taken by different photographers, both individually or representing press agencies, and then further edited by Marker (the final colophon mentions also the collaboration of Juliette Caputo as assistant). What has motivated me to select this particular book as my case study relates more to its exceptionality than to its exemplarity. It is an utterly dissonant book when compared to the wider panorama of books published on Portugal during those years. In almost all other examples, independently of the possible influence of Portuguese official institutions in their making processes, we are commonly confronted with a strong promotional tone. They all cannot avoid demonstrating the country's particularities, highlighting places or habits that, even if uncommon, are expected to operate like teasers for the reader. On the contrary, this book (and I mean specifically Villier's words) constitutes one of the most unflattering examples I have come across. One could say that for the most part, books on countries published in the *Petite Planète* series possess a common unorthodoxy towards the conventional national discourses and this one is not immune to the global spirit of the collection; but Villier's exaggeration and pejorative attitude were so strong that it was even mentioned in another travel book, published nine years later, as being very unfair and full of sarcasm (Ganne, 1966).

Generally, some disdain is to be detected throughout the text where every traditionally glorified episode of the Portuguese past is exposed only to reveal its absurdity and irrelevance. The images in their turn, occupy a somewhat more moderate and interesting position. First of all, in contrast with the text, it looks like most photographs were not specifically produced for this publication. Although I was not able to identify the original context of every one of them, the fact that a large amount is associated with press agencies immediately raises not only the possibility (but not the inevitability) of a connection with photojournalistic discourses but also of an eventual use or re-use within different places and circumstances. More concretely however, there is evidence that some of the pictures had already been published before: it is the case of some images by Cartier-Bresson which had first been included in the famous book *Les Européens* (Cartier-Bresson, 1955) or others by Jean Dieuzaide, which had also previously appeared in the book *Le Portugal* (Bottineau, 1956).

In fact, the origin of the photographs is so immensely diverse that one cannot point to a single photographer who shapes the visual discourse of this book more significantly than others. If there is such thing as the authorship of the pictorial text, I am persuaded it lies with Marker's editing work for he assembled very different photographs and graphic material in a suggestive manner (which already points to the photo-essays he would develop and publish some years later), reflecting at the same time Marker's personal interests and political inclinations. But finally, how does this choice of images actually interact with the text by Villier? Far from saying that they function as mere illustrations of the text, I also don't want to claim that images have any primacy above words. I rather prefer to regard them as independent discourses which of course have foreseeable points of contact. I consider that Marker's own words taken from the beginning of his photo-essay *Le dépays* make also sense in this particular case:

> The text is no more a commentary for the image than images are illustrations of the text. They are two different series of sequences

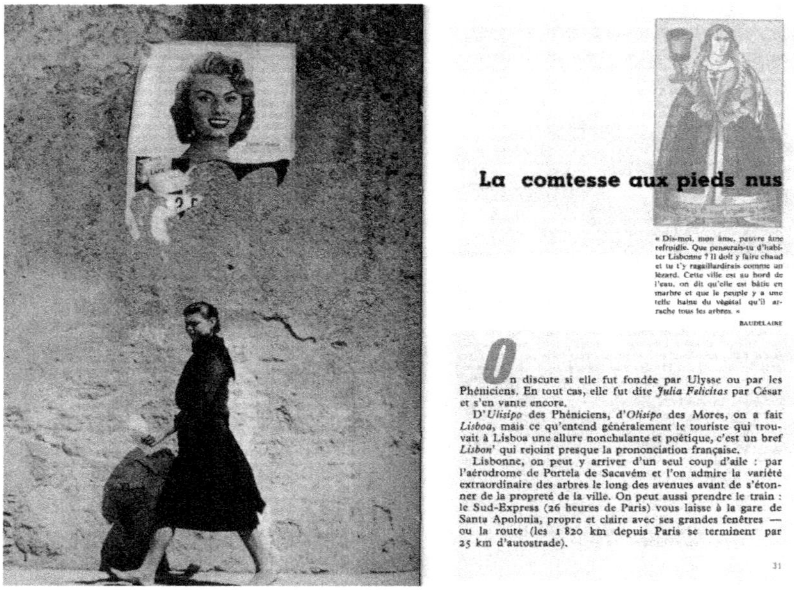

La comtesse aux pieds nus

« Dis-moi, mon âme, pauvre âme refroidie. Que penserais-tu d'habiter Lisbonne ? Il doit y faire chaud et tu t'y ragaillardirais comme un lézard. Cette ville est au bord de l'eau, on dit qu'elle est bâtie en marbre et que le peuple y a une telle haine du végétal qu'il arrache tous les arbres. «

BAUDELAIRE

On discute si elle fut fondée par Ulysse ou par les Phéniciens. En tout cas, elle fut dite *Julia Felicitas* par César et s'en vante encore.

D'*Ulisipo* des Phéniciens, d'*Olisipo* des Mores, on a fait *Lisboa*, mais ce qu'entend généralement le touriste qui trouvait à Lisboa une allure nonchalante et poétique, c'est un bref *Lisbon'* qui rejoint presque la prononciation française.

Lisbonne, on peut y arriver d'un seul coup d'aile : par l'aérodrome de Portela de Sacavém et l'on admire la variété extraordinaire des arbres le long des avenues avant de s'étonner de la propreté de la ville. On peut aussi prendre le train : le Sud-Express (26 heures de Paris) vous laisse à la gare de Santa Apolonia, propre et claire avec ses grandes fenêtres — ou la route (les 1 820 km depuis Paris se terminent par 25 km d'autostrade).

31

Fig. 5.1 Agnès Varda, 1956, *in* Villier, *Portugal* (Paris: Seuil, 1957). © Agnès Varda.

> that inevitably cross each other and interact now and then. But it would be pointless and tiring to have one confront the other (Marker in Alter, 2006, 10).

I will not be able to analyze here every line and picture of the entire book but I will however select some images and some of these fruitful contact points which, I believe, are significant and reveal the particular position this book seems to occupy.

Let us begin with the image that opens the chapter on Lisbon (fig. 5.1). It is a very beautiful and interesting image by Agnès Varda that appears on the page next to the title of the chapter, in a display that makes the title function equally as the caption of the image: *The barefoot countess* [*La comtesse aux pieds nus*]. This expression is a direct allusion to a 1954 film directed by Joseph L. Mankiewicz starring Ava Gardner and Humphrey Bogart, entitled *The Barefoot Contessa* that deals (like every construction of a national identity) with the fine balance between truth and appearance. It tells the story of Maria Vargas, a Spanish barefoot dancer (raised in a very modest family that could not even afford to buy her a pair of shoes) who lives a true Cinderella's dream: after achieving a great success as movie star in Hollywood, she becomes a 'contessa' by falling in love and marrying an Italian Count. Her dream life will however be very brief and shall lead her to a tragic end. Apart from this reference to the film in the title of the chapter, which is never directly mentioned by Villier, a further reading of the text allows us to clearly identify the woman in the picture as being a personification of the city of Lisbon. While this extrapolation may seem abusive at first sight, it has a reasonable explanation. In Portuguese popular expressions and in several fado songs, Lisbon is often called the 'queen of river Tagus' but Franz Villier reacts against this epithet arguing that we should question the established nobility title: 'we can discuss the title, duchess, marchioness or just countess, but barefoot in any case [*on peut discuter du titre, duchesse, marquise ou seulement comtesse, aux pieds nus en tout cas*] (Villier, 1957, 48).' He justifies his own designation by saying that Lisbon is indeed one of the European capitals where we can find the greatest amount of people walking barefoot on the streets. The introductory image destroys thus a common popular label of Lisbon and is, above all, a direct point to the economic situation of the Portuguese.

In Agnès Varda's photograph we see a popular woman who enacts an oppositional dialogue with another woman that figures above her: Sophia Loren in an

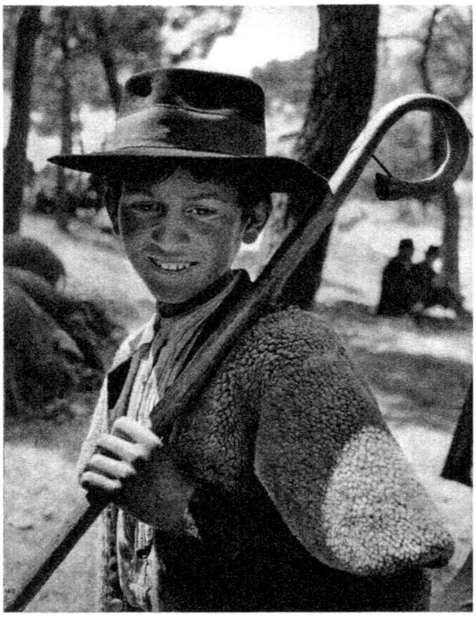
Fig. 5.2 Yan, 'En Alentejo' *in* Bottineau, *Le Portugal*, (Paris: Arthaud, 1956).

advertisement image for Lux soaps. In symbolic terms, the reading seems not so difficult to make: the Portuguese woman appears as a kind of anti-glamorous counterpart of the starlet and the social-economical contexts of both figures could not be more antagonized. Nevertheless, in this confrontation between reality and imagery, she is the living protagonist of the picture, while Sophia Loren is nothing but an image (even an aspiration?) in a half-torn poster. I believe that the presence of the semi-destroyed poster can be openly interpreted: not only does it allude to the inadequacy and non-sustainability of such a lifestyle in that existing reality, but it also performs the conflict present in every book about national identities that always implies a reconciliation between the actual reality and the artificiality of a mediated representation, between the truth of what exists and the forgery of what is produced to be consumed. But yet, and no matter how the combination of the two women can be understood, what interests me here is how their much dissociated realities, these two different times come together in the very same photograph.

The mixture of the two different times is particularly interesting because I want to suggest that the photographic images present in the *Petite Planète* book (and the text as well) tend to go against a national conception of time, invented, encouraged and used by the dictatorial regime of Salazar as a central part of the Portuguese imaginary. In almost all travel books, and especially in those produced in collaboration with Portuguese governmental institutions such as the National Secretariat of Information (*Secretariado Nacional de Informação*) or the Houses of Portugal in several foreign countries, visual images strengthen to a certain nationalist discourse, particularly in that they forge and build a 'mythical time'. This mythical time is predominantly a past time and it is achieved in pastoral images that promote Portugal as country where the visitor can find, contrasting with the

West's attraction to all manifestations of modernity, the picturesque and uncorrupted ancestral traditions still very vividly present in everyday life (figs 5.2 and 5.3). It is of course an ideological time that is at stake. By inscribing the Portuguese people within the frame of an immemorial past, this fabricated mythical time manages to hide from view a contemporary reality that could, on the one hand, inspire political changes, while on the other, aims to legitimate the socio-economic situation of Portugal by aestheticizing the condition of the country, whose population was actually rural, uneducated and poor.

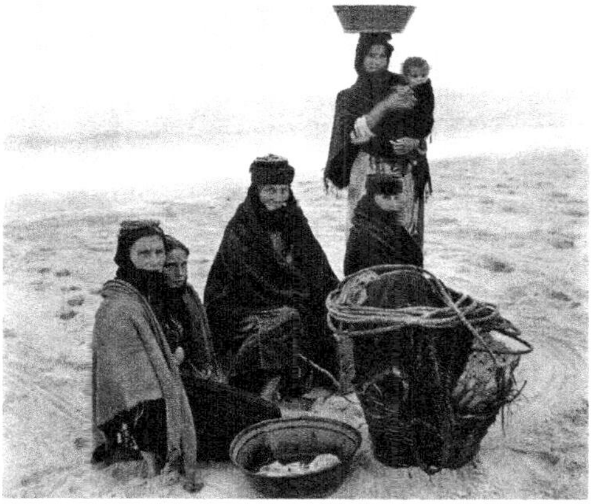

Fig. 5.3 Yan, 'Femmes de Nazaré' *in* Bottineau, *Le Portugal* (Paris: Arthaud, 1956).

This strategy becomes very explicit if we take as an example some pictures of the fishing village of Nazaré, a place that was turned into a mandatory stop both for tourists and photographers. Usually fishermen and their women appear visibly at work but somehow detached from present circumstances. In pictures, they are reduced to types, to archetypical figures, to 'nobodies' that embody a legendary time, for their existence is nothing but a replication of the same practices and rhythms that for ages ruled the lives of their ancestors (fig. 5.4). In addition, the visual representations of Nazaré generally serve a twofold political intention: not only do they legitimate aesthetically the undeveloped state of the country but they also represent, more often than not, an obvious connection with the glorious past of the Age of the Discoveries (approximately during the 15th and the 16th centuries). These fishermen were visually appropriated as a national fiction: they symbolize and are the living proof of the inevitability of the Portuguese adventure in the sea. They personify the evidence of a maritime fate, of an Atlantic nostalgia for they are presented as part of a great historical genealogy, as direct heirs of the famous sailors of the past. They are an actualization (and perpetuation) of Portugal's greatest national epopee.

As we return to Franz Villier's book, we find a positive refusal of this bond with historical narratives. Although he acknowledges that Nazaré is indeed 'the capital

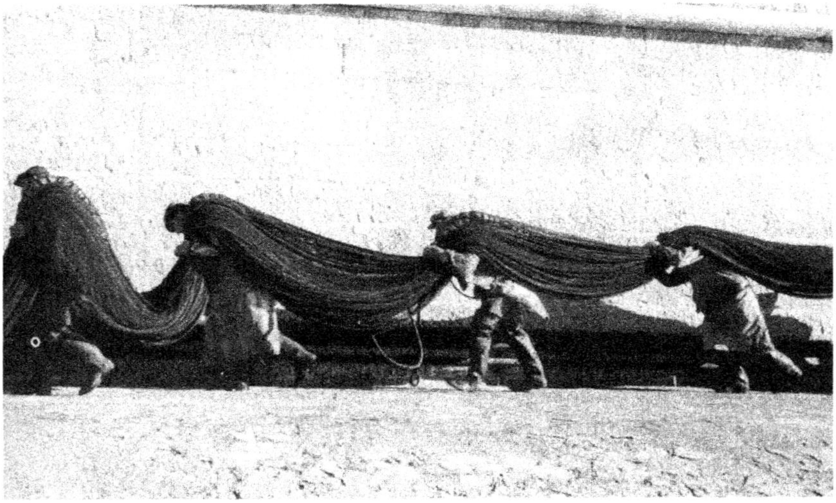

Fig. 5.4 Unidentified photographer, 'Nazaré' *in Tour du Monde* – Portugal (Paris:1961).

of fishing and fishermen for the tourist in love with the picturesque [*la capitale de la pêche et des pêcheurs pour le touriste épris de pittoresque*] (Villier, 1957, 58),' there is only one image unquestionably captioned as Nazaré's to be found in the book (fig. 5.5). In the picture we see in fact a fisherman but he does not play a part in that temporal mythology I have just referred to: aside from his figure, the picture also shows a car, people from another social level and we don't even have a glimpse of the hyper-connoted sea. The photograph reveals, if not a more real, at least a more present and contemporary environment.

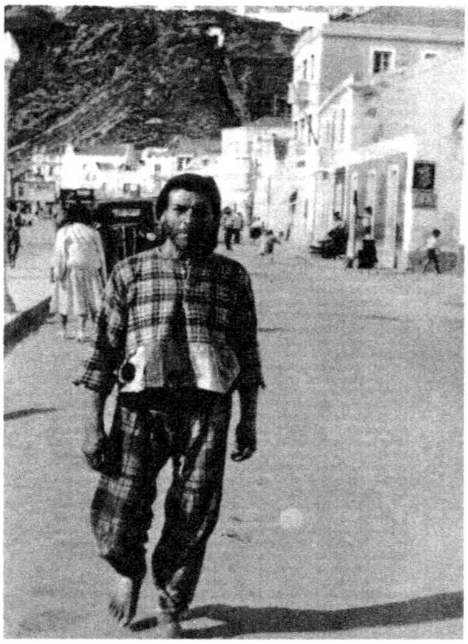

Fig. 5.5 Papon, 'Pêcheur de Nazaré' *in* Villier, *Portugal* (Paris: Seuil, 1957).

Villier's words and Marker's choice of the photographs ostensibly expose their awareness of the strategy used by Salazar's state to promote a nationalist discourse. Being overtly opposed to the political color of the country, they seek to escape all formulas and labels used by the governmental institutions. Furthermore, there is a visible concern with the revelation of the social and cultural situation of the Portuguese, observable in how the book denounces the incongruence between this reality and the propagandistic images of the country. If we can identify such a thing as a goal of the book, this goal is to deconstruct and to go against the hegemony of these glorifying national fictions. 'As his oeuvre reveals,' Nora M. Alter writes about Marker, 'his operative principle is to ignore ultimately constraining and divisive national and cultural identities and boundaries...His aversion to any conformity and to any mode of patriotism may be related to a social philosophy that aligns with those who are oppressed and abused by authoritarian regimes, regardless of nationality (Alter, 2006, 6).' This reaction however, is not without danger: particularly in Villier's text, the refusal of every possible reference to that golden historical past sometimes gives over to a very arrogant discourse whose aim is only to reduce and diminish Portugal to a complete platitude, where there is nothing remarkable enough to point out and where even the period of the Discoveries is interpreted as a mere consequence of geographical chance, performed by a country that was never able to be an empire.

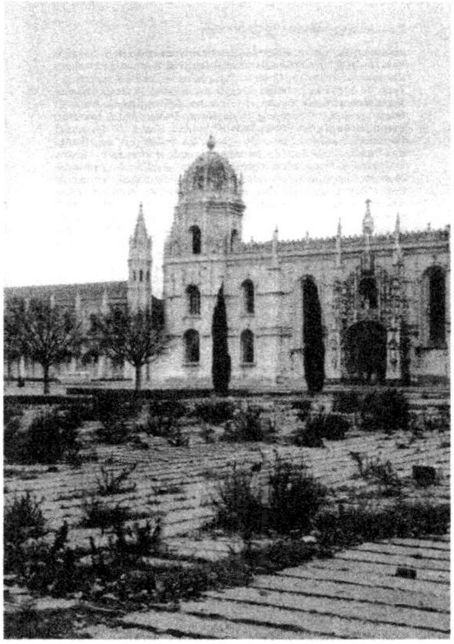

Fig. 5.6 Chris Marker, 'Monastère des Jerónimos' *in* Villier, *Portugal* (Paris: Seuil, 1957). © Chris Marker.

I would like to conclude now with some examples of representations of Lisbon present in Villier's book, which are a reply to the almost authoritarian power of historical narratives of the past. Those images of Lisbon do not adhere to the common imagery that usually just depicts popular and picturesque lifestyles in poor neighborhoods. On the contrary, these photographs tend to offer a more urban reality, with cars, cafés and people moving around in their ordinary routines. What we see is first and foremost, a resolute non-cooperation with the official mythical time, which becomes even more evident as we pay attention to the way historical monuments are depicted.

In a tour to Lisbon, touristic tradition will suggest that the traveler should at least pay a visit to two emblematic sites: the monastery of Jerónimos and the tower of Belém. These monuments, like history in general, are part of a national specificity that the government of Salazar knew very well how to exploit. In the *Petite Planète* book, however, they appear in a quite surprising manner: the monastery of

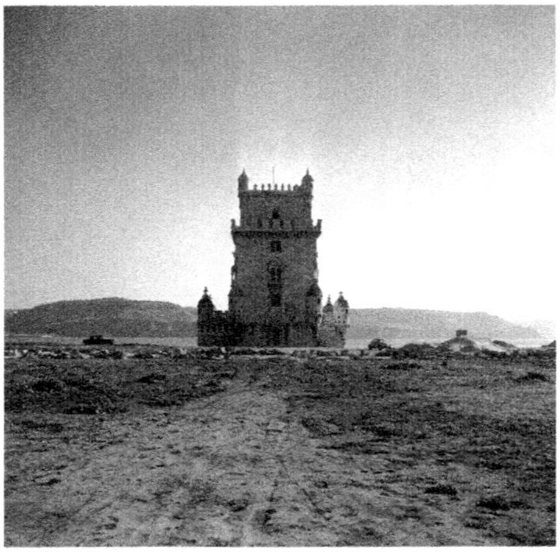

Fig. 5.7 Agence Roger Viollet, 'Tour de Belém' *in* Villier, *Portugal*, (Paris: Seuil, 1957). © Agence Roger Viollet.

Jerónimos appears as being much less important than some bushes growing wild in a neglected area in the foreground (fig. 5.6) and the tower of Belém emerges almost in the background, surrounded by mud in a picture with very poor visibility conditions (fig. 5.7). The pictures I have mentioned look just like snapshots taken from an ordinary traveler's point of view and do not seem to have any great deal of technical quality. The fact that they were included in a carefully constructed travel book makes them seem all but accidental. They suggest an unexpected gaze, intended to be more faithful and less disappointing when compared to reality. If in other photographs, in other travel books of these years, one can detect the effort put into monumentalizing and faking the dimensions and the dignity of some places by means of cropping or standpoint, what the pictures in this book do is no less manipulative. These images ridicule the places as monuments and ridicule what they symbolize in a certain national fiction at the same time that they propose an alternative vision to the official praising and eulogizing images. In this sense, the Jerónimos image (fig. 5.6) holds an additional meaning because it was exactly in front of the monastery, where we can only see the bushes now, that one of the major propagandistic operations of 'Estado Novo' had been set some years before, in 1940: the *Exhibition of the Portuguese World* [*Exposição do Mundo Português*], a major exhibition designed to celebrate nationality formation (1140) and restoration (1640) of Portugal, where Portuguese history and colonial enterprise were pompously put on display. Now, in the same location, the desolated sight of an abandoned space seems to silently question the future continuation of that great Portuguese empire.

In Chris Marker's selection of photographs, the link with history and with time is therefore never absent: it is just built the other way around. These visual constructions do not cooperate with the building of history based in dreamlike national discourses. They are committed to stop the turn towards the past because, the book seems to tell its readers, Portugal should be concerned with the actual, contemporary time, maybe with the time of Sophia Loren. But ultimately, it is also evident that by exposing the fakery and masquerade of these national fictions, the photographs we find in this particular book, form also another type of artificial visual narrative, equally fictionalized, where the new and present time they seem to propose is, of course, no less ideological.

Acknowledgements

The author acknowledges the useful discussions with Jan Baetens and the financial support from FCT, Portugal.

Bibliography

¬ Nora M. Alter, *Chris Marker* (Urbana and Chicago: University of Illinois Press, 2006).

¬ Benedict Anderson, *Imagined Communities* (London and New York: Verso, 1983).

¬ Roland Barthes, *Mythologies* (Paris: Éditions du Seuil, 1957).

¬ Yves Bottineau, *Le Portugal, Les Beaux Pays* (Paris: Arthaud, 1956).

¬ Henri Cartier-Bresson, *Les Européens* (Paris: Éditions Verve, 1955).

¬ Gilbert Ganne, *Portugal, L'Atlas des Voyages* (Lausanne: Éditions Rencontre, 1966).

¬ W. J. T. Mitchell, 'What is an Image?', *New Literary History*, 15, 3 (1984): 503-37.

¬ Anandi Ramamurthy, 'Spectacles and illusions: photography and commodity culture', in Liz Wells (ed.) *Photography: A Critical Introduction* (London and New York: Routledge, 1996).

¬ Allan Sekula, 'On the Invention of Photographic Meaning', in Victor Burgin (ed.) *Thinking Photography* (London: Macmillan Press, 1982), 84-109.

¬ William W. Stowe, *Going Abroad. European Travel in Nineteenth-Century American Culture* (Princeton: Princeton University Press, 1994).

¬ Anne-Marie Thiesse, *La création des identités nationales. Europe XVIIIe-XXe siècle*, *Points Histoire* (Paris: Éditions du Seuil, 1999).

¬ Franz Villier, *Portugal*, *Petite Planète* (Paris: Éditions du Seuil, 1957).

6 Time and Order: Self-Reflective Strategies in Photo Essays

Maren Polte

Ever since databases like SmugMug, Flickr or locr have given every internet user the chance to store and retrieve pictures, photography has become a medium of communication able to reproduce the world almost in its totality. Pictures and reality are facing each other. It is taken for granted that everything can be pictorialized and the instruments of doing so can be made available for almost any situation.

'Anything visible can also be turned into a picture', Gottfried Böhm says in his book *Wie Bilder Sinn erzeugen* (Böhm, 2007, 11). And, one has to add, most things that can be made into pictures, have been made already. To take on this enormous universe of pictures, often described as a deluge, a new analytical tool kit is needed. In the Anglo-Saxon world, the phenomenon is the subject of 'visual studies', or 'cultural studies'. In a German-speaking context, there is a trend to prolong traditional art history into 'Bildwissenschaft', adapting the scope of the discipline to the new conditions.[1]

But what exactly are those new conditions? They have been described as a 'pictorial turn' (Mitchell, 1992, 89-94) or 'iconic turn' (Böhm, 1994, 11-38). The terms echo Richard M. Rorty's 'linguistic turn' of 1967 (Rorty, 1992 [1967], 1-39) for a text-based understanding of the world that in the meantime has been increasingly overshadowed by the pictorial onslaught. It is this shift from text to picture that led art theory to try to resuscitate in new terminology some sort of 'imaginative' thinking, a reflection on and in pictures.

The larger part of the sheer mass of pictures is of a technical nature, i.e. the result of a production process involving technical means. These 'apparatuses themselves', Villem Flusser states, 'are the products of applied scientific texts (Flusser, 1997 [1983], 13).' Analyzing technical pictures, therefore means analyzing their foundations first, which are cultural, language-based codes. In practice, however—and despite ample evidence to the contrary—the technical picture is being taken as a mirror of the information it entails. It is seen as belonging to the same dimension of reality as the object shown, not as a symbol or a text-based code that needs to be de-coded. A technical picture such as a photograph is misunderstood as an instrument of *Erkenntnis* (recognition). It seems to deserve the same trust as primary perception with our five senses.

This parallelism blurs the line between the pictorial and the real worlds. Once visually fixed, one person's experience is turned into the experience of countless others. A multitude of world views is being made available, already arranged into certain structures. Structures in this context are however not subject to strict terminology, as technical pictures—as well as all others—suspend terminological thinking and replace it with imagination. Yet this imagination represents cultural codes, not a given reality.

For several decades now, artists have been addressing these codes—the information, historical content and imaginative powers of technical pictures—in their works. From a creative position, and using artistic rather than theoretical means, they have explored the role and purpose of pictures in our society. The results are of course not available in the form of terminological concepts. Nevertheless, they represent an analytical response, which tries to get the recipient involved in a reflection on the world of pictures. The following text addresses the auto-reflective strategies employed by a number of artists from a German, or German-speaking, context. It is suggested that they provide, in their own photographic ways, a most valuable and instructive supplement to the theoretical explorations of the same problem ('What is a picture?', 'How does a picture produce meaning?') undertaken by Gottfried Böhm and other leading representatives of 'Bildwissenschaft'.[2]

It will become apparent that different concepts of organizing visual material into systems of aesthetical order also imply different approaches to time. Time is photography's great absentee, photographs are essentially 'stills'—what is left of reality after time has been squeezed out. The fourth dimension can only be presented indirectly or through a succession of pictures. For photo essays, taking a few steps down the long way from 'stills' to 'movies' is a natural option, of which the photographers dealt with here make strikingly different use.

Bildordnung (Pictorial Order)

Instead of adding to an already comprehensive visual catalog of the world, many artists are using prefabricated or existing picture material to consider the different usages and their limitations. The aim is not an exploration of the essence of photography or individual moments of the camera at work. The artists rather use photography as a huge stock of visual patterns and arrangements: breaking them up, and assembling new ones.

In Germany, Hans Peter Feldmann has been pursuing this strategy since the late 1960s. The bulk of his material is, as Thomas Weski puts it, 'stolen' (Weski, 2003, 104-105). Feldmann collects all sorts of everyday stuff but particularly pictures, amateur snapshots, self-made photographs taken out off their original context and re-arranged. Printed in small—in terms of circulation as well as size—magazines and other publications, they carry a potential double meaning: concerning themselves but pointing to something beyond as well.[3]

A lack of information is immediately apparent. In their original context, these pictures serve as illustrations to texts. This need not be in writing, they can also be part of an oral narrative. They can be articles in the press, commercial manuals, or texts from somebody's private life. Whatever the text is—it is needed in order to 'load' the pictures and render them complete.

Once those textual indicators are absent, as is the case in Feldmann's pictures, they will automatically be substituted with imaginative thinking, which reconnects technical pictures to cultural codes. If a picture shows smiling people in front of a monument, the spontaneous assumption will be: holidays. If what we see is a formal setting with a woman in a long white dress and with flowers in her hand we add the missing elements of a wedding scene. Policemen point to some incident or crime, and so forth.

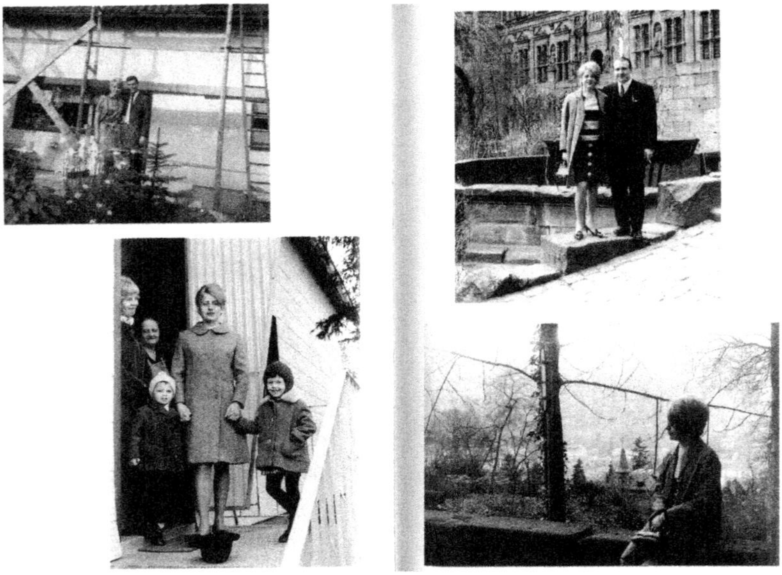

Fig. 6.1 Hans-Peter Feldmann, images of the series *Porträt*, 1994. © of the book by Schirmer/Mosel, Munich, 1994.

Another decoding level is provided in the context arranged by the artist. Not all of Feldmann's publications are as homogeneous as his *Porträt* published in 1994 by Schirmer/Mosel in which 324 photographs document the life of one woman between 1943 and 1993 (fig. 6.1). In this case, our collective memory allows us to spin a narrative tale right across the pages, identifying locations and relating views and events to our own personal experience. If, however, a funny snapshot, a view of a demolished industrial site and the portrait of a concentration camp prisoner are placed side by side (fig. 6.2), the contextual gaps in between are difficult to bridge. The combination somehow does not seem to be 'right'. Every picture remains in isolation, demonstrating that it is impossible to decode it as such. Presented in sequence, the pictures remain elements of a narrative that, in the absence of an explanatory framework, has to be imagined by the beholder.

Feldmann's book *Ferien* [*Holidays*] (Vienna, 1994) is a collection of pictures which the reader is supposed to arrange and paste onto the pages herself. His smaller picture booklets also suggest a much larger narrative frame, which cannot be pinned down in terms of chronology, specific persons or objects. It is diachronic, ubiquitous and in constant change of its personnel, ignoring identities of color, faith, age, origin. A viewer used to western habits is invited to reflect upon the different usages of photography, mass media pictorializing and thus to specific ways of representing the world in pictures.

This approach led Feldmann to become the co-founder, in 1994, of the magazine and art project *Ohio, Photographie wie noch nie*. Its idea is to publish material, paper and collections which would never make it into a public archive. Each issue presents one collection, stripped of all additional information about the original context. The pictures—private shots, archive pictures, documentaries, digital files—are reproduced without any commentary. It is the pictures and nothing but the pictures. Uschi Huber and Jörg Paul Janka have been *Ohio*'s publishers since 1995. They are constantly on the look-out for photographic lost-and-found material, which can then be put in a new order. Whatever genre a picture might have belonged to is ignored. The same applies to qualitative hierarchy. The artistic picture is not in any way superior to the shots by amateurs or reporters. In the no-comment presentation, the quality of the individual picture is highlighted as they have to speak for themselves.

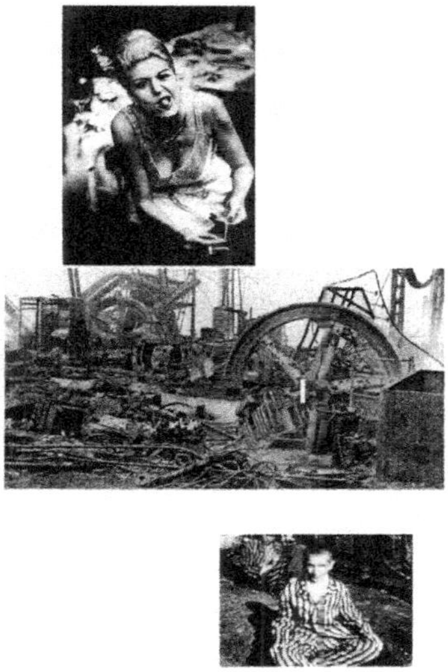

Fig. 6.2 Céline Duval and Hans-Peter Feldmann, doublepage of one *cahier d'image* from the *cahier d'images* publication series (undated).

Psychograph

Ohio #15 (fig. 6.3) presents a collection of photographs by the late Jens Hagen, a writer, activist and musicologist from Cologne, who died in 2004.[4] It is just a selection from some 1,000 35mm shots taken in 2002, when Hagen stayed at a hospital in the city of Koblenz (figs 6.4-6.7). Removed from his normal environment and with a very restricted mobility, he uses the camera to establish a sort of rapport with his new surroundings. He cannot move well but his eyes are even more agile for that and what they see is frozen by the camera. The photographs are ordinary analog shots, machine-processed like millions of others in some big department store. Hagen labeled the prints carefully and kept them in strict chronological order. Huber and Janka picked a sample of 200 from the lot. They dropped

Figs. 6.3 - 6.7 *Ohio #15, Photos von Jens Hagen*, 2007. © for the photos Jens Hagen and VG Bild-Kunst 2007, for the arrangement in the magazin Ohio Photomagazin, Cologne, 2007 (Courtesy of Uschi Huber, Jörg Paul Janka).

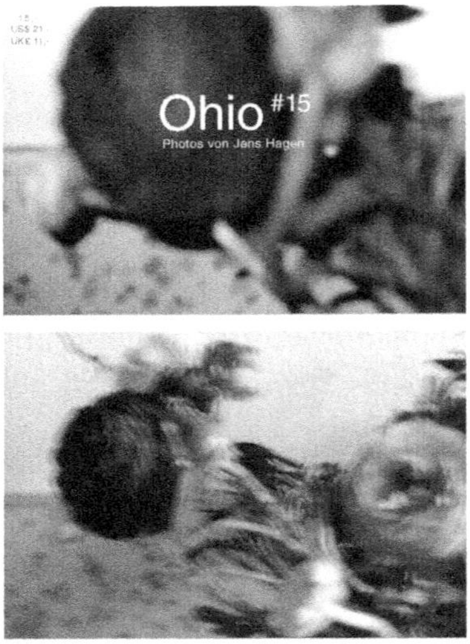

Fig. 6.3

the captions but kept the chronological order—the pictures alone, stripped of the anecdotical annotations, are left to tell the whole story.

Hagen took a lot of pictures, seemingly on the spur of the moment, and following the old Kodak motto: 'You press the button, we do the rest'. The result is a pictorial diary of a special period in his life, a psychological study of an environment that could be described, in Foucault's terminology, as a *crisis-* or *deviation-heterotopia* indicating a secluded area for people with out-of-norm conditions or behavior (Foucault, 1990 [1967], 40-41). They include psychiatric hospitals, prisons, homes for the elderly but also normal hospitals—spaces safely separated and distanced from society's mainstream living modes.

Hagen spent time in such an environment during his stay at the hospital, uprooted from 'normal' life. It was impossible for him to pursue his usual daily routines

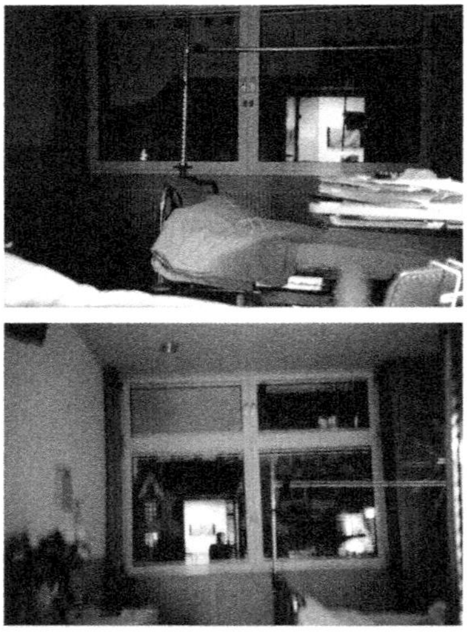

Fig. 6.4

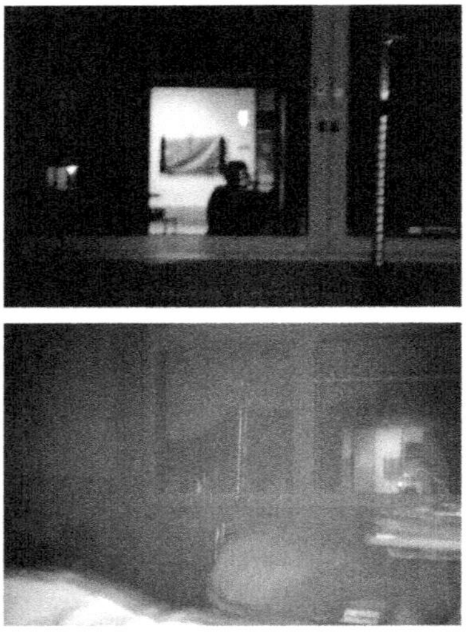

Fig. 6.5

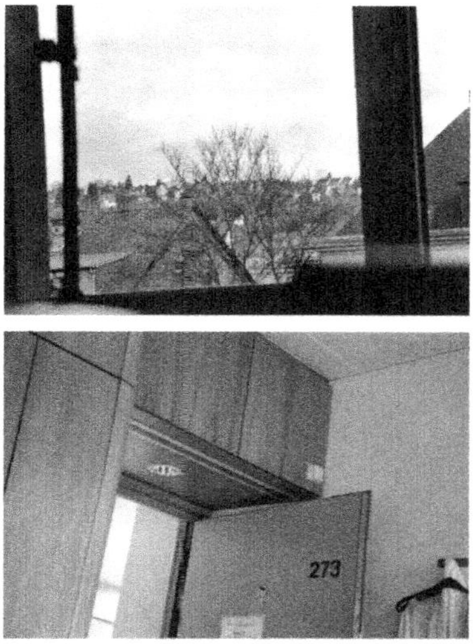

Fig. 6.6

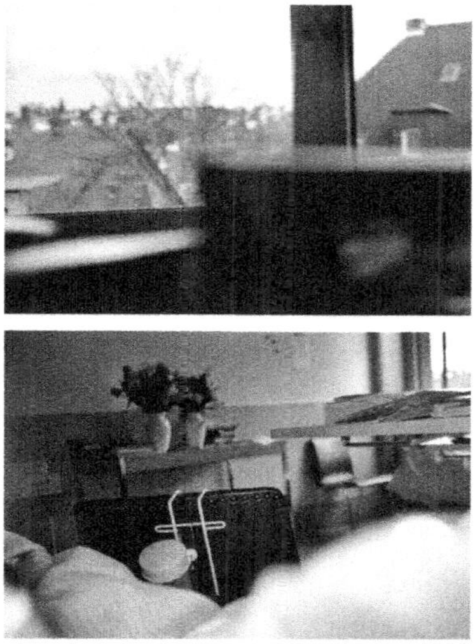

Fig. 6.7

and social functions. His own activities suspended and his actions determined by others, a different attitude towards the flow of time set in. Time would no longer be shaped by personal productivity and rhythm. Nor would it be something 'neutral', flowing by unnoticed. Instead, it was externalized, marked by a succession of meals, doctor's visits and medical treatments. They constituted a new structure, in which the loss of self-determination could be experienced both as a shortage and an over-abundance of time. Wolfgang Hagen reacted by exploring systematically the surroundings and limited space to which his life was now restricted.

The published sequence of pictures starts with a glimpse of the dark hospital room (fig. 6.4). There is a bed and a bare radiator beneath the thermopane windows through which other buildings are visible. The room looks sterile, there is nothing personal, with the exception of a stack of papers on a folding table. What light there is comes through the open door from the corridor. The scene is a carefully chosen entrée to an anonymous location—and to the people living there in anonymity.

The following pictures are out of focus, the perspective is off-balance, the contours of things are vague in a foggy light. One and the same subject is presented in a series of only slightly different angles. It is as if Hagen had been looking for dissolving forms to echo the loss of the reliable formal structures of his life. For the viewer as well, the usual visual guarantors of stability are gone. The third shot captures the photographer himself mirrored by a window, a dim silhouette visible against the background of the lit corridor. The window is not a passage to the world outside. The person on the inside is reduced to a sketchy outline, without individual features, let alone means of emotional expression.

After this he vanishes completely. The inner and outer worlds dissolve into each other, the visual narrative abandons the descriptive and psychological approaches, turning to a dreamlike surrealism. The room loses its physical qualities and turns into a manifestation of feelings and imaginations. On the following pages, some minor developments and changes are registered, such as springtime arriving and fir-tree branches being replaced by tulips. But there is nothing pointing to the patient's and photographer's personal situation, his health in particular. The order of the collection is purely psychological. The pictures, as selected by Huber and Janka, present the location as an externalization of a state of mind. Photography becomes psychography—a vehicle of emotions.

The suppression of the annotations opens up the imaginative space for the viewer who is free to proceed from the limitations and banality of the pictures to her own psychological narrative rather than just follow that of the photographer. Hagen's approach is direct and spontaneous. A moment of precise observation is followed by hasty and superficial impressions. The camera follows the ups and downs without making any effort to fashion the result into something more stylish or artistic.

The original rhythm is preserved in the Huber/Janka selection. The reproductions are only a fraction bigger than a 10 x 15cm print. There are four pictures on a double page, only exceptionally one photograph is blown up to cover a whole page. The standard unit is a four-pictures block, not a single shot. There are no viewing instructions but the magazine is clearly not meant to be thumbed through. Photography is put on display as a useful practical tool, a means of survival both intellectual and emotional.

Fading Tracks

Moll 31 (1995) (fig. 6.8), the first photography book by the Berlin-based artist Wiebke Loeper, is a different story, despite being a picture diary as well.[5] The protagonist is identical with the publisher, half of the material existed already prior to the book, as pictures from the family photo album. This is all about tracks, about the foot-prints of a personal life, woven into a comprehensive narrative of private, urban and political elements. This is photography as a medium of personal historiography.

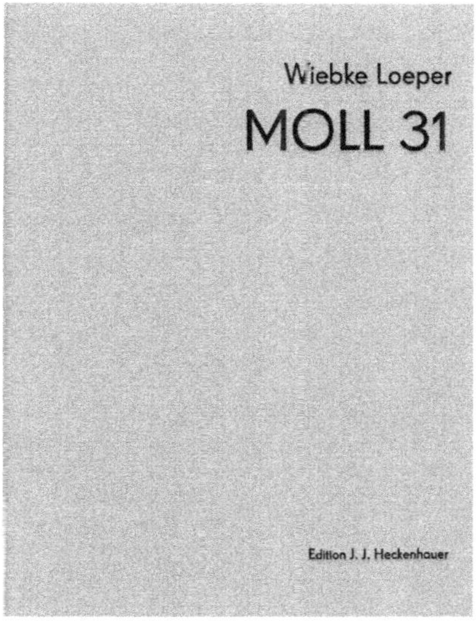

Fig. 6.8 Cover of the book Wiebke Loeper, *Moll 31*, 2005. © Wiebke Loeper, Edition J.J. Heckenhauer, 2005.

Wiebke Loeper was born in 1972 in what at the time was still Communist East Berlin. She was trained at the Leipzig Hochschule für Grafik und Buchkunst, home of the 'Leipzig School' of painting. After German re-unification and restructuring of the academy, the academy's department of photography also enjoyed wide acclaim, thanks to professors such as Joachim Brohm, Tim Rautert or, later on, Peter Piller. Wiebke Loeper attended Joachim Brohm's classes in the 1990s. Like many in the aftermath of the collapse of East Germany, she was primarily interested in the social and political changes of the time and their repercussions on individual biographies. Unlike the prominent representatives of the 'Düsseldorf School' of photography, who concentrated on the perfection of single, over-size pictures devoid of any personal context, her works are serial and saturated with biographical content. Most take the form of an artist's book, such as *Hello von Bloomer. Viele Grüße aus Wismar* (Berlin, 2000), *Gold und Silber lieb ich sehr* (Berlin, 2000) or *Moll 31*.

The title refers to the address of the Berlin house where Loeper grew up. It had been co-designed and built by her father Herwig Loeper, who was one of the architects involved in what was called the 'sanitation' of the East German capital city. The richly ornated turn-of-the-century buildings were replaced by sober, uniform architecture supposed to give the inner city a 'modern', no-frills look. The old bricks-and-stucco facades gave way to concrete slabs, the apartments were equipped with radiators and proper bath-rooms. Mollstraße No. 31 was one of those new houses, a 18-storey high-rise close to Alexanderplatz, in the heart of East Berlin. The Loepers, moving in a short time before their daughter Wiebke was born, were among the first inhabitants.

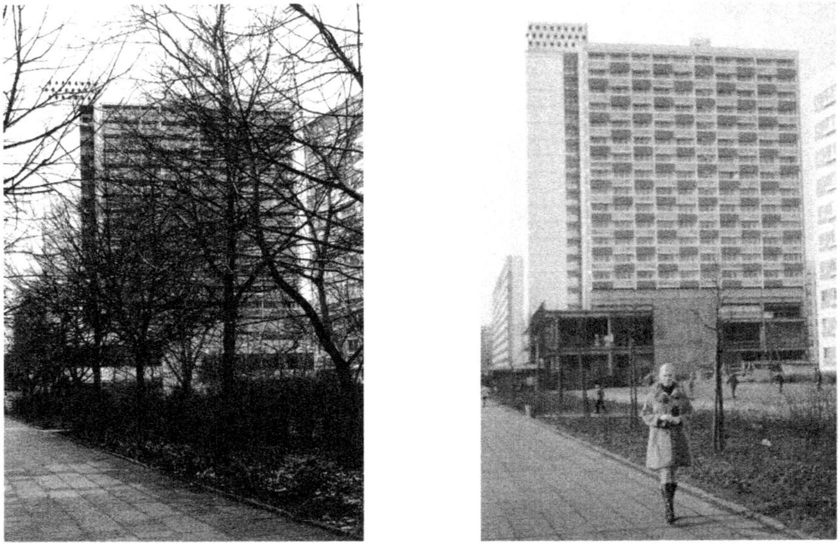

Fig. 6.9 Wiebke Loeper, images from the series *Moll 31*, 2005. © Wiebke Loeper 2005.

They occupied an 'experimental' flat on the 17th floor, with variable inside walls, a concept first developed at the Bauhaus in the 1920s. A total of 24 apartments were designed that way, to allow tenants to adapt the lay-out of their living quarters to changing family needs. As it turned out, the idea was better than its implementation—as was the case with the whole state in which the house was built. It was erected all too hastily on sandy soil and began to tilt in 1989. Just two decades after construction, at the time of the opening up of the Berlin Wall, the building had to be evacuated. The Loepers moved out as well. In the end, another thirteen years elapsed before the house was finally knocked down. In the meantime, the slowly rotting structure served as a shelter to animals and city vagabonds.

Before demolition, the photographer returned to her childhood home to capture and preserve what was left of the past. She took pictures of the rooms where she grew up, of the spots where she sat, slept, took a bath and stumbled along as a toddler. Pictures from the Loeper family album helped her to remember and mentally reconstruct the erstwhile living situation. In the book, the two perspectives—the intimate views of family life and the neutral documentary—are presented on an equal footing. One pictorial record is full of life and individual stories, the other is a sober register of what is left once life itself has vanished. There is a time gap of up to twenty years between the two. It is left to the viewer to bridge this undefined space.

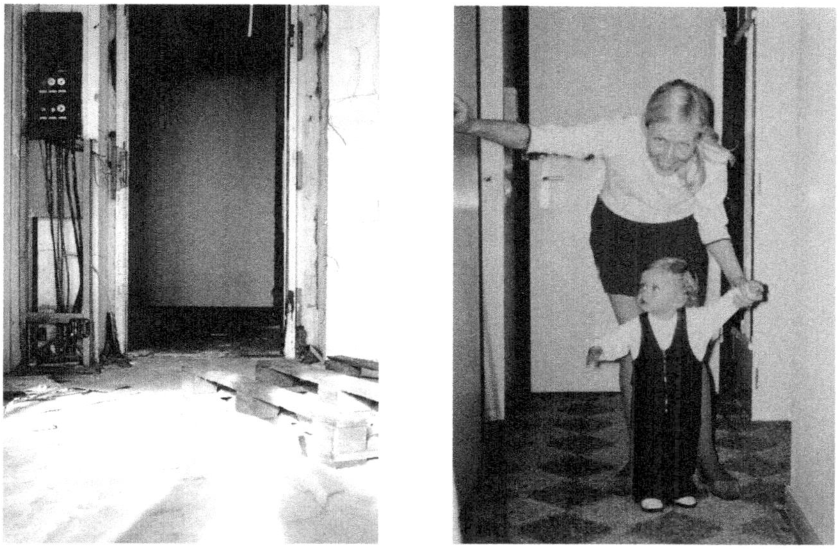

Fig. 6.10 Wiebke Loeper, images from the series *Moll 31*, 2005. © Wiebke Loeper 2005.

The journey back in time starts with a long shot showing Bärbel Loeper, the photographer's mother, in front of the freshly completed building, a pretty blonde woman in a short fur-rimmed coat, her daughter not yet born (fig. 6.9). On the opposite page we get a view of the building taken from exactly the same spot twenty years later. The red and white grid facade is hardly visible any more through the maze of branches of the trees that have grown to full size in front of it. The blonde woman is gone. Wiebke's mother, as we learn from a view of her tombstone 38 pages later, died at the age of only 37. Her daughter had to cope not only with the loss of her mother but with that of her first home as well—and indeed with the collapse of her home state, the German Democratic Republic, and all its utopian ambitions and hopes. Individual biography, architectural and political history are inextricably woven into each other. The term 'short-lived' applies to all three.

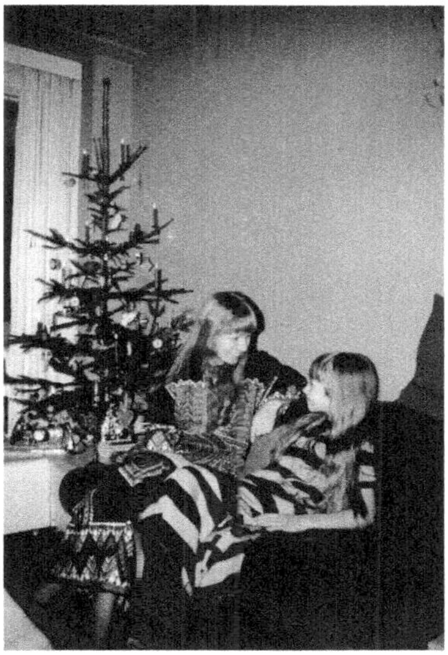

Fig. 6.11 Wiebke Loeper, images from the series *Moll 31*, 2005. © Wiebke Loeper 2005.

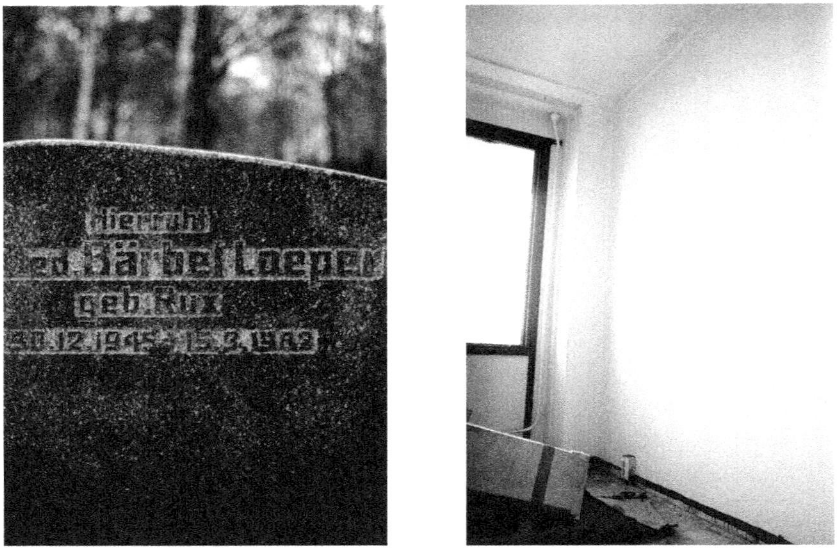

Fig. 6.12 Wiebke Loeper, images from the series *Moll 31*, 2005. © Wiebke Loeper 2005.

The following pages show the interior of the flat (fig. 6.10), with the movable walls already gone for good, leaving an open space where they once formed a narrow corridor between rooms. Even the door to the apartment is missing, everything is accessible for everybody. A snapshot of little Wiebke running down the corridor holding mama's hand is an idyllic memory the scene of which is already half-destroyed when the daughter returns to the spot. Later, Bärbel and Wiebke Loeper are seen sitting in front of a Christmas tree, the last view of the mother (fig. 6.11). The following page shows the scripture on her tombstone, the only indication of what happened (fig. 6.12). Life still went on for a while in those rooms, until the people disappeared and even the rooms themselves started to decompose.

The book is partly a family chronicle in pictures, partly a documentation of a decaying piece of architecture. Both elements are the narrative frame to what is the real story of the book and happening between the pictures of the past and the present. *Moll 31* is a pictorial tale about vanishing and perishing as the inevitable fate of everything that lives—and not just of that. Here, a period, a whole life, an ideology shaping the lives of a people, a life's work, a supposed architectural highlight all disappear. It is a very private story, but with a universal meaning. The collective picture codex evoked by Loeper is the key to, and vessel of, countless individual stories, stored for retrieval through memory.

Photography is supposed to be the giant storage house, in which everything can be saved from death and destruction and preserved for eternity. That is the promise: shoot pictures, beat time. Loeper has a disillusionment to offer. The camera is not just a tool of preservation but a recording machine for the process of vanishing as well. Hers is a morality tale in the Baroque 'vanitas' tradition, a somber counterpoint to, and warning of, a naive optimism about the camera and its power.

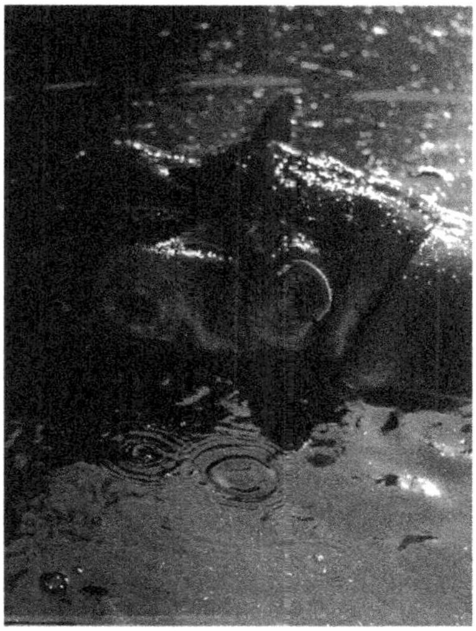

Fig. 6.13 Peter Fischli, David Weiss, cover of the book *Sichtbare Welt*, 2000. © Peter Fischli, David Weiss, Verlag der Buchhandlung Walther König, 2000 (Courtesy of Galerie Eva Presenhuber, Zurich).

Visible World

Sichtbare Welt is the title of a multi-media work by Peter Fischli and David Weiss, the Swiss artist duo. Like much of their art, this work exists in different forms: as a video installation, a collection of slides and as a book. The following analysis deals with the latter.

As a book, *Sichtbare Welt* (2000) is a massive proposition: 360 pages, 3 cm thick, almost DIN A 4 size, it weighs 1,5 kilogram (fig. 6.13). On each page, there are eight 5.2 x 7.8 cm pictures. This is a colorful world, full of splendor and beauty, romantic and exotic places, nature and culture (figs 14-17). It is, both in the psychological and physical sense, anything but lofty. It puts on display real things as recorded and collected by the artists. Since 1987, they have been shooting pictures in their home country as well as abroad: cities, airports, people, animals, parks and landscapes in different corners of the world. The photographs, 2,800 in all, take us on a global sight-seeing trip, from one 'picture opportunity' to the next. The artists themselves are entirely absent, no attempt at recording an event or telling a story is being made. The style of presentation is that of a travel feature or publicity photography. Photogenic quality is the decisive criterion. There is no looking behind scenes or probing beneath surfaces. This is a world without problems, human suffering and political catastrophes.

Figs. 6.14 - 6.17 Peter Fischli, David Weiss, images from the series *Sichtbare Welt*, 2000. © Peter Fischli, David Weiss, Verlag der Buchhandlung Walther König, 2000 (Courtesy of Galerie Eva Presenhuber, Zurich).

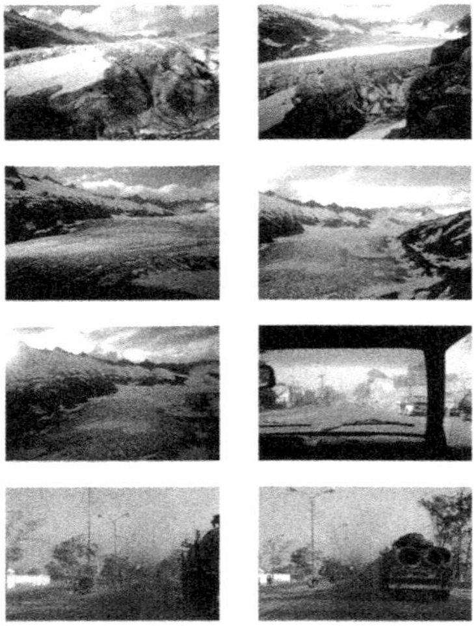

Fig. 6.14

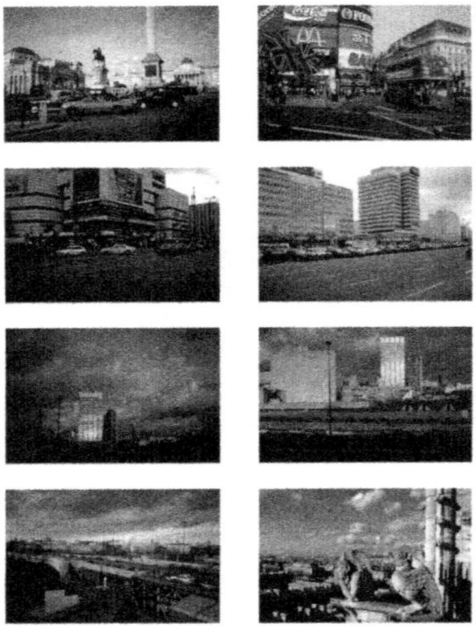

Fig. 6.15

The sequence of the pictures does not follow chronological or topographical order—a view of Trafalgar Square may be followed by Notre Dame (fig. 6.15, 6.16) and then by a jump to a different continent. Color and lighting are the determining factors. We may get one scene in a variation of lights and/or exposure times before being taken to a completely different location shown in a similar style. A palm tree beach is followed by a big city skyline, after a sunset lake there is an Indian summer forest, a winter landscape and a red-and-yellow dusk. Bangkok, Milan, Los Angeles, New York, London and Paris sit side by side, just as desert, snow, jungle, small gardens, mountains and dusty roads become neighbors on one page (see fig. 6.14). Airport scenes scattered in between reinforce the impression of the reader/viewer being taken on a virtual jet-setter's trip around the globe. We become a modern Phileas Fogg traveling around the world in 3,000 pictures. Justin Hoffman has noted the encyclopedic approach adopted by Fischli/Weiss, who go out of their way to place the camera in the standard position for each shot (Hoffmann, 1989, 39).

The result is an unfettered invitation to stay on the outside of things, to joy-ride an endless loop of attractive surfaces, seeing everything but perceiving nothing. The viewer is simply overwhelmed by a tsunami of visual material. The book demonstrates our helplessness to cope with the pictorial onslaught confronting us every day. *Sichtbare Welt* is not a book about the world but about pictures of the

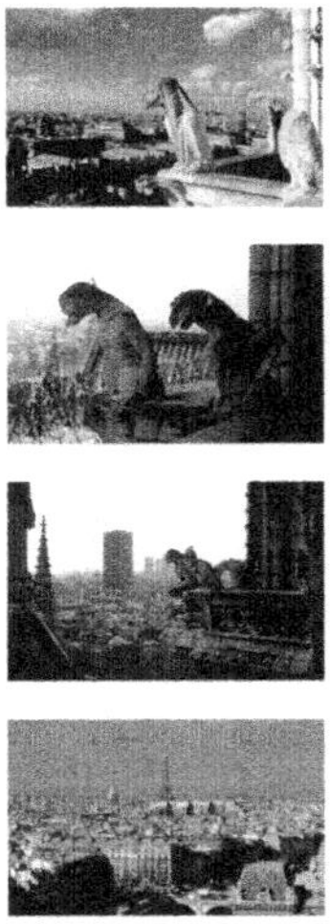

Fig. 6.16

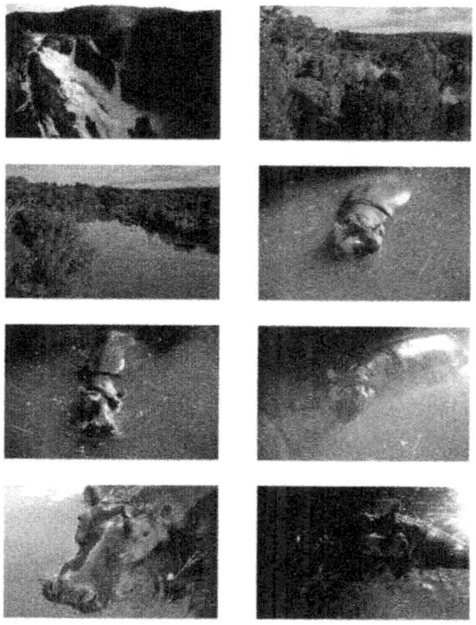

Fig. 6.17

world. It follows and replicates all the well-known and obvious views of technical and commercial photography. Its photographs are, so to speak, second degree pictures. They do no aspire to capture the world anew but to assemble and arrange systematically existing pictures in a way which will expose how little there is to be seen. What we are trained to take as reliable renditions of 'reality' is in fact a form of info-tainment, the product of a ruthless and artificial filtering process.

Fischli/Weiss have a highly developed sensitivity for the entropy of systematic order. As in all their works, they have arranged their material in *Sichtbare Welt* with an engineer's precision into groups and sequences. Nothing is accidental, everything owed to rational categorization. But the resulting order is just a fake, it does not lead to recognition and understanding. It is form without substance—a satirical play with meaning which is constantly being constructed, only to collapse just as regularly.

As opposed to Fischli/Weiss's slapstick approach, Feldmann, the editors of *Ohio #15* and Wiebke Loeper all rely on order as an instrument of meaning. Whenever they irritate the viewer, it is to make her search for deeper layers of significance in the composition and presentation. She is invited to detect and construct new connections between the individual pictures. Isolated, they cannot be understood, Feldmann claims. They need to be situated into a context or sequence. Even when stripped of their original private context, the snapshots in Feldmann's *Porträt* are automatically perceived as samples of a cultural code which will determine their de-coding and imaginative reloading by the viewer. Without cultural knowledge, the photographs could not be interpreted.

In Feldmann/Duval's *cahier d'image,* the referential frame is large and the referential game wide open. In comparison, *Ohio #15* presents a much stricter and narrower concept of order. It has to substitute for the essential information originally given by Wolfgang Hagen in his own accompanying notes. The order and arrangement of the pictures is the only clue to what is going on. Only the shots themselves allow the viewer to realize that the camera was used by somebody to help him survive in a difficult situation which has swallowed all elements of normal life.

In *Moll 31,* time is what happens between the pictures. They create an empty space that needs to be filled with the viewer's narrative speculation. The photographs are referential points providing dates and recognizable situations from which an individual story can be reconstructed. In it a much wider historical context is embedded—the story of a generation. Loeper is the only one creating a narrative, and thus chronological, order. It consists of an almost brutal 'then-and-now' dichotomy, with time the black hole in between. The passing of time in general, and of specific historical times in particular, is the central focus of Loeper's essay. The opposite is true for Hagen, the hospitalised patient fighting his illness with a camera. In the confined space of the hospital room and with nothing much happening, the special quality of time is indirectly visualized by Huber's and Janka's selection. For Hagen, time—i.e. the reliable progression and continuation of everything, including himself—has catastrophically disappeared. His life is no longer a river quietly flowing on but spinning round in a deadly vortex. The camera is Hagen's main tool of survival, a means to carry him through a situation in which time stands still and pictures just render different views of the same overpowering existential situation: fatal illness.

While both Loeper and Hagen take an—almost literally—dead serious attitude, Fischli/Weiss treat time, as well as everything else, firmly tongue-in-cheek. At first glance, *Sichtbare Welt,* with its endless rows of pictures each similar to its predecessor, almost seems like a flip book, like the individual frames of a film roll. But this, the promise of a coherent narrative, is again nothing but illusion, a trap into which the two artists merrily lead the viewer. Her expectation to be taken on an exciting trip is disappointed time and again. Stories seem to be starting constantly, only to collapse after the turn of the next corner. There is no chronological, let alone biographical, order linking those pictures. For Fischli/Weiss, the disappearance of time is not a tragic individual fate but a man-made, cultural process. In the hopelessly overpopulated pictorial world of today, they seem to be saying: even time isn't what it used to be.

Art reflecting art is a hallmark of modernism, and photography has been taking part in the exercise for quite a while now. A late arrival on the scene, it was pushed to do what literature, music or painting had done already by the rapid expansion of its physical and technical means and the omnipresent consequences of this process. Self-reflection in photography did not just follow the same intrinsic logic of all the different forms of art. To a large extent, it was technology-driven.

The way photography turned on itself for introspection is, however, anything but uniform. The four examples discussed in this essay demonstrate an impressive variety self-relection, of pictures reacting to a world full of pictures. Never veering off to the merely conceptual, the approaches range from the funny to the serious, from the critical to the affirmative, from satirical playfulness to architectural construction. These photographers employ a remarkably varied set of tools. When it comes to the structures of a society constantly reproducing and re-inventing itself in pictures, they are reflecting the questions raised by their theoretical counterparts just as competently—and emotionally more powerful.[6]

Notes

[1] Concerning the impossibility of translating 'Bildwissenschaft' into English, see Bredekamp, 2003, 418-419. For the same reason, Hans Belting has proposed to use the term 'Iconology' in a more open, interdisciplinary sense than in Erwin Panofsky's understanding (Belting, 2005, 302-319).

[2] The three leading theorists in terms of 'Bildwissenschaft' in the German-speaking countries are Hans Belting (Belting, 2001, 2005, 2007), Gottfried Böhm (Böhm, 1994, 2007) and Horst Bredekamp (Bredekamp, 2003, 2004). Apart from them, a lot of research in this field has been published in anthologies edited by Klaus Sachs-Hombach (like Sachs-Hombach, 2004). For a 'Bildwissenschaft'-overview see Schulz, 2005.

[3] Between 1968 and 1974 he edited around 35 of those booklets. In 1974 he founded the publishing house 'Drei Möwen-Verlag', since 1998 he publishes as well in 'Feldmann-Verlag' and others.

[4] After the death of Jens Hagen his wife, Dorothee Joachims, has given Huber and Janka the possibility to publish Hagens archive.

[5] *Moll 31* was first published as artists' book in 1995 with handprinted photographs and letterpress printing in an edition of 9 + 4 copies as volume No. 13 in the Berlin Edition LIANE. 2005 Edition J.J. Heckenhauer re-edited the book in a limited edition of 750 copies.

[6] See note 2.

Bibliography

¬ Gottfried Böhm, 'Die Wiederkehr der Bilder', in Gottfried Böhm (ed.), *Was ist ein Bild?* (Munich: Wilhelm Fink Verlag, 1994), 11-38.

¬ Gottfried Böhm, *Wie Bilder Sinn erzeugen. Die Macht des Zeigens*, (Berlin University Press, 2007).

¬ Hans Belting, *Bild-Anthropologie. Entwürfe für eine Bildwissenschaft* (Munich: Wilhelm Fink Verlag, 2001).

¬ Hans Belting, 'Image, Medium, Body: A new approach to Iconology', *Critical Inquiry* (Winter 2005): 302-319.

¬ Hans Belting (ed.), *Bilderfragen. Die Bildwissenschaft im Aufbruch* (Munich: Wilhelm Fink Verlag, 2007).

¬ Horst Bredekamp, 'A Neglected Tradition? Art History as *Bildwissenschaft*', *Critical Inquiry* (Spring 2003): 418-428.

¬ Horst Bredekamp, 'Drehmomente. Merkmale und Ansprüche des Iconic Turn', in Christa Maar and Hubert Burda (eds) *Iconic Turn. Die neue Macht der Bilder* (Cologne: DuMont, 2004): 15-26.

¬ Hans-Peter Feldmann, *Porträt* (Munich: Schirmer/Mosel Verlag, 1994).

¬ Peter Fischli, David Weiss, *Sichtbare Welt* (Cologne: Verlag der Buchhandlung Walther König, 2000).

¬ Michel Foucault, 'Andere Räume' ('Des espaces autres', 1967), *Aisthesis. Wahrnehmung heute oder Perspektiven einer anderen Ästhetik* (Reclam Verlag Leipzig, 1990), 34-46.

¬ Vilém Flusser, *Für eine Philosophy der Photographie,* Edition Flusser Bd. III (1997 [1983]).

¬ Justin Hoffmann, 'Die Fotografien von Fischli und Weiss', *Artis* (July-Aug, 1989): 36-39.

¬ Uschi Huber, Jörg Paul Janka (ed.), *Ohio Photomagazin*, no. 15/2007, (Cologne: Ohio Verlag, 2007).

¬ Wiebke Loeper, *Moll 31* (Tübingen/Berlin: Edition J.J. Heckenhauer, 2005).

¬ W.J.T. Mitchell, 'The Pictorial Turn', *Artforum* (March 1992): 89-94.

¬ Richard M. Rorty, 'Metaphilosophical Difficulties of Linguistic Philosophy', in Richard M. Rorty (ed.) *The Linguistic Turn. Essays in Philosophical Method* (Chicago/London: University of Chicago Press, 1992 [1967]), 1-39.

¬ Klaus Sachs-Hombach (ed.), *Wege zur Bildwissenschaft. Interviews* (Cologne: Halem Verlag, 2004).

¬ Martin Schulz, *Ordnungen der Bilder. Eine Einführung in die Bildwissenschaft* (Munich: Wilhelm Fink Verlag, 2009).

¬ Thomas Weski, 'In indirect speech', in Helena Tatay (ed.) *Hans-Peter Feldmann—272 Pages*, exh. cat. (Barcelona: Fundació Antoni Tàpies, 2001/2002; Paris: Centre national de la photographie, 2002; Winterthur; Fotomuseum Winterthur 2002; Cologne: Museum Ludwig, 2003), 104-105.

part 3

Cinematic Time / Duration and Fragment

7 The Eclipse of Time

Victor Burgin

On February 15, 1961, the 'path of totality' of a solar eclipse passed through North-Central Italy. Michelangelo Antonioni travelled to Florence to film the event. He later said: 'In that darkness, in that icy cold, in that silence so different from other silences, in that almost complete motionlessness...I speculated whether even sentiments are arrested during an eclipse (Antonioni, 1963, x; Chatman, 1985, 72-73).' Antonioni's film *L'eclisse* [*The Eclipse*] was released in 1962, a year after the appearance of *La notte* and two years after *L'avventura*—the films which together with *The Eclipse* form a *de facto* 'trilogy'. The story told in *The Eclipse* can be simply summarized: A young woman leaves an older man with whom she has been living. On a visit to the Rome Stock Exchange to see her mother, who is playing the stock market, she meets a young stock broker and drifts into an affair with him. The film follows the course of their relationship up to the point when they arrange to meet each other again: 'At eight o'clock. Same place.' These words from Piero (Alain Delon) are the last words spoken in the film. The camera follows Vittoria (Monica Vitti) as she leaves Piero's office and enters the street. The camera then returns to watch Piero as he sits at his desk, ignoring the telephones that have begun to ring. Here, the film's depiction of the story of Vittoria and Piero ends, but the film does not end here. It continues for a further seven minutes.[1]

The seven minute sequence with which *The Eclipse* ends is a montage of shots filmed in the streets of the modern 'EUR' (Esposizione Universale Roma) district on the South-Western periphery of Rome.[2] In broadly schematic terms the first part of *The Eclipse* is a chronologically linear narrative—without, for example, such devices as the 'flashback'. The closing sequence is a descriptive concatenation of shots of a place which succeed one another according to no narrative imperative. In the first part of the film, Vittoria and Piero adopt as their meeting place an intersection at which a house is being built; a wooden fence surrounds the construction site, and just inside the fence is a pile of bricks and a barrel of water. The first time the couple linger there Vittoria throws a small piece of wood into the water in the barrel. When they next meet there, Piero discards an empty book of matches in the water. In the final seven minute sequence we see the wood and the match book cover still floating on the surface of the water. There is also a shot of the pile of bricks, and of the façade of the half-built house screened by reed matting. These shots attach the coda to the narrative that precedes it, but there are other shots that seem to have no such relation to the story. So, for example, in a comprehensive study of Antonioni's cinema, Seymour Chatman refers to the final sequence as 'a kind of minidocumentary of EUR' and 'a portrait of the suburb' (Chatman, 1985, 81-82). It is only with repeated viewings that it becomes apparent that the camera never leaves the immediate environment of the intersection, and that each one of the fifty-seven shots that comprise the sequence contains a more or less legible clue to its belonging in that same magnetic space. A young Italian photographer told a friend of mine that she has a DVD copy of the last seven minutes of *L'eclisse* that she carries with her wherever she travels. The author of a substantial study of *The Eclipse* says that if he were 'compelled to choose between eliminating the coda or all of *L'eclisse* up to the point of the coda [he] would choose the latter (Rosenfeld, note 4).' If this choice were exercised, what kind of object would remain? In the terms of conventional cinematic genre the coda may be classified neither as a fiction film nor a documentary. Evening descends during the course of the sequence, which ends with a close-up of a brilliant streetlight against the blackness of night, but although this imposes a temporal order on the shots one would not say that the sequence tells the story of nightfall. Again, if the sequence is indeed to be considered, in Seymour Chatman's terms, a 'minidocumentary of EUR' then it is a singularly uninformative one—for example, we learn nothing of the origin of the district in Benvenito Mussolini's plan for an international exhibition to celebrate twenty years of fascism, nor do we learn much about the social composition of those who inhabit the EUR today. With no story to tell, the coda most resembles a random assemblage of photographs.

I am in a nondescript neighborhood in a city unfamiliar to me. I came with the intention of making photographs, but now I am here I feel at a loss. Nothing seems especially interesting. Nevertheless I begin to photograph, hoping that some sense of purpose will emerge as I do so. But although I continue to take photographs, even as the light fades and darkness falls, nothing happens. This is the feeling I have during the last seven minutes of *The Eclipse*. I know I am looking at a film, but I have the impression of a series of photographs.[3] It is not that the shots appear to *be* photographs, it is rather that the world in the shots appears as if it were *being photographed*. Nevertheless time passes in these shots, and a photograph—it is generally agreed—excludes time. In his book of 1983 *L'Acte Photographique* Philippe Dubois tells a personal anecdote. He was five years old, and running a race against other children under the eyes of an assembly of parents and other family members. He was far ahead of the others, and close to the finishing line, when he noticed his father pointing a camera at him 'in order to fix the exploit for posterity'. The young Dubois stopped dead in his tracks. While the other runners streamed by behind him he remained motionless, and never did complete the race. The incident provides him with the image of the course of time, in the form of the race, continuing to unfurl *behind his back* as he faced the camera. 'To the eyes of photography', he comments, 'time no longer flows'; the photographic act 'guillotines duration' to establish a sort of 'outside time' [*hors-temps*]. I similarly feel that time passes behind the back of the images that make up the coda of *The Eclipse*, even while I also have the impression that they contain time. I can resolve the apparent contradiction only if I allow that time is not a singular thing.

Commonsense tends to assume a duality of temporalities, and in doing so echoes two distinct philosophical traditions. In the first of these, originating in Classical antiquity but deriving mainly from Newton, time is an objective fact: uninfluenced by objects and events, time, together with space, is the 'container' in which objects and events take place. A uniform and unidirectional flow, time is an absolute and invariable condition of the physical universe; it is quite simply part of the way things are. In an alternative tradition, deriving mainly from Kant, Newtonian mechanics describes not the way things are, but rather the way in which we may have knowledge of them: time—again like space—is an *a priori* form of our innate intuition of 'things in themselves', which by themselves have neither spatial nor temporal properties. In introducing the human subject into the consideration of time, Kant opened the way to such modern philosophical and psychological formulations as those of Bergson and Freud. Everyday language routinely distinguishes between time as it is 'in reality' and time as it appears to us. For example, we say that time 'passes quickly' if we enjoy what we are doing, or 'passes slowly' if we do not. Few would dispute that subjective time and 'clock time' are different things. But the 'clock time' of modern life is a specifically historical version of Newtonian cosmology, it is the invention of industrial capitalism.

Time has a history. Early agrarian societies were governed by such things as the alternation of day and night, the succession of the seasons and the movement of the planets; periods of daylight were measured by the sundial. The first mechanical clocks appear at the turn of the 13th and 14th centuries in response to the needs of Church, State and commerce to govern and profit through the synchronization of human affairs. In this period, the fundamental unit of mensural time was most intensively debated in relation to music, where early attempts to establish the pulse of time quite literally proposed the duration of a heart beat. The subsequent history of the concept of time is one of its progressive alienation from any condition of nature. Modern time, the time of modernity, is consolidated in the 19th century with the national, then international, synchronization of clocks brought by the coming of the railway and the telegraph, and continues with the introduction into the work place of such things as the punch-card time clock, the assembly line and Taylorism. As the human body is forced to the temporally constant and predictable rhythm of machines, so the working day is detached from natural rhythms: first with the advent of electrical lighting, and more recently with mobile telephones and remotely networked computers. Clock time is money. When, in Antonioni's *L'eclisse*, a minute of silence is called for at the Rome Stock Exchange following the death of a colleague, Piero mutters to Vittoria in mild irritation: '...a minute, here, that costs millions'.[4]

The clock time of capital flows behind the last seven minutes of *The Eclipse*. The time of the images in the coda is different from that in which the preceding narrative takes place, but this different time is not confined to the coda, it also interrupts the course of the narrative. Such an alternation of temporalities is not unique to Antonioni's cinema. I think, for example, of the films of Yasujiro Ozu. In the work of either of these directors a shot may run on beyond the time necessary to establish the dramatic sense of a scene, producing what in conventional terms would be considered a redundant image, 'surplus' footage that would conventionally be consigned to the cutting room floor. Such images may emerge when the actors have exited the frame, and the anticipated transition to the next scene appears delayed as the camera lingers on the now vacant space. An analogous effect is achieved in Ozu's films by a cut away from the action to an 'irrelevant' object or view. An example of this occurs in Ozu's film of 1949 *Late Spring,* at the close of a scene between Noriko (Setsuko Hara) and her father (Chishu Ryu). Father and daughter are staying at a traditional Japanese inn. They have laid down to sleep on the floor of their room, and in the darkness have exchanged some desultory observations about the day's events. After a short silence Noriko addresses a further remark to her father, but he does not reply. Turning her head towards him she sees that he has fallen asleep. She turns back and, gazing towards the ceiling, smiles fondly. There is a cut away to a vase, which the immobile camera frames for six seconds, and then a cut back to Noriko, whose expression now turns to one of sadness; a second cut to the vase, with the same framing, fills the last ten seconds of this scene before the cut to the next scene. Commenting on the cut away to the vase Gilles Deleuze writes: '...this duration of the vase is precisely the representation of that which remains, across the succession of changing states (Deleuze, 1985, 28).' The final seven minute sequence of *The Eclipse* seems composed almost entirely of such 'gratuitous' shots 'out of time' that appear to owe more to what we conventionally think of as photography than to cinema.

Only thirty-nine seconds into the beginning of *The Eclipse* Antonioni reminds us of the proscenium apparatus that frames the history of visual representations in the West. The fundamental stasis of painting and theater is to be historically surpassed with the advent of photography and cinemaphotography, which although they will not free objects from the frame will liberate the frame itself. In a 1960 interview, Antonioni describes his discomfort on arriving for the first day of filming his first full-length feature film (*Cronace di un Amore*, 1950) and finding the camera fixed to its stand: 'I felt paralyzed...The next day, I called for a dolly, and I began to follow my characters...('Entretien avec Michelangelo Antonioni', quoted in Leprohon, 1963, 25).' Antonioni describes his relation to the film camera here almost as if he were a 'street photographer', and his remarks may recall the park scene in his film of 1966 *Blow-Up*, where the camera follows Thomas, the photographer, as Thomas follows and photographs the couple in the park. Speaking in 1958, Antonioni says: 'One of my preoccupations when I am shooting is that of following a character until I feel the need to let him go...When everything has been said, when the scene appears to be finished, there is what comes afterwards. It seems to me important to show the character, back and front, just at that moment—a gesture or an attitude that illuminates all that has happened, and what results from it ('Colloquo con Michelangelo Antonioni', quoted in Leprohon, 1963, 96).' Again, Antonioni's use of cinema here is consonant with photography—in this case with the idea of the 'decisive moment', which in turn is continuous with the history of Western representations. Between the 16th and 18th centuries, a body of doctrine was assembled in response to the problem of how best to depict a narrative in a painting. With only a single image at his or her disposal, it was agreed that the painter should isolate the *peripeteia*—that instant in the story when all hangs in the balance.

The difference between the shots in the coda and most of the narrative that precedes it broadly corresponds to Deleuze's distinction between the movement-image and the time-image. It might seem that this distinction applies only to film. It accords with common sense to assign the still image to photography theory and the moving image to film theory. But to equate movement with film and stasis with photography is to confuse the representation with its material support. A film may depict an immobile object even while the film strip itself is moving at twenty-four frames per second; a photograph may depict a moving object even though the photograph does not move.[5] Writing in 1971 the photographer and filmmaker Hollis Frampton envisaged an 'infinite film' that would consist of a spectrum extending from the stasis of an image resulting from a succession of completely identical frames, to the chaos of an image produced by a succession of totally different frames (Frampton, [1971] 1983, 114). An interest in movement for its own sake may be found in early 20th century avant-garde film and photography, and in painting under the impact of film and photography; but it is not movement as such that fascinates most people but purposive movement, movement with causes and consequences. What cinema audiences find most interesting about characters on the screen is not their movements (albeit these have their own, primarily erotic, interest) but their acts. Activity however is not necessarily bound to movement. Peter Wollen illustrates this point with reference to a book of photographs by André Kertèsz entitled *On Reading* (Kertèsz, 1971). Wollen observes that although all the people in the photographs are motionless they are nevertheless doing something. He writes: 'They are not simply static or frozen in place. They are all in the process of reading'; thus, 'We can see that activity is not at all the same thing as movement (Wollen, 1984).' Chris Marker's film *La Jetée* is perhaps the most widely commented example of a work that disjoins action from movement and contradicts the idea of a fundamental opposition between film and photography.[6] Some of the images in the film are shot with a still camera, others are derived from film footage. *La Jetée* rejects any radical opposition between film and photography in favor of a choice between equally available options. It moreover demonstrates that a distinction between film and photography based on the difference between simultaneity and succession is founded on a misrecognition. Although a photographic exposure may be made 'in the blink of an eye', the experience of looking at the resulting image belongs to the subjective register of *durée* rather than to the mechanical abstraction of the 'instant' in which the image was recorded on film (see Bellour, 1987; Mulvey, 2003).

On the evidence of the calendar clock that appears in the first scene at the stock exchange, and the date of the newspaper seen in the final sequence, *The Eclipse* covers a period of about two months. The subjective impression while watching the film is that the action takes place in the space of a few days. The only thing certain is that the film itself runs for about two hours. A film has both a diagetic time and a running time, which is usually the time of its viewing; a photograph has only the time of its viewing. We expect to be told the running time of a film or video; we do not usually ask: 'How long is the photograph?'—but the question is not entirely irrelevant. Photography renders a 'moment' in terms of space and suspends it as if out of time. The material support of the spatial image however, whether silver print or digital, is itself subject to entropy, and will eventually decay. The photograph does not stop time, but rather suspends a moment between parentheses until the time when time returns. During this entropic time of the photograph the subjective time of the viewer intervenes. A friend told me that, after moving house, she found herself going through some photographs she had long ago put aside and forgotten. She described her shock on coming across an old photograph of her mother. She recalled that, as an adolescent, she had disliked this photograph because she felt it made her mother look old, and so she had hidden it away. She was now surprised to see the radiantly beautiful young woman in the image—a woman much younger than she herself now was. The undisclosed 'winter garden' photograph of Roland Barthes' mother as a child prompted Barthes to write a book devoted to photographs that contain a wounding detail. We may turn to psychoanalysis for an explanation of the mechanisms by which a detail in a photograph may trigger an apparently incomprehensible affect in the viewer, but the precipitating cause is made possible by the inherent contingency of the photograph.

Left to its own devices the camera accords as much attention to a discarded sandwich wrapper as it does to the sublime landscape that the litter defaces. Just as a photograph recognizes no hierarchy in the world within its frame, so the final seven minutes of *The Eclipse* bestows no hierarchal order on the shots that comprise it. Antonioni has referred to the final sequence of *The Eclipse* as 'seven minutes where only the objects remain of the adventure (Strick, 1963, 17).' That it is not the vocation of objects to be actors in an adventure is precisely what the final sequence recognizes. When, on the occasion of her second meeting with Piero at the corner by the building site, Vittoria pushes apart her floating piece of wood and Piero's match book cover, the surface of the water is a stage for her personal drama. But Vittoria's intentionality alone imposes allegorical meaning on the objects in the water barrel; with the eclipse of her desire the world of objects is revealed as indifferently contingent, and it the contingency of the world that reasserts itself in the final sequence. As Wittgenstein expresses it: 'In the world everything is as it is and happens as it does happen. *In* it there is no value (Wittgenstein, *Tractatus*, 6.41).' When a similar perception of things is presented in Jean-Paul Sartre's novel of 1938 *Nausea* it is explicitly tied to language and to time. The protagonist Roquentin finds that words lose their grip on the things they name: 'I murmur: "It's a seat"...But the word remains on my lips: it refuses to go and rest upon the thing (Sartre, 1965, 180).' With the loss of linguistic organization, the contingency of being-in-itself [*en-soi*] breaks through in its unique temporal place: the present. Roquentin writes:

> The true nature of the present revealed itself: it was that which exists, and all that was not present did not exist. The past did not exist. Not at all...Things are entirely what they appear to be—and *behind them*...there is nothing (Sartre, 1965, 139-140).

In his comment on the cut away to the vase in Ozu's film, Deleuze writes that the shot is 'the representation of that which remains, across the succession of changing states.' Noriko sees the father she loves asleep, as if dead. Deleuze's otherwise abstract formulation is to be understood in relation to the dramatic context in which the shot of the vase takes place: the vase represents a contingent order of being *en-soi*, and a temporality which is indifferent to ephemeral human life. The sense of the final sequence in *The Eclipse* is similarly bound to its context, the preceding narrative that is its *pre-text*. There is however a significant difference between the two examples, a difference allowed by, although not guaranteed by, the difference between a sequence and an isolated shot: just as the type of 'gratuitous' shot that makes up the coda also intervenes in the preceding narrative, so the temporality of human affairs enters the final sequence.

Most of the fifty-seven shots that make up the final sequence of *The Eclipse* are of unpopulated details of the urban environment: the shadow of a tree on tarmac, the façade of an apartment block, a bus turning a corner, and so on. Other shots have people in them: a dark-haired woman stands at the pavement edge on an empty street; a grey-haired man also seems to wait for someone or something; some people descend from a bus and the camera follows a man who is reading a copy of the Italian national weekly *L'Espresso* as he walks away, the headlines read 'THE ATOMIC RACE' and 'THE PEACE IS WEAK'.[7] *The Eclipse* was released in the same year as the Cuban Missile Crisis. The front page of the periodical also has a reference to an article on Alain Resnais' film of 1961 *L'année dernière à Marienbad* by the investigative journalist, novelist and critic Camilla Cederna (d. 1997). The headline reads 'Camilla Cederna à Marienbad: ...où des couloirs interminables ...' (a line from the film). Camilla Cederna is the model for the character of the journalist Maria Feletti in Dario Fo's play *Accidental Death of an Anarchist*, which was first produced in Milan in 1970. The play was a response to the events surrounding the suspicious death while in police custody of the anarchist Giuseppe Pinelli, after he was arrested in the aftermath of the 1969 Piazza Fontana bombing in Milan. The bombing of the bank was yet to come, but Camilla Cederna's reputation as an investigative reporter was already established, and the original Italian audience of Antonioni's film would have been aware of it. The front page therefore introduces contemporary culture and national and international politics into a parade of contingencies indifferent to human temporalities. Nevertheless the punctual political anecdote is not contextualized or explained. The headline in shot twenty-seven of the coda takes its place in an ensemble that includes the close-up of the earlobe of an old man in shot forty-two, and the shadow of a tree in shot nine. The punctual, whether *punctum* or mere punctuation, remains discrete—no causality is suggested, no connections are made between the points: whether historical, moral or merely rhetorical. As a consequence, subjective association and reflection are facilitated.

The sequence runs its course and I am left in the wake of its time. I am left with much the kind of feeling I had after reading Marguarite Duras' story *Le ravissment de Lol V. Stein* (1964), the feeling of an indeterminate space and time within which a story was unfolding that had nevertheless always-already taken place, and which would repeat indefinitely. It is perhaps significant that Duras' story revolves around a moment in a ballroom where Lol sees her lover dancing with another woman. The dancers turn as if out of time, but nevertheless in motion. Meaning has drained from the event, leaving only its contingency, and leaving Lol to perpetually turn their image in her mind in the space around the void. In her book of 2002 *The Emergence of Cinematic Time* Mary Anne Doane speaks of the difficulties early film photographers had in determining the duration of an event, in deciding how far meaning could extend into the surrounding 'vast and uncontrollable, and ultimately meaningless, realm of the contingent (Doane, 2002, 12).' Antonioni abandons his protagonists to contingency seven minutes before his film runs out. One critic remarks that he seems literally to have lost interest in them. In her book of 1984 *L'ennui et ses discours*, Michèle Huguet remarks:

> ...the subject experiencing boredom is not suffering from an absence of desire, but from its indetermination, which in turn forces the subject to wander, in search of a point of fixation (Huguet, 1984, 215; cited in Petro, 1995, 271).

On an evening in Rome, many years ago, I left my hotel and took a taxi to the opening of an art exhibition. After the opening I was driven to dinner in a restaurant, and after dinner to a bar where the party continued. From the bar, another drive across town took me to a gathering in a private house. There, in the early hours of the morning, with no idea of where I now was, I asked how I might best find my way home. I was led to a window. There, across the street, was my hotel. In the first sequence of *The Eclipse* Vittoria, in the early morning, opens the curtains in her lover's apartment upon the view of a large concrete water tower; we do not see the tower again until it appears in the background of a shot in the last sequence. In a moment of surprised recognition a path through space and a time folds back on its beginning. The figure traced by the camera around a closed path in the final sequence of the film is a mise-en-abyme of the closed path the entire film takes in its unreeling. These paths that circle in space might also be seen as describing a circle in time. The narrative portion of *The Eclipse* begins with Vittoria opening the curtains upon the morning light, the coda ends with darkest night. But we might easily view the coda as a prelude to a repetition of the same, in which the same woman opens the same curtains onto the same morning. Time is not one thing, nor is it only linear. Speaking to students at Paris 8, St. Denis, in 1982, Deleuze distinguished between two kinds of film director: 'A realist is interested in intermediaries...he is interested in neither the beginning nor the end. But the others are only interested in the beginning and the end because it is the same thing. It is in the same movement that the world is born and is already ended.'

The invention of photography was consistent with the project of the industrial revolution to transfer complex and time consuming manual tasks to the automatic operation of a machine. As a consequence of its inception as a mechanical means of recording appearances, photography tends to be discussed mainly in positivist terms: the active phenomenon of perception is reduced to a passive optics of vision, and a naïve realism reduces the photographic image to an unmediated record of reality. The idea that the photograph is 'outside' of time implies a similarly positivist picture of time, a reductive *spatialization* of temporality to clock time. In clock time, as Henri Bergson writes: 'Outside of me, in space, there is never more than a single position of the hand...for nothing is left of the past positions.' Roquentin, we may remember, concurs: 'The past [does] not exist. Not at all.' Clock time, however, is only one aspect of the phenomenon of temporality. Bergson continues:

> Within myself a process of...interpenetration of conscious states is going on, which constitutes duration (durée). It is because I endure in this way that I picture to myself what I call the past...at the same time as I perceive the present.

The photograph is not outside of time, but it may produce the effect of an eclipse of clock time. Left to its own automatic devices, the photograph withdraws from participation in clock time, which then 'passes behind its back'. To the extent that it withdraws, that which Bergson considers the *real* time of *durée* comes to the foreground—and also the contingency of the world. Such photographic practices as advertising and reportage deploy their rhetorical techniques against the inherent 'contingency effect' of the photograph, placing the photograph in the service of consensual meanings—venal or moral—preconstituted in the increasingly unified clock time of global markets, the media and global history. It is again due to the tenacity of the positivist attitude that the issue of indexicality returns so consistently in discussions of photography. There may well be an ontological essence to the photograph, just as there may be an ontological essence to the phoneme. But what is essential in photography, as in language, resides not in its materiality but in its *use*. I am sitting in a café in Marco Polo airport, in Venice. In a corner opposite, a group of young people have immured themselves behind baggage, tables and chairs. One of them, his back to me, has held up a digital camera and is cycling through images of their holiday together. Shot succeeds shot, with intermittent close-ups and occasional pans and zooms. I think of the view from my hotel room where, each night as I opened the shutters, I would see images passing erratically and silently on a television screen in a room across the deserted square. The young man passes the camera around the circle of friends, who laugh and add their own commentary as they recall their time together. What sense does it make to say that these images are out of time? I have the fantasy that one of the group, let us call him or her 'X', is secretly enamored of 'Y', but who is already attached to 'Z'. One of the images shows 'X' and 'Y' laughing together, a couple within the frame if not in reality. Perhaps 'X' will find a way of keeping this image; perhaps it will then be put away and forgotten, only to be found again by chance some forty years from now. Perhaps 'X' will then look with bemused wonder upon the melancholy miracle of this image 'out of time'. I can only guess what material form the photographic image will take forty years from now. It is a further tribute to positivism that the photographic image is so often identified with its material support, a support that today has become volatile and mutable. Because of this new-found mutability, however, it is perhaps now easier to conceive of the photographic image as, precisely, an *image*. As Georges Didi-Huberman reminds us:

> The image can be, at one and the same time, material and psychical, external and internal, spatial and linguistic (*langagière*), morphological and formless, plastic and discontinuous... (Didi-Huberman, 2000, 114).

In the spirit of positivism we might say that the young people in Marco Polo airport used photographs to 'document' their holiday—we might equally say that they used them to advertise it. What is apparent is that they used photographs to tell the story of their time together. Paul Ricoeur has argued that 'time becomes human to the extent that it is articulated through a narrative mode (Ricoeur, 1985,

52).' In the only article Clement Greenberg wrote about photography he judged that the specificity of photography resides in its ability to tell a story (Greenberg, 1964). This seems a contradictory idea from a critic who insisted that an artistic practice can only progress through the attention it gives to that which marks it as individual, that which differentiates it from other art practices. Surely the ability to tell a story is properly specific to literature. When asked why she did not tell the story in her novel *Love* more simply, Tony Morrison replied that her aim was to 'reproduce the way we perceive life'. Greenberg suggests that the inevitable role of the photographic image is to tell a story. Morrison implies that the role of her stories is to evoke an image. We can bridge the apparent incommensurability of these positions only if we understand the image not simply in terms of its optical definition but in its extensions. For example, Bergson writes: 'Perception is never a simple contact of the mind with the object present; it is completely impregnated with memory-images which complete and interpret it (Bergson, 1999, 146).' This is the aspect of *durée* that Bergson calls *interpenetration*. In a commentary on Bergson, Gilles Deleuze writes: 'The real and the virtual coexist and enter into a narrow circuit that takes us constantly from one to the other (Deleuze, 2002, 184).' What Deleuze calls the 'virtual' component of the image will include public knowledge of what is being looked at—historical, philosophical, political, technical, aesthetic, and so on; it will include personal memories, fantasies and feelings; and it will include narratives.

The grand legitimating narrative of late capitalism is woven with the clock time of *The Eclipse*. The story of the relationship between Vittoria and Piero is its conventional vehicle. Handsome, hard-working and successful, his life is devoted to the pursuit of the pleasure of consuming, trading up and moving on—stocks, motor-cars and women. Piero is the complete Don Juan of late capitalism. The Lacanian theorist Alenka Zupancic has observed: 'Don Juan can fuck as much as he likes, but, finally, it is he who is being fucked by the signifier, that is, by the famous list that he has to fill up with as many names as possible.' The names cried out on the floor of the Rome stock exchange in Antonioni's film are a roll-call of the companies then driving Italy's post-war 'economic miracle': Mediobanca, Pirelli, Generali, Fiat... When a joyrider drives Piero's Alpha Romeo into a lake and dies, Piero views the event exclusively as an opportunity to acquire a BMW; when Vittoria comes into sight he instantly dumps his girl-friend. All objects are equal before the Law in the symbolic order of late capitalism, and Piero obeys its only super-ego imperative: consume them all and enjoy. We are now near the end of Antonioni's film, the two protagonists have made love in Piero's office. As Vittoria prepares to leave, the two agree to meet each other again. Piero says: 'At eight o'clock. Same place'—the spatio-temporal coordinates of a promise. Something inherent in the sexual relation, says Freud, resists satisfaction. Lacan says, 'Il n'y a pas de rapport sexuelle'. Antonioni wonders—with a note of anxiety—'whether even sentiments are arrested during an eclipse'. Freud's biographer, Ernest Jones, gave a name—'aphanisis'—to the fear of the loss of sexual desire. Lost, perhaps stolen...in a 1940s movie Ava Gardner sings 'Love is pure gold, and time a thief.'[8] In the clock time of late capitalism our desire is extracted from us along with our labor, and sold back to us in the form of the commodity. The eclipse of this time may allow at least the possibility of a reconfiguration of desire, perhaps even the possibility of imagining a different form of society.

Notes

[1] At least two versions of the final sequence of *The Eclipse* are described in the literature on the film. José Moure, in his book on the cinema of Antonioni, gives a one-and-a-half page description of the final sequence in which he mentions about forty shots (Moure, 2001, 82-83). The issue of *L'Avant-Scène Cinéma* devoted to *The Eclipse* lists precisely forty-four shots (*L'Éclipse*, 1993, 103-107). A closely detailed article by Mirella Jona Affron confirms this number (Affron, 1981). However, a version of the screenplay published in 1963 describes fifty-seven shots (Antonioni, 1963, 356-361), and in a book on Antonioni, Sandro Bernardi refers to the 'fifty-seven shots and seven minutes that constitute the final sequence (Bernardi, 2006, 114)'—this accurately describes the sequence that may be found on the 2007 DVD release of the film upon which I base my own remarks here (*L'Eclisse*, Optimum Releasing, 2007—the exact time of the sequence is 07min 11 sec). Nor are these 'two versions' the only versions to have been released. It is reported that the producers of *The Eclipse* cut fourteen shots from the closing sequence of the film, and that the US distributor then made further cuts (Perry and Prieto, 1986, 109).

[2] The 'EUR' building complex was begun by Benito Mussolini in 1935 but with the intercession of the war was left largely incomplete, and was still under construction when Antonioni filmed there in the early 1960s.

[3] The camera moves in only thirteen of the fifty-seven shots that comprise the final seven minute sequence, and when it does so I have the feeling of looking for the next 'photograph'.

[4] The names cried out on the floor of the exchange are a roll-call of the companies then driving Italy's post-war 'economic miracle': Mediobanca, Pirelli, Generali, Fiat...Between 1958 and 1963 industrial output in Italy increased by over 10 percent per year—a rate surpassed only by Japan and West Germany. In *The Eclipse*, released in 1962, Antonioni stages a market crash. In reality, an economic slump

began the year after the film was released from which Italy would not recover until the 1980s. *The Eclipse* is a film which resonates well with the present condition of a world where market values and relations have not only penetrated the economic, social and cultural life of the planet, but also suffuse both the conscious and unconscious registers of subjectivity.

[5] See, for example, Hollis Frampton's film *A Casing Shelved*, which consists of a static shot of a book case; and the photographs in Eadweard Muybridge's *Animal Locomotion*.

[6] Other, very different, examples is provided by Hollis Frampton's film *Nostalgia*.

[7] "LA GARA ATOMICA", "LA PACE È DEBOLE".

[8] *One touch of Venus* (dir. William A. Seiter, 1948).

Bibliography

¬ Mirella Jona Affron, 'Text and Memory in Eclipse', *Literature/Film Quarterly*, vol. 9, no. 3, (1981): 139-151.

¬ Michelangelo Antonioni, *Screenplays of Michelangelo Antonioni* (London: Souvenir, 1963).

¬ Sandro Bernardi, *Antonioni: Personnage paysage* (Saint-Denis: Presses Universitaires de Vincennes, 2006).

¬ Raymond Bellour, 'The Pensive Spectator', trans. Lynne Kirby, *Wide Angle*, vol. 9, no. 1, (1987): 6-10.

¬ Henri Bergson, *Matière et mémoire* (Paris: PUF, 1999 [1939]).

¬ Seymour Chatman, *Antonioni, or, The Surface of the World* (Berkeley, Los Angeles and London: University of California, 1985).

¬ 'Colloquo con Michelangelo Antonioni,' *Bianco e Nero* (June, 1958).

¬ Gilles Deleuze, *Cinéma 2: L'Image Temps* (Paris: Minuit, 1985).

¬ Gilles Deleuze and Claire Parnet, *Dialogues* (Paris: Flammarion, 2002).

¬ Georges Didi-Huberman, *Devant le Temps* (Paris: Minuit, 2000).

¬ Mary Anne Doane, *The Emergence of Cinematic Time* (Cambridge, Mass. and London: Harvard, 2002).

¬ 'Entretien avec Michelangelo Antonioni,' *Cahiers du Cinéma*, no. 112, (October, 1960).

¬ Hollis Frampton, 'For a Metahistory of Film: Commonplace Notes and Hypotheses' (1971), in *Circles of Confusion: Film, Photography, Video; Texts 1968 - 1980* (Rochester, N.Y.: Visual Studies Workshop, 1983), 107-116.

¬ Clement Greenberg, 'Four Photographers', *New York Review of Books* (23 January, 1964).

¬ Michèle Huguet, *L'ennui et ses discours* (Paris: PUF, 1984).

¬ André Kertèsz, *On Reading* (New York: Penguin, 1971).

¬ *L'Éclipse, L'Avant-Scène Cinéma*, no. 419 (February, 1993).

¬ Pierre Leprohon, *Michelangelo Antonioni* (New York: Simon and Schuster, 1963).

¬ José Moure, *Michelangelo Antonioni: Cinéaste de l'évidement* (Paris: Harmattan, 2001).

¬ Laura Mulvey, 'The "pensive spectator" revisited: time and its passing in the still and moving image', in David Green (ed.) *Where is the Photograph?* (Brighton: Photoforum, 2003).

¬ Ted Perry and Rene Prieto, *Michelangelo Antonioni: A Guide to References and Resources* (Boston: G.K. Hall, 1986).

¬ Patrice Petro, 'After Shock/Between Boredom and History', in Patrice Petro (ed.) *Fugitive Images: From Photography to Video* (Bloomingdale and Indianapolis, Indiana, 1995), 265-284.

¬ Paul Ricoeur, *Time and Narrative*, vol. 1, (Chicago: University of Chicago Press, 1985).

¬ David Saul Rosenfeld, 'Michelangelo Antonioni's L'Eclisse—a broken piece of wood, a matchbook, a woman, a man', http://www.davidsaulrosenfeld.com/

¬ Jean-Paul Sartre, *Nausea* (London: Penguin, 1965) [*La nauseé*, Paris: Gallimard, 2002 [1938].

¬ Philip Strick, *Antonioni* (Loughton: Motion, 1963).

¬ Ludwig Wittgenstein, *Tractatus Logico-Philosophicus*, trans. C.K. Ogden (New York: Dover Publications Inc.: 1999).

¬ Peter Wollen, 'Fire and Ice', *Photographies*, no. 4 (Avril, 1984).

8 Suspended Relationships: The Montage Photography Books of Moshe Raviv Vorobeichic

Andrea Nelson

> The flashlike act of connecting elements not obviously belonging together. Their constructive relationships, unnoticed before, produce the new result. If the same methodology were used generally in all fields we would have *the* key to our age—**seeing everything in relationship**.
>
> László Moholy-Nagy (1947, 68)

In 1931, Lithuanian photographer Moshe Raviv Vorobeichic published two strikingly different photography books: *Ein Ghetto im Osten (Wilna)* and *Paris*. *Wilna* is a carefully edited sequence of sixty five photographic compositions that depict everyday life in Vilnius's historic Jewish quarter (fig. 8.1).[1] Mass produced as a volume for the *Schaubücher* series by the Swiss publisher Orell Füssi, this low-priced book was designed for a non-specialist, middle-class audience. The entire series of collectible 'look' books was intended to be both entertaining and educational, and in order to keep the modern reader's attention, the volumes covered a variety of topical themes from winter Olympic sports to Russian revolutionary films (Starl,

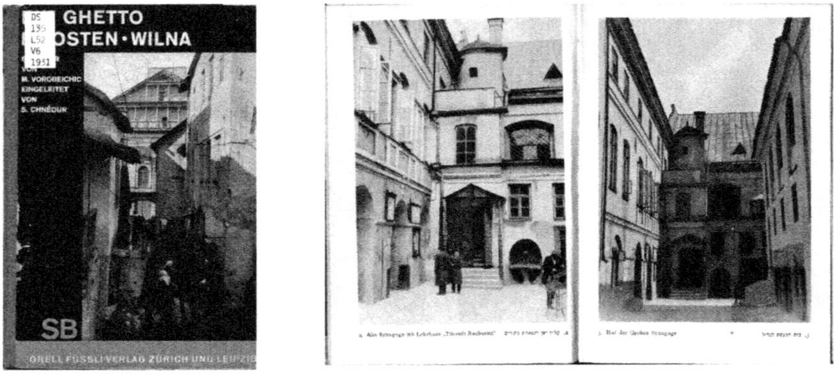

Fig. 8.1 Moshe Raviv Vorobeichic, cover and page layout, *Ein Ghetto im Osten (Wilna)*, Schaubücher 27 (Zurich/ Leipzig: Orell Füssli Verlag, 1931). © Orell Füssli Verlag.

1996, 47).[2] Overall, each volume adheres to a fairly standardized format; every book begins with an introductory essay followed by a sequence of around sixty to ninety photographs, each numbered and titled with a short descriptive caption.

Similar to most modern photography books, the *Schaubücher* were understood to be a new perceptual technique and were designed to communicate knowledge visually in a precise and efficient manner. Therefore it is the photographic sequence and not the written essay that conveys the narrative of the book. True to form, *Wilna* opens with a short, poetic analysis by the Jewish author Salman Chnéour followed by Vorobeichic's photographs. However, what makes this book unlike any of the others in the series is the manner in which Vorobeichic constructs his photographic sequence. Vorobeichic presents the quarter's cultural traditions and architectural spaces through the modern prism of montage. He develops a complex visual narrative through page spreads that present multiple photographs, photomontages, and graphic design elements in active relation to one another. Therefore, rather than following a strict cause-and-effect narrative progression, the reader is required to interact with the book by constructing meaningful transitions and connections between these visual elements. In addition, unlike the other *Schaubücher*, *Wilna* was published in several bilingual versions, including Hebrew and Yiddish, and Hebrew and German (Dmitrieva, 2004, 69).

Vorobeichic began working on his second photography book, *Paris*, immediately after he completed the maquette for *Wilna*. While *Wilna* brought the photographer back to his childhood home and the familiar spaces and memories of his youth, *Paris* depicts the chaotic, fast-paced rhythms of the cosmopolitan center he had been living and working in since the fall of 1928. Published under the pseudonym Moï Ver, *Paris* was produced as a limited edition artistic book with

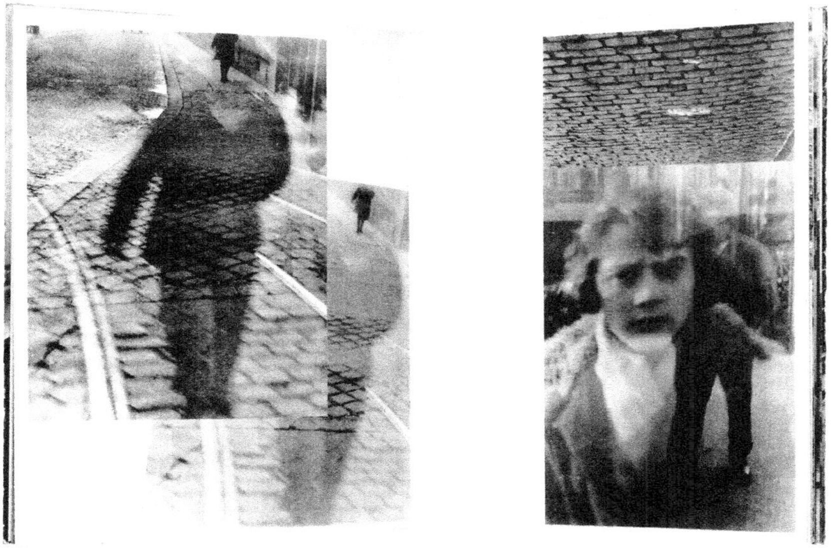

Fig. 8.2 Moï Ver [Moshe Raviv Vorobeichic], page layout, *Paris* (Paris: Éditions Jeanne Walter, 1931). National Gallery of Art Library, David K. E. Bruce Fund. Courtesy of Yossi Raviv.

only 1,000 copies printed by Éditions Jeanne Walter.[3] With a short introduction written in French by painter Fernand Léger, *Paris* was designed for a more specialized audience of bibliophiles and avant-garde photography enthusiasts. Often described in cinematic terms, *Paris* is a dynamic narrative sequence of eighty photographs that contains no additional written text or captions (fig. 8.2). Each double-page layout includes multiple photographs organized in a cut-and-paste montage fashion. However, its most distinctive feature is that almost every single photograph is, itself, a complexly layered image. Reminiscent of montage film frames, Vorobeichic produced these enigmatic photographs by the superimposition of several negatives, many of which were tilted or reversed. This process creates page spreads that simultaneously appear to set the still photograph in motion and still the filmic sequence.

These two books—one perceived as a documentary record, the other as a fine art object—reveal not only the variety and popularity of modern photography books, but also the porous boundaries defining such projects. Despite their differences, *Wilna* and *Paris* both stand out from other photography books published in the early 1930s because they are doubly grounded in the practice of montage, that is, they use photomontages as the constituent components of their montage page spreads. Moreover, structured by the logic of montage, both *Wilna* and *Paris* appear to answer directly Walter Benjamin's desire for a more 'perceptible history' by taking readers on a discontinuous journey through city streets and marginal spaces where the past and present collide. Benjamin asks: 'Must the Marxist understanding of history necessarily be acquired at the expense of the perceptibility of history?...The first stage in this undertaking will be to carry over the principle of montage into history (Benjamin, 1999, 461).' Because he believed that history, as a constellation of events and experiences, emerges through breaks in the linear movement of time, Benjamin called for a complete rethinking of the narrative, spatial, and temporal structure of history based on the process of montage. His methodology re-evaluated those people, events, objects, and spaces that had previously defined the discipline, insisting that history should be comprised of the seemingly random, visual elements of everyday life. These elements, aspects that had been forgotten or suppressed in traditional accounts, work to interrupt established narratives of history by opening up another possibility for history that is fundamentally visual. By offering a sequence of kaleidoscopic, overlapping views that suggest the experience of unfolding time while simultaneously suspending it, Vorobeichic's photography books combine fragments and overlooked details of the social and cultural environment in a way that fosters a new understanding of photographic time and the construction of history. Therefore, just as a reader may flip back and forth through the pages of a book, multiple narratives circulate through Vorobeichic's photography books, potentially working against positivistic constructions of history. Their sequences, which involve an intertwining of motion and stasis, diachronic and synchronic time, engage readers in acts of analogical perception, a mode of relational reading.

Witnessing the Streets of Wilna

In 1927, after studying painting for several years in the Department of Fine Arts at the Stefan Bathory University in Vilnius, Vorobeichic dramatically altered the course of his artistic training. He moved to Dessau, Germany, in order to attend the Bauhaus, an experimental art and design school founded by architect Walter Gropius after the First World War. When Vorobeichic arrived the students were enthralled with photography. This exuberant photo-culture was both a reflection of the unprecedented popularity of photography in society at large, but also of the excitement generated by Bauhaus educator László Moholy-Nagy. Moholy-Nagy's theories and photographic projects epitomize what has been termed 'New Vision' photography. By breaking with normalized viewing habits, he sought to de-familiarize the subject matter of his photographs in order to challenge viewers not only to see in a 'new' or different manner, but also to think about the effects of modern technologies on human perception. Inspired by these ideas, students and other faculty members created photographs that disregarded traditional conventions in an attempt to make photography productive rather than just reproductive. Vorobeichic was also enrolled in the required preliminary course under Josef Albers where he studied carefully the external appearances and interior structural qualities of a wide variety of objects. This comprehensive analysis of form and color was set within a framework that stressed both creative contact with and an economical use of materials. By the end of the semester-long course, Vorobeichic had produced several color, material, and architectural studies in addition to singular montages and advertisement posters for the theater and cinema (Molderings, 1987, 52). At the Bauhaus, Vorobeichic also continued to paint and draw, taking courses on form and color taught by Russian painter Wassily Kandinsky and Swiss painter Paul Klee.

Clearly this environment, which coupled inter-media practice with an inquisitive treatment of surface texture and form, influenced Vorobeichic's artistic development. As a sequence of densely layered montages that exercise visual apperception, I want to focus on how Vorobeichic's photography books are, in part, a practical application of Moholy-Nagy's theoretical discussions of photography and vision. Learning to 'see everything in relationship' had been crucial to Moholy-Nagy's pedagogical theories beginning in the mid-1920s and was a theme that permeated his work throughout his lifetime. His first book *Malerei Photographie Film* (1925) [*Painting Photography Film*] is an instructional guide to modern visual literacy that shaped the future production of photography books as well as the public display and critical analysis of photography.[4] With its innovative mixture of photographic reproductions, graphic design, and theoretical writings, *Malerei Photographie Film* constructs a discourse of photography by first visualizing the mechanics of perception itself. The guide does not dictate to readers how to see, but rather engages them in a theoretical discussion about vision, a discussion that not only acknowledges but also demands their individual attention and participation. His career-long focus on perception led Moholy-Nagy to contend in his last book, *Vision in Motion* (1947), that the 'flashlike' or instantaneous act of relational reading occurs in a space-time dynamic. As a new way of perceiving, vision in motion is, 'vision in relationships', that is, 'seeing matters in a constantly changing moving field of mutual relationships' rather than a fixed viewpoint (Moholy-Nagy, 1947, 114).[5]

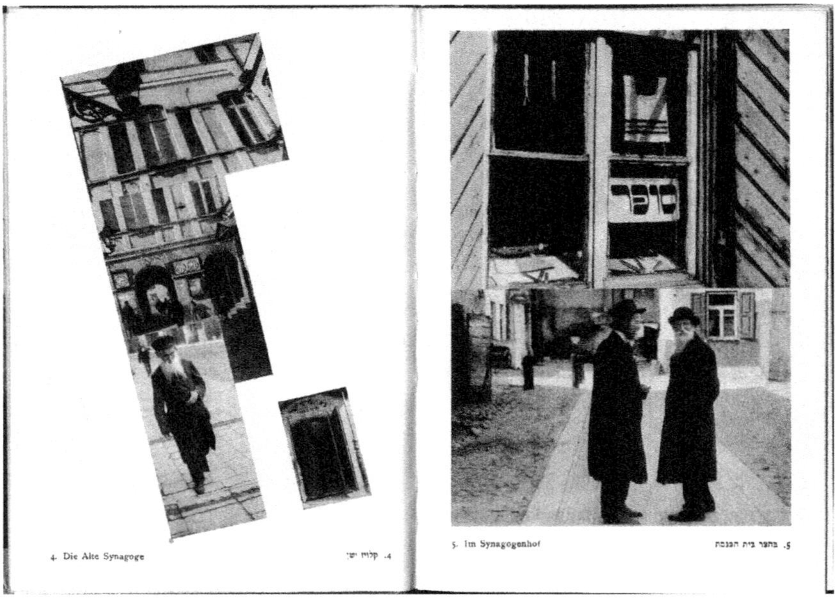

Fig. 8.3 Moshe Raviv Vorobeichic, page layout, *Ein Ghetto im Osten (Wilna)*, Schaubücher 27 (Zurich/Leipzig: Orell Füssli Verlag, 1931). © Orell Füssli Verlag.

Cultural historian Louis Kaplan argues that with his theory of vision in motion, Moholy-Nagy is critiquing fixed modes of representation and traditional historiographic structures. Kaplan states: 'the simultaneity that accompanies vision in motion or, synonymously, the overlaying and superimposition of space onto the axis of time, provides the extra dimension which shakes up the historical order and any integral claim to a *proper sequence* [emphasis added] (Kaplan, 1995, 3).' The act of reading, including the reading of history, involves both physical observation and abstract perception, which Moholy-Nagy understood to be a 'creative performance—seeing, feeling and thinking in relationship and not as a series of isolated phenomena' (Moholy-Nagy, 1947, 12). Within this context, *Wilna* and *Paris* operate more as primers for visual literacy than cultural guidebooks.

Yet *Wilna* also produces for the general public an authoritative witness to the lives and experiences of a marginalized social group through its careful sequencing and editing of photographs and written text. With the opening page spreads (fig. 8.3), Vorobeichic defines *Wilna* as an examination of a living cultural space, not a formal study of architectural monuments or a series of social typologies. These compositions, which directly link the human element of the quarter with the culturally identifying institutions of the synagogue and religious school, establish the foundation of the narrative. His use of New Vision techniques, particularly

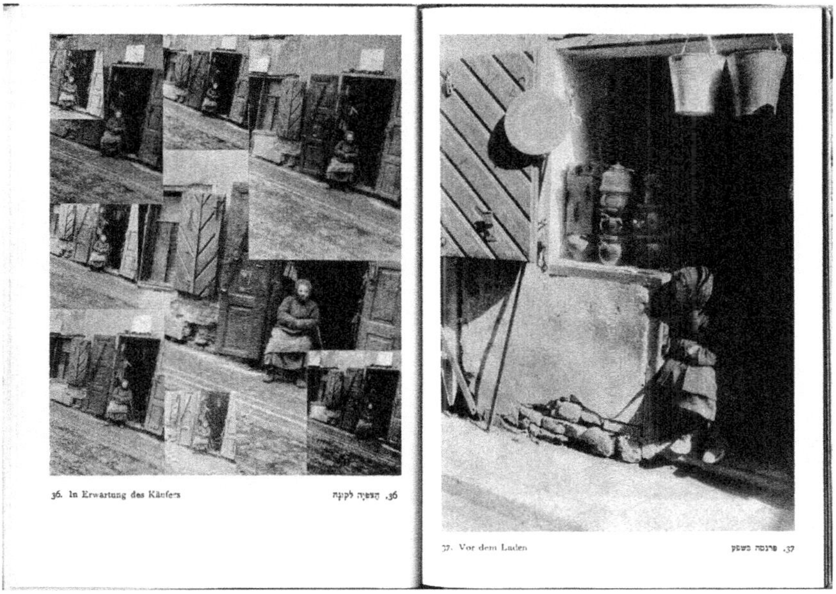

Fig. 8.4 Moshe Raviv Vorobeichic, page layout, *Ein Ghetto im Osten (Wilna)*, Schaubücher 27 (Zurich/ Leipzig: Orell Füssli Verlag, 1931). © Orell Füssli Verlag.

photographs taken from different vantage points, frames the interaction between people and architectural spaces as one that is grounded in tradition yet ever changing. Throughout the book, Vorobeichic explores the city by combining photographs that vividly contrast views of proximity and distance. By doing this, he does not easily map out and organize the informational space of his photography book, but rather establishes *Wilna* as a study of multiple aspects read in relation to one another. While some pages are composed of single, uncut photographs, others are composed of highly manipulated photomontages, many of which repeat the same image. For example, the dynamic repetition of an image taken from varying distances (fig. 8.4) works to re-animate a timeless, almost nostalgic street scene, yet at the same time, it freezes any movement forward, stopping time and therefore the onrush of progress associated with modernity. The entire narrative is saturated with optimistic visions of the future and mournful memories of the past, a paradoxical stance made palpable through Vorobeichic's montage practices.

Vorobeichic's use of montage creates a visual dissonance, a dislocation between subject matter and technique that attempts to thwart proscribed readings of otherness. Rather than creating a de-historicized, omniscient view of the quarter through social documentary practices, Vorobeichic uses montage to depict the flux of daily life set within the more stable rubric of tradition. Montage, with its juxtaposition

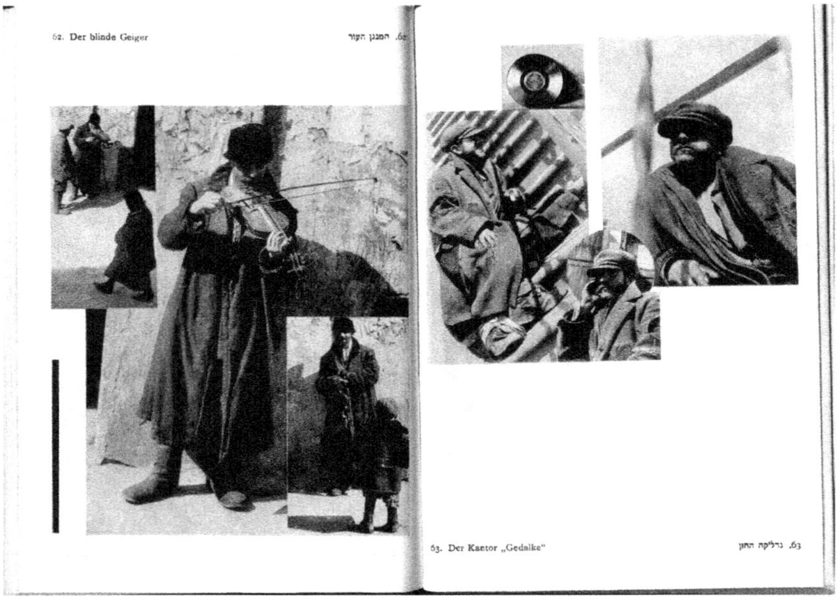

Fig. 8.5 Moshe Raviv Vorobeichic, page layout, *Ein Ghetto im Osten (Wilna)*, Schaubücher 27 (Zurich/Leipzig: Orell Füssli Verlag, 1931). © Orell Füssli Verlag.

of different viewpoints, works against the concept of totality; it questions the existence of a singular truth so often associated with the documentary photograph. In his essay, Chnéour compares Vorobeichic to a theater director, arguing that he is able to shape the reader's understanding of the Jewish quarter by capturing 'expressions and details at the right moment to give the viewer an idea of the depth of the subject.' Chnéour adds: 'he has enlarged and accented the details not normally noticed by the hurrying passerby. With scissors he has cut out squares and circles, their narrow focus becoming especially meaningful, crammed with the contents of the Jewish lane (Chnéour, 1931, 4-5).' However, Chnéour claims that the effectiveness of Vorobeichic's sequence is due to both the photographer's personal vision and the documentary qualities of the photographs themselves, writing: 'The photobook brings us reality and authenticity...It shows the true Jewish existence and with its ethnographic material, is a handbook for everyone (8).' Therefore, for Chnéour truth is embedded in the photographs' transcription of reality, but it can only be revealed through the disruptions of montage editing. *Wilna* does rely on the presumed authenticity of the photographic trace in order to provide a certain evidentiary force, yet its narrative points backward as much as it does forward and is more concerned with issues of memory and revelation than with any ideal notion of progress. Because his photographs provide a representation of Jewish life in Vilnius informed by memories and past experiences, they are not purely disinterested, and therefore 'objective' views of the quarter. In fact, *Wilna* reconciles Vorobeichic's own nostalgia for the past with an uncertainty about the quarter's present and future. I would argue that this can be seen in a page spread that juxtaposes a montage of three photographs of a blind violinist in the street to a photomontage of a several men listening to a phonographic recording of a cantor (fig. 8.5). Here, not only do aspects of a traditional, unchanging past collide with the modernization of culture, but also Vorobeichic's memories work to interpret his present situation. Vorobeichic recalled that 'the old man playing his fiddle in the lane' was one of the vivid memories of Vilnius he had while on a trip to a synagogue library in Dessau as a Bauhaus student (Dmitrieva, 2004, 74-75).[6] Such experiences inspired and framed his later photographic coverage of the town and the construction of his first photography book.

Important to understanding how a montage structure informs both the design and reading of Vorobeichic's books is the change in the conception and practice of montage that began in the late 1920s. By this time, serial works constructed largely with intact photographs were replacing singular cut-and-paste photomontages, such as those made by Dada artists. In his 1928 essay 'Against the Synthetic Portrait, for the Snapshot', Soviet photographer and graphic designer Alexander Rodchenko argues that the single photograph or 'synthetic' portrait is unable to adequately represent the full likeness of an individual. His response was to produce a series of snapshot photographs that revealed the sitter in different situations and therefore different moments in time. These portraits, intended as a series, are comparative in nature and depend upon relational reading for their meaning. A few years later, photographer and critic Sergei Tret'iakov voiced a similar argument, claiming that traditional, posed portraits monumentalize the sitter and focus the viewer's attention on the physical attributes of the individual rather than revealing how he is connected to his social environment. Tret'iakov set forth two of his own solutions, the photo-series and the extended photo-observation, as a way to construct a more comprehensive image of a collective subject. The photo-series, while similar to Rodchenko's definition of the snapshot portrait, is more grounded in the practice of the photo-essay. In fact, Tret'iakov's treatise is, partly, a review of Max Alpert and Arakii Shaikhet's photo-essay 'A Day in the Life of a Moscow Working-Class Family' published in *Proletarskoe foto* in 1931. Tret'iakov explains that the photo-series is 'a momentary cross-section that cuts through the entire skein of relationships that entangle the individual' while the extended photo-observation, by following its subjects over a longer period of time, notes 'every moment of growth and change in their condition (Tret'iakov, 2006, 77).' In theory, the extended photo-observation would provide a more sustained argument because it could visualize the development of a process, that is as Tret'iakov states, to see the subject 'in a state of flux, in contradiction (77).' Such an examination follows a mode of perception akin to cinéma vérité, which Tret'iakov believed gave form to the dialectical-materialist method that 'sees the person as a product of the reality that surrounds him and as a force that transforms this reality (73).'[7] *Wilna* does not document the city and its inhabitants over a period of years, but rather is made up of photographs that Vorobeichic took during a trip to visit his family in 1929. Instead of spending more time walking the streets of Vilnius, Vorobeichic's observation of the town involved a melding of his past memories with the present moment. As a book, *Wilna* presents a deeper analysis than that of a photo-essay and seems to fall somewhere in between the photo-series and the extended photo-observation.

As part of Vorobeichic's journey through Vilnius, a section of the book focuses on the different generations of Jews living there. Informal, montage portraits of the elderly, young children, religious leaders, and the destitute underscore the diversity of the quarter. These photographs make demands on the reader because they possess an unfixed identity, one that is both historical and timeless; densely coded and transparent; highly specific and universal. Vorobeichic's sequence is at once memory and reality, with its gateways and maze of winding, medieval streets, the quarter is a space full of promise and a space of confinement. He visualizes this experience with layouts that compare active streets full of commerce to empty streets, layered one on top of the other in order to create a dream-like crossroads. Chnéour points out that *Wilna* acts as an archive and a miniature museum. Both share with the photograph the mission of preserving a past for the future. Archival systems are concerned with genealogies and have nostalgic tendencies; they construct their own origins and produce events as much as they record them. According to Jacques Derrida, the archive comes into being at the moment when there is a structural breakdown in memory; it is—in comparison to Michel Foucault's reliable and systematized archive—feverish, fragmentary, and traumatized (Derrida, 1996, 91). *Wilna* is an anonymous archive; the photographs and titles do not provide specific names of any of the individuals but rather provide more general thematic titles, such as 'streets' or 'twilight'. The photography book's archival desire, its ability to store and preserve information between its covers nevertheless remains embedded in a shifting cultural context. The photograph, and in turn the photography book, embodies two different conceptions of space and time. It not only re-presents the duration and space of its inscription but also as a representation holds open a duration and space of its reading, not to mention the gap in-between.

Benjamin's analysis of how historical materialism is able to disrupt the linear path, or time, of historical movement is centered on the idea of a suspended break. He writes: 'To thinking belongs the movement as well as the arrest of thoughts. Where thinking comes to a standstill in a constellation saturated with tensions—there the dialectical image appears (Benjamin, 1999, 475).' This montage model of history depends on a visual metaphor that embodies both rupture and stasis. As Gerhard Richter explains: 'the dialectical image is lodged in the paradox that, on the one hand, all images must "freeze" and arrest movement in order to become legible while, on the other, dialectics, in both the ancient sense of continuous disputation and in the modern Hegelian sense, by definition never can be frozen or brought to a complete standstill (Richter, 2007, 61).' Benjamin's dialectical image reveals how the photograph is both articulated and traversed by the past and the present, it is, as Richter points out, a relational stance that is always at odds with itself, it 'constitutes the scene, space, and form of a certain temporal rupture in which time and space are out of joint (62).' Thus, similar to the narrative structure of a photography book, Benjamin's model on one hand disrupted temporality, but on the other, had the capacity to show events over time, to suggest duration and development in a more visual and spatial manner.

These suspended images are marked by their fracturing of time with what Benjamin calls the image's historical index. As literacy theorist Eduardo Cadava explains, this use of the term 'index' does not mean an image belongs to a 'specific time,' that is, the time of its production, but that it only comes into *legibility* at a specific time (Cadava, 2001, 38-39). An image's historical index allows us to move back and forth in our search for meaning because a photograph's context includes not just the historical contexts in which the image was produced but also that of the reader's. Therefore, if the truth can be read, it is through the traces of what is no longer present before us and history is read only in its transitory state, a state that consists of both arrested moments and fleeting traces. Photography books present a series of images that are inscribed in a photographic space and time that disrupts one's understanding of both space and time. Their pages simultaneously construct and displace a sense of continuous time by creating a relational web of different fragments of experience, laying out the transitory state of history with a montage of images, which individually contain and interact with several contexts. Through them we can see how by intending to witness history, they often testify to the disappearance and destruction of testimony and memory. For Cadava, the photograph itself is always an image of ruin, often speaking of death and the impossibility to represent the truths and histories of what it depicts. Yet, he argues the photograph bears traces and has potential to speak. While it reveals that it can no longer really show anything, it nevertheless bears witness to what history has silenced and to what we are still responsible for today (36).

So, how does one read Vorobeichic's montages of Vilnius with their intense details of crumbling buildings and men sleeping in the streets, of workers, busy markets, and children playing? Vorobeichic had no way of knowing that this area would soon be destroyed and many of its inhabitants displaced or killed when he produced what would become one of the few visual archives of this cultural environment. Today, *Wilna's* historical index involves the context of the late 1920s suspended with that of the 21st century. It involves the desire to educate vision and to record everyday life as well as the impossibility of recovering a neutral past, of trauma, and the limits of photography as a witness. Alfred Döblin described Vilnius's Jewish community during the mid-1920s as diverse and politically divided. Known as the Jerusalem of Lithuania, the city was a center of both Jewish socialism and Zionism, and in 1925, it became home to the Jewish Historical Institute (YIVO). However, restrictive policies and discrimination under Russian, and later Polish, rule combined with the hardships experience during the First World War and a new worldwide depression led to the economic impoverishment of the Jewish quarter as reflected in *Wilna* (Weeks, 2005, 143). The sequence is also marked by the Holocaust; an impending catastrophe in 1929, it has already past for the contemporary reader, whose knowledge of the atrocities is also informed by the continuation of genocide in the 20th and 21st centuries. The project, ultimately, concerns images of ruin and powerfully bears witness to the enigmatic relationship between death and survival, destruction and preservation, mourning and memory that, as Cadava maintains, is found in every image (Cadava, 2001, 35).

Seeing the City of Paris

Late in the summer of 1928, Vorobeichic left Germany and moved to Paris. While his first sustained interaction with photography began at the Bauhaus, the school had yet to establish an official photography workshop. Perhaps due to this lack of technical training, Vorobeichic decided to attend the École Technique de Photographie et de Cinématographie. In addition, a strong network of émigré photographers and artists, many of whom were Eastern European Jews, existed in Paris at the time. Once in Paris, Vorobeichic quickly developed relationships in the Parisian avant-garde arts community. He participated in Fernand Léger's evening courses at the Académie Moderne and within the year he was working as a free-lance photojournalist for the Globe-Photo agency, publishing his work in both popular magazines and art journals.[8] He also began immediately to photograph the city as he experienced it, focusing particularly on the working-class neighborhood where he lived. This consistent examination of the city, not as a tourist, but as a new émigré, would eventually lead to the production of his second photography book, *Paris*.

Paris precedes several popular photography books that examine the city in a creative, more subjective manner. No longer tourist guidebooks highlighting the great monuments of the city, books such as Ilya Ehrenburg's *My Paris* (1933), Brassaï's *Paris de Nuit* (1933), and André Kertész's *Paris Vu par André Kertész* (1934) were personally observed fragments of the city's inhabitants and architectural spaces (Sichel, 1992, 105). These photographers sought to make visible an untouched, almost mythical Paris that was hidden beneath the chaos and change of modernity. They followed the model established by Parisian photographer Eugène Atget, whose photographs of the old quarters of Paris were published posthumously in book form in 1930. Atget was concerned with documenting the ordinary streets and daily life of Paris, particularly those places and aspects of culture that were under threat by the onslaught of modernity. In their own private journeys through the city, these later photographers captured the complexity and ambivalence of the urban experience, often infusing it with a surreal mood. Noted photography critic Pierre Mac Orlan called this disquieting yet powerfully emotive element the 'social fantastic' (Mac Orlan, 1989, 32). Photographs by Brassaï and Kertész exude this characteristic with their accidental and un-manipulated moments; however, as a sequence of densely layered montages, *Paris* is conceptually different from these projects. Most writers quickly cite the formal differences, yet none have addressed

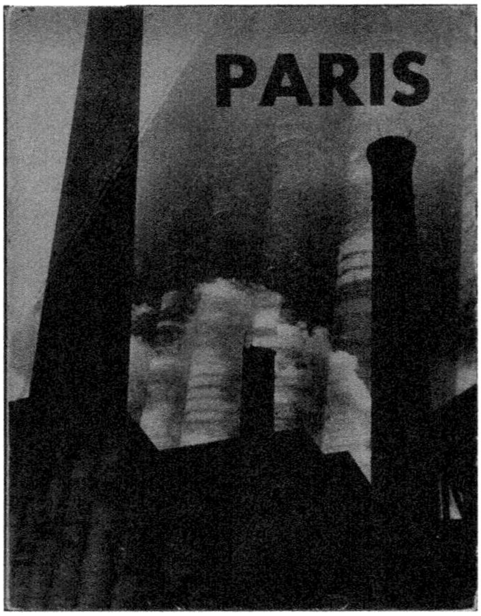

Fig. 8.6 Moï Ver [Moshe Raviv Vorobeichic], cover, *Paris* (Paris: Éditions Jeanne Walter, 1931). National Gallery of Art Library, David K. E. Bruce Fund. Courtesy of Yossi Raviv.

how Vorobeichic's use of montage engages with social and political issues pertinent to the time period. In an era of growing nationalism and economic uncertainty, Vorobeichic presents Paris as thoroughly modern, a city where factories, smokestacks, and transportation systems epitomize the experience of rupture and change brought about by advanced industrialization. Neither a celebration of technology as manifested in the period's machine aesthetic, nor an extended journey to uncover a lost past, *Paris* is a dialogue concerning class and cultural identity.

The cover of *Paris* (fig. 8.6) features the neo-classical Parisian Bourse fading out behind the outline of three smokestacks. Vorobeichic does not encapsulate the city through a representation of one of its well-known monuments; rather, he presents Paris as an industrialized, capitalist center with an imperialist history. What at first appears to be a juxtaposition of modern and classical architectural forms, a call for simplicity and functionalism in opposition to ornament and historicism, develops into a more complex association concerning the role of industrialization and capitalism in the early 1930s. Industrial smokestacks, or the chimneys from which combustion products are exhausted into the open air, are components of modern industrial furnaces and power plants but were in use as early as the mid-17th century. Free standing chimneys of brick and stone, the forerunners to those reinforced concrete and steel imaged on the cover of *Paris*, were already in use when, in 1807, Napoléon Bonaparte commissioned architect Alexandre-Théodore Brongniart to design the Bourse. The grand and imposing Corinthian columns of the Bourse mimic the smokestacks and link the expansion of capitalism to Napoleonic imperialism. A third layer of clouds creates a sense of depth to the cover, but also obscures the reader's vision, making it hard to decipher the buildings. This scattering of clouds can also be read as combustion waste, thereby calling attention to the natural world as one that both influences human behavior

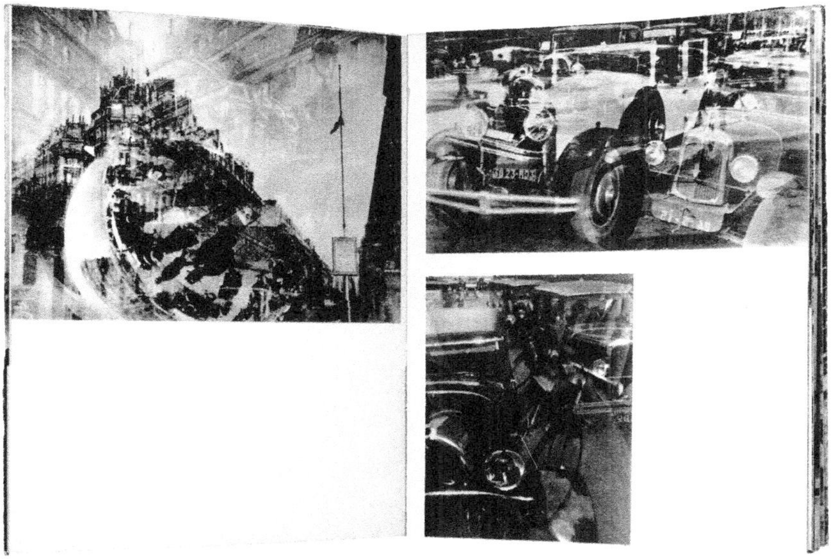

Fig. 8.7 Moï Ver [Moshe Raviv Vorobeichic], page layout, *Paris* (Paris: Éditions Jeanne Walter, 1931). National Gallery of Art Library, David K. E. Bruce Fund. Courtesy of Yossi Raviv.

and is greatly affected by it. The unabashed celebration of technology that had dominated the 1920s was, by 1930, in serious question, as a sense of dystopia regarding the future sustainability of both rural nature and urban industry gained momentum. With this richly layered cover, Vorobeichic's immediately entangles readers in a web of complex issues regarding how society will balance nature, humanity, and the power of technology.

Similar to *Wilna*, *Paris* presents a complex site of witnessing that interrupts the vision of its readers, making them more aware of the act of perception. It demands close reading, at first chaotic, its pages exercise and challenge vision with a sequence of photographs, which like the world, is fragmentary and full of mundane things. Vorobeichic's images simultaneously project surface reflections of the world and dream-like states. The opening sequence contrasts the overwhelming density and size of the city with minute details of its streets. Swirling rooftop views depict multiple layers of buildings, which are juxtaposed to photomontages of brick roads marked with streetcar tracks. For Vorobeichic, the city is densely layered with people, advertisements, and automobiles (fig. 8.7). In this page spread, Vorobeichic attempts to visualize the multitude of sensory experiences found in the urban environment. On the left is a kaleidoscopic view of a busy street where pedestrians seem to be caught in a whirlwind of commotion. Facing this page

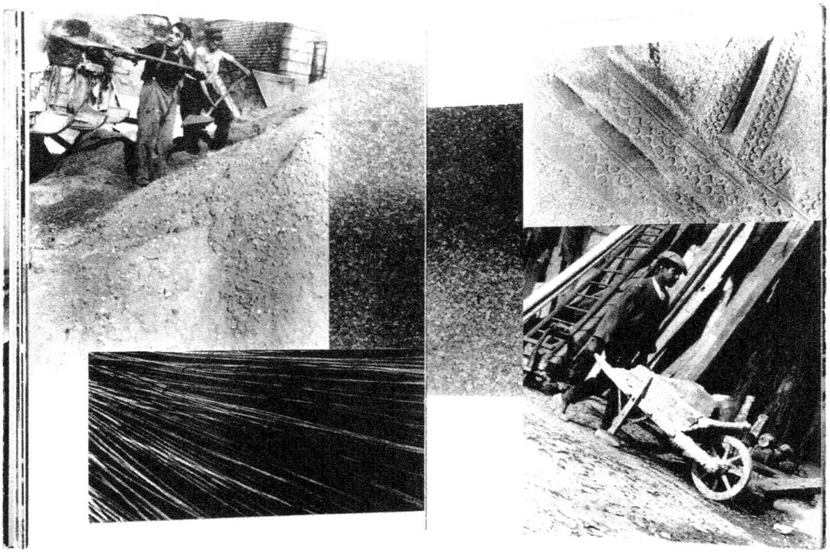

Fig. 8.8 Moï Ver [Moshe Raviv Vorobeichic], page layout, *Paris* (Paris: Éditions Jeanne Walter, 1931). National Gallery of Art Library, David K. E. Bruce Fund. Courtesy of Yossi Raviv.

are two photomontages, one above the other. The top displays various models of expensive cars while the bottom features a man riding a bicycle placed at an angle to a mirage-like succession of parked cars. Taken by itself, this layout could read as a celebratory statement of progress made possible by advancing technology, particularly in the field of transportation. One only has to turn the pages to find additional layouts depicting the expansion and development of the subway and streetcar systems in the outer rings of the city. Surprisingly, in the 2004 reprint of *Paris*, one folded sheet comprising four pages was bound out of sequence.[9] Thus, the swirling street scene found on the left of the original layout was replaced with an image of a worker pulling a cart superimposed over several photographs of streets lined with cars. This reordering creates a page spread more focused on the juxtaposition of various modes of transportation within the city. In either case, Vorobeichic tempers the modern ideal of technological progress by examining the discrepancies between access and choice of transport in Paris, both of which were deeply entrenched in social and economic status.

In a noticeable break from the hectic city streets, Vorobeichic assembles close-up details of the river Seine seen from different viewpoints. As a defining aspect of the city, the Seine is often romanticized. Its curving trajectory bisects the city; the stairways and paths built along its banks are the sacred spaces of lovers, clochards, and painters. Vorobeichic, however, presents the famous river unemotionally

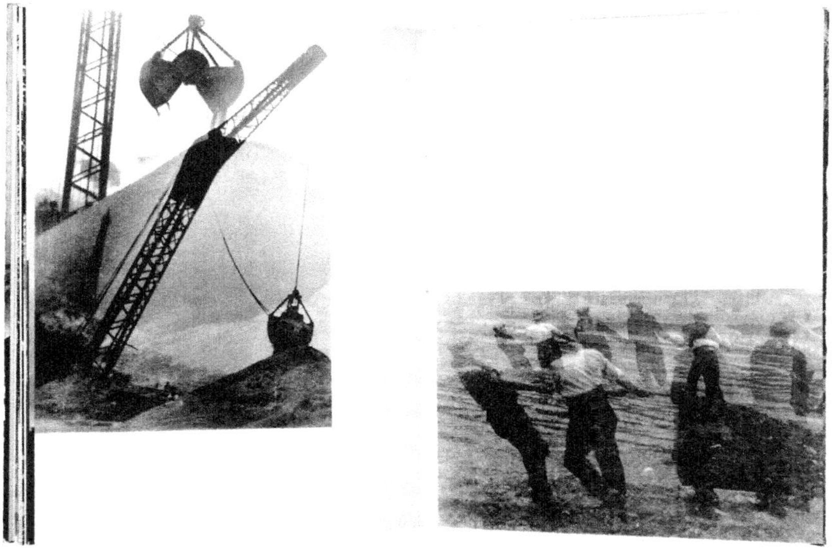

Fig. 8.9 Moï Ver [Moshe Raviv Vorobeichic], page layout, *Paris* (Paris: Éditions Jeanne Walter, 1931). National Gallery of Art Library, David K. E. Bruce Fund. Courtesy of Yossi Raviv.

through a constructivist montage of abstract photographs of rippling waters and fragments of the riverbank. In a following page spread (fig. 8.8) he examines a construction site by juxtaposing workers with the indexical marks that they and their tools leave in the dirt. These seemingly random observations of objects and everyday activities bear strong similarities to the material studies Vorobeichic conducted at the Bauhaus. They also invite contemplation on photography as an indexical practice—one that is dependent upon a physical referent in order to be understood as a direct emanation of the real, but one that is also a chemical process that can only produce the simulation of surface appearances.

With its concentration on the outer arrondissements of the city, *Paris* engages pointedly in a dialogue about labor. Several page spreads contrast masses of workers to factory owners and financiers while others compare modern machinery with manual labor. For example, one page spread juxtaposes towering cranes fitted with digging equipment with a montage of workers pulling on ropes (fig. 8.9). Here the past appears quite literally to collide with the present, bringing to mind *Wilna's* examination of the fate of tradition in the face of modernity. While cranes are modern symbols of industrial might, essential to the building of skyscrapers, the demand for human labor in the city was still high. In this respect, Vorobeichic's montage is reminiscent of Umberto Boccioni's anachronistic painting *The City Rises* (1910), where Boccioni paints the frenetic construction of a city by human and animal labor rather than the sleek, modern machinery embraced by the Italian Futurists. While inspired by new technologies, Boccioni conveys the swirling action of the men and horses through a rough, post-impressionistic brushstroke. Using a more traditional style, movement and energy is visualized through dashes of paint rather than an overlapping succession of repeating images produced by stop action photography. In comparison, Vorobeichic's photomontages possess both painterly and mechanical effects. With their haunting atmosphere they share with Atget's work an ability to suspend the moment when particular ways of life are about to disappear. Yet rather than just revealing an image of the past that, however oddly, still exists in the present, Vorobeichic constructs a cognitive process similar to one explicated by social philosopher Georg Simmel. As a student of Simmel, cultural critic Siegfried Kracauer explains: '[Simmel's] manner of thinking functions both to connect and to dissolve: the former in that he reveals connections everywhere between seemingly separate things; the latter insofar as he makes us aware of the complexity of many supposedly simple objects and problems (Kracauer , 1995, 233).'

Vorobeichic's montage layouts, some of which superimpose the faces of workers over smokestacks and conflate fashionable high-heel shoes with wooden workers' clogs, look like frozen montage film frames, and as filmic images, they have much in common with the materialist cinema of Sergei Eisenstein. Eisenstein believed that film is a dialectical system, which through its form (a sequence of montage frames synthesized by the viewer) revealed the materialist structure of thought. Eisenstein defined cinematic montage as a process of collision, which created dialectical thinking in the viewer. In his essay 'The Dramaturgy of Film Form (The Dialectical Approach to Film Form),' Eisenstein argues that montage should not be understood as a series of images blended together in a continuous progression, but rather as the gap between the two frames, the point of collision, writing: 'montage is not an idea composed of successive shots stuck together but an idea that DERIVES from the collision between two shots that are independent of one another...each sequential element is arrayed, not *next* to the one it follows, but on *top* of it (Eisenstein, 1988a, 163-164).' Eisenstein differentiated himself from fellow Soviet filmmaker Dziga Vertov by stipulating that his approach had what Vertov's 'montage of separate sequences' lacked, an overarching purpose. While noting that Vertov's practice was concerned with more than vision, that it was about contemplation, Eisenstein maintained that it was not active enough to instill predetermined emotions and thoughts in its viewers, claiming that too much complexity produces 'a chaos of perception rather than a distinct emotional tension (Eisenstein, 1988b, 187).'

Eisenstein essentially, and somewhat hypocritically, charged Vertov with favoring form over content. By 1930, aesthetic contemplation of formal relationships for their own sake was disparaged by a variety of critics and practitioners who desired the realism and social impact of documentary approaches. In general, such distrust was grounded in the perceived subjectivism of the array of meanings produced by montage. This was especially the case in the Soviet Union, where by 1931, the official criticism labeled both Vertov and Eisenstein as formalists who made films that were incomprehensible to the masses. Yet, as Rosalind Krauss has argued, Eisenstein understood the space between documentary and artistic film as analogous to the space of political action (Krauss, 1973, 62). As two separate practices, documentary and artistic film call for a depoliticized mode of viewing history, where history is either the passive recording of events (the thesis of documentary) or the contemplation of an autonomous ideal (the antithesis provided by art). However, synthesis, through the use of intellectual montage, breaks open a way out of this political inaction.

What is at stake is the accessibility of meaning: who controls it, how it is produced, and how well it can be comprehended. Vorobeichic's photographs through their juxtapositions create spatial and temporal displacements that do not possess a stable meaning. He presents readers with a mesh of moments, not imaged in succession, but superimposed. However, by delaying the cinematic montage, *Paris* presents an alternative to both the purely static singular photograph and the fluency of film. Vorobeichic constructs series that are simultaneously a linear experience of events unfolding in time and a non-linear web of association and meaning. His sequences allow the reader to stop and reflect, to question how contemporary experience is defined by both a rush to the future and a disappearance of the past. His photographs present an uncertain temporality that offers, according to Roland Barthes, a level of psychic engagement that is impossible in film. Vorobeichic's photography books stop the flow of cinema, comparable to the act of delaying cinema, making us more aware of time's relation to both stillness and movement. As Laura Mulvey explains, delaying cinema is essential to any textual analysis of it, which has been made all the more accessible to the public with the advent of video and digital technologies. She writes: 'The process of repetition and return involves stretching out the cinematic image to allow space and time for associative thought, reflection on resonance and connation...key moments and meanings become visible that could not have been perceived when hidden under the narrative flow and the movement of film (Mulvey, 2006, 146-147).'

Ci-Contre

While living in Paris, Vorobeichic maintained several of the artistic connections he had made at the Bauhaus, even stopping to give Moholy-Nagy a copy of *Paris* on a trip to Berlin. Likely encouraged by the success of the photography-book genre, Vorobeichic set out to publish a third photography book titled *Ci-Contre*. A French expression for the illustration on the facing page of a news story, 'ci-contre' denotes the organization of the double page layout where opposing tensions are in active relation to one another. With *Ci-Contre*, Vorobeichic organizes 110 photographs onto forty one double-page layouts. In this book, he is less concerned with documenting a specific place or topology than with developing thought-provoking analogies. As a method of reasoning from the known to the unknown, from the visible to the speculative, and from the individual to the cultural, analogy allows human beings to construct bridges between what they know and what they do not know. It is a means to learn and intuit new knowledge, but it is also critical to how one understands the past. People use analogies everyday to translate familiar terms, concepts, and images from one context to another. By producing visual analogies, *Ci-Contre* instructs readers to think about the myriad possibilities of meaning by spurring them to see similarity in dissimilarity. This third photography book, which remained unpublished during Vorobeichic's lifetime, may well have been the final installment of a trilogy of photography books covering the past (*Wilna*), present (*Paris*), and future (*Ci-Contre*).[10]

Through their multiplicity of viewpoints, strange juxtapositions, and analogical associations, Vorobeichic's books visualize the disintegration of traditional forms of experience. In their dream-like quality, his photographic sequences appear to manifest only the traces of history, those forgotten fragments of which Benjamin writes about. The photography book's relation to time is somewhere in-between that of the singular photograph and the projected filmstrip. Unlike the singular photograph's relation to time, where the trace of one moment is inscribed onto a light sensitive surface, thus becoming a fragment of the past that persists in the present, the photography book presents numerous photographs in a sequence bound between two covers, its parts both relate to and construct a larger whole. Yet, such books do not possess film's inherent link to duration, its ability to construct a continuous present. In comparison to film, which as a rapid sequence of visual stimuli more often works to hide its narrative breaks, photography books are dependent upon such breaks, because they require readers to be more involved in constructing their own reception of the work, leading to a more active and critical apperception. Within their covers, Vorobeichic's photography books suspend chronological time, turning seriality into co-presence, thereby challenging the naturalness of the status quo.

Acknowledgements

I would like to thank Yossi Raviv for his generous granting of permission rights and for kindly discussing his father's history with me from his home in Tel Aviv.

Notes

[1] The artist Moshe Raviv Vorobeichic, born Moses Vorobeichic in the village of Lebedevo, just outside of Vilnius, worked under the names Moï Ver and Moshe Raviv. Moï Ver is derived from the French *Moïse* and the Russian *Verobeichic*. Members of Vorobeichic's family reside today in Israel, the United States, and Canada. I would especially like to thank Yossi Raviv for discussing his father's history with me from his home in Tel Aviv. Wilna, now called Vilnius, is the capital of Lithuania and has been variously referred to as Vilne, Vilna, and Wilno. Vorobeichic first exhibited his photographs of Vilnius at a Zionist congress in Zurich where they caught the eye of Emil Schaeffer, editor of the *Schaubücher* series.

[2] The *Schaubücher* were in production from 1929 to 1932; their format was shaped by early 20th-century travel and cultural photography books, especially Karl Robert Langewiesche's *Blaue Bücher* series. According to the publisher, the series was developed for the contemporary person who has little time to read, but would still like to be well informed.

[3] Orell Füssli published around 12,500 copies of *Wilna*.

[4] The core of the book consists of a sequence of seventy photographic reproductions organized as double-page spreads. See Andrea Nelson, 'László Moholy-Nagy and Painting Photography Film: A Guide to Narrative Montage,' in *History of Photography*, 30, no. 30 (Autumn, 2006): 258-269.

[5] Moholy-Nagy wanted to make clear that his concept of vision in motion (space-time), while influenced by a popular understanding of Einstein's theory of relativity, was not just a scientific issue, but

also a major aesthetic and psychological factor that affected the nature of modern societies and their cultural practices (Moholy-Nagy, 1947, 266).

[6] Vorobeichic's daughter, Maya Raviv, recounts this event in her unpublished manuscript, 'Time Accelerates Itself'. Vorobeichic recalled: 'The sights I had left behind in far away Vilna came to mind. The image of the pupil bent over his book in the old prayer house, the old man playing his fiddle in the lane, the child at his game of hopscotch.'

[7] Tret'iakov notes that while not that long ago photographs were deemed unsuitable for artistic books, today a book without them appears inauthentic.

[8] Vorobeichic worked also for the Parisian newspaper *Soir*, and his photographs covering events in Poland, Spain, and Palestine were printed in several popular illustrated magazines of the time, including *Vu*, *Arts et Métiers*, *Espirit*, *Bifur*, and *Varieté*.

[9] The 1931 edition of *Paris* from the National Gallery of Art, Washington follows the exact sequence as the 1931 edition from The Art Institute of Chicago and the 1931 edition from The Museum of Modern Art. Therefore I believe this to be the original sequence of the book. At this time, I can only suspect that something happened during the publication of the 2004 reprint to change the original order.

[10] In March of 1932, art historian Franz Roh told Vorobeichic that while he intended to publish *Ci-Contre* as part of the *Fototek* series, problems with the publishers had left the entire series suspended indefinitely. After 1933 correspondence between Roh and Vorobeichic broke off and in 1934, Vorobeichic immigrated to Palestine. Assuming that *Ci-Contre* was lost during the war, Vorobeichic tried to reconstruct the book from his negatives. However, by 1950, he gave up on the project and stopped photographing altogether in order to start an artists' colony in northern Israel. To Vorobeichic's own surprise, Roh had kept the original photobook and it passed into the possession of collectors Ann and Jürgen Wilde, purchasers of Roh's estate. The Wildes, in collaboration with the Pinakothek der Moderne, Sammlung Moderne Kunst, Munich reprinted the photography book and held an exhibition of Vorobeichic's photographs in 2005.

Bibliography

¬ Walter Benjamin, *The Arcades Project*, trans. Howard Eiland and Kevin McLaughlin (Cambridge/London: Harvard University Press, Belknap Press, 1999).

¬ Eduardo Cadava, 'Lapsus Imaginis: The Image in Ruins', *October*, 96 (Spring, 2001): 35-60.

¬ Salman Chnéour, 'Die Judengasse in Licht und Schatten', in *Ein Ghetto im Osten (Wilna)* (Zurich/Leipzig: Orell Füssli Verlag, 1931), 4-8.

¬ Jacques Derrida, *Archive Fever: A Freudian Impression*, trans. Eric Prenowitz (Chicago: University of Chicago Press, 1996).

¬ Marina Dmitrieva, 'Die Wilna-Fotocollagen von Moshe Vorobeichic', in Marina Dmitrieva and Heidemarie Petersen (eds) *Jüdische Kultur(en) im Neuen Europa Wilna 1918-1939* (Wiesbaden: Harrassowitzverlag, 2004), 69-84.

¬ *Ein Ghetto im Osten. Wilna. 65 Bilder von M. Vorobeichic. Eingeleitet von S. Chnéour* (Zurich/Leipzig: Orell Füssli Verlag, 1931).

¬ Sergei Eisenstein, 'The Dramaturgy of Film Form (The Dialectical Approach to Film Form)', (1929) in Richard Taylor (trans. and ed.) *S.M. Eisenstein Selected Works, Volume One, Writings 1922-1934* (London/Bloomington: BFI Publishing/University of Indiana Press, 1988a), 161-180.

¬ Sergei Eisenstein, 'The Fourth Dimension in Cinema' (1929), in Richard Taylor (ed. and trans.) *S.M. Eisenstein Selected Works, Volume One, Writings 1922-1934* (London/Bloomington: BFI Publishing/University of Indiana Press, 1988b), 181-194.

¬ Louis Kaplan, *Moholy-Nagy Biographical Writings* (Durham, NC: Duke University Press, 1995).

¬ Siegfried Kracauer, 'Georg Simmel', in Thomas Y. Levin (ed. and trans.) *The Mass Ornament: Weimar Essays* (Cambridge, MA/London: Harvard University Press, 1995), 225-258.

¬ Rosalind Krauss, 'Montage "October": Dialectic of the Shot', *Artforum*, 11, no. 5 (January, 1973): 61-65.

¬ Pierre Mac Orlan, 'L'Art littéraire d'imagination et la photographie', *Les nouvelles littéraires* (Paris: September 22, 1928) and 'Éléments de fantastique social', *Le Crapouillet* (Paris: March 1929), in Christopher Phillips (ed.) *Photography in the Modern Era: European Documents and Critical Writings, 1913-1940* (New York: Metropolitan Museum of Art/Aperture, 1989), 27-33.

¬ László Moholy-Nagy, *Vision in Motion* (Chicago: Paul Theobald, 1947).

¬ Herbert Molderings, 'Wer ist Vorobeichic?', *Fotogeschichte*, 7, no. 26 (1987): 50-56.

¬ Laura Mulvey, *Death 24x a Second: Stillness and the Moving Image* (London: Reaktion Books, 2006).

¬ Gerhard Richter, 'A Matter of Distance: Benjamin's *One-Way Street* Through the *Arcades*', in *Thought Images Frankfurt School Writers' Reflections from Damaged Life* (Stanford, CA: Stanford University Press, 2007), 43-71.

¬ Kim Sichel, '*Paris vu par André Kertész*: An Urban Diary', *History of Photography*, 16, no. 2 (Summer, 1992): 105-114.

¬ Timm Starl, '"Schaubücher" Eine Bildbandreihe 1929 bis 1932', *Fotogeschichte*, 16, no. 61 (1996): 47-59.

¬ Sergei Tret'iakov, 'From the Photo-Series to Extended Photo-Observation', *October*, 118 (Fall, 2006): 71-77. [Originally published as 'Ot fotoserii—k dlitel'nomu fotonabliudeniiu,' *Proletarskoe foto*, no. 4 (1931): 20-43.]

¬ Theodore R. Weeks, 'The Transformation of Jewish Vilna, 1881-1939', in Leonard J. Greenspoon, Ronald A. Simkins, and Brian J. Horowitz (eds) *The Jews of Eastern Europe. Studies in Jewish Civilization,* Volume 16 (Omaha, NE: Creighton University Press, 2005), 143-164.

¬ Moï Ver, *Paris: 80 Photographies* (Paris: Éditions Jeanne Walter, 1931).

9 'An image of an image': Photography and Robert Morris's Continuous Project Altered Daily

David Green

In his seminal essay 'Art and Objecthood', published in 1967, Michael Fried launched his now famous attack on minimalism or, as he referred to it, literalist art, at the same time launching a trenchant defense of the principal tenets of modernist painting and sculpture. Fried's major criticism of minimalism was that it seemed to aspire to a form of 'objecthood' that was neither painting nor indeed sculpture, but instead was defined by its lying between the individual arts and thus falling into a category he defined as 'theater'. Whereas the historically defined technical, material and aesthetic criteria provided modernist painting and sculpture with the basis for their continuing possibilities for a reflexive exploration of the medium, 'theater' could claim no such determining conventions. In their absence, the category of theatricality was not defined 'internally' by any combination of formal or aesthetic factors but solely by its mode of apprehension. Indeed, 'Art and Objecthood' is to be read as an argument in which, ultimately, it is the fundamental difference between the encounter of the viewer and the modernist work of art and the experience of the spectator of the minimalist object that matters most.

However, crucially for Fried, the distinction revolved around the issue of time. In the case of minimalism the work of art's self sufficiency was surrendered to the infinitely varied experience of the individual viewer moving through both space *and* time and thus involving a sense of duration. Stressing the interaction between the viewer and the object, Fried argued that minimalism surrendered the autonomy of the work of art: it needed the viewer to complete it. Towards the end of the essay he summarizes the nature of the experience that minimalism offers:

> Here finally I want to emphasize something that may already have become clear: the experience in question *persists in time*, and the presentment of endlessness that, I have been claiming, is central to literalist art and theory is essentially a presentment of endless or indefinite *duration*...The literalist preoccupation with time—more precisely, with the *duration of the experience*—is, I suggest, paradigmatically theatrical, as though theater confronts the beholder, and thereby isolates him, with the endlessness not just of objecthood but of time; or as though the sense which, at bottom, theater addresses is a sense of temporality, of time both passing and to come, *simultaneously approaching and receding*, as if apprehended in an infinite perspective...(Fried, 1998a, 166-167).

The sense of endlessness and the preoccupation with duration that characterize minimalism stand in sharp contrast to modernist painting and sculpture. Here the viewer's encounter with the work of art is marked by a directness and immediacy such that any sense of place and time is suspended.

> It is as though one's experience of [modernist painting and sculpture] has no duration—not because one in fact experiences a picture by Noland or Olitski or a sculpture by David Smith or Caro in no time at all, but because *at every moment the work itself is wholly manifest*...It is this continuous and entire *presentness*, amounting, as it were, to the perpetual creation of itself, that one experiences as a kind of *instantaneousness*, as though if only one were infinitely more acute, a single infinitely brief instant would be long enough to see everything, to experience the work in all its depth and fullness, to be forever convinced by it (Fried, 1998a, 167).

Much later Fried felt it necessary to clarify that his use of the concept of 'presentness' was intended to convey 'something other than *mere* instantaneousness' and that the latter term was never to be taken 'literally' (Fried, 1998b, 46). Yet, reading 'Art and Objecthood' one is struck by the connotations of Fried's chosen terminology. It is, I think, possible to see how Fried's characterization of the type of experience proper to the modernist work of art—as one in which it appears as 'instantaneously present' and with a directness and immediacy such that its identity is made available and wholly manifest in a single moment to a stationary viewer—bears an analogy to the nature of the photographic image; and how, conversely, the stress upon the notion that the viewer's experience in the case of minimalism was one predicated upon the passage of time and a sense of duration, could appear as its direct antithesis and be aligned with the medium of film.

Others have drawn attention to the importance of the issue of temporality that lies at the heart of Fried's analysis (Lee, 2004; Meyer, 2001). Yet the particular interpretation that I am offering here draws some considerable measure of support through comparison to Robert Morris's essay 'The Present Tense of Space' published nearly a decade later in 1976, the principal arguments and terminology of which seems to make direct reference back to 'Art and Objecthood'. (Fried's essay was itself a response to Morris's views on recent developments in sculpture expressed in two essays, 'Notes on Sculpture', published the previous year and it would seem that 'The Present Tense of Space' was a belated contribution to the debate between the two). In this essay Morris sets out to identify and define a tendency in late 20th century sculpture in which the experience of the viewer existing and enduring in real space-time and interacting in a continual and evolving manner with the sculptural work of art was such that there was an 'intimate inseparability of the experience of physical space and that of an ongoing immediate present (Morris, 1993a, 177).' The kind of work that Morris primarily had in mind, and examples of which illustrate his essay, were environmental forms of sited 'sculpture' in which the work is assimilated into either an architectural or landscape setting through which the viewer moves and who is thereby engaged in a continual process of experiencing the space from a constantly shifting series of viewpoints. The state of being that such work engenders, which foregrounds the 'presentness' of real space-time, is contrasted by Morris to the mode of experience involved in the encounter with modernist sculpture.[1] In the latter the experience of the viewer is a kind of frontal confrontation with an independent static object which, insofar that it is presented as 'specific, singular, dense, articulate, and self-contained, it has already removed itself from space' and thereby removed itself also from the realm of temporal duration (185). The contrast between the two models of sculpture that Morris offers is thus also a contrast between two modes of experience and perception and he elaborates upon their difference in terms of the self's presentation to itself as either 'I' or 'me':

> The 'I' is that part of the self at the point of time's arrow which is present to the conscious self. The 'me' is that reconstituted 'image' of the self formed of what ever parts—language, images, judgements, etc.—which can never be coexistent with immediate experience but accompanies it in bits and pieces...As there are two types of selves known to the self, the 'I' and the 'me', there are two fundamental types of perception: that of temporal space and that of static, immediately present objects. The 'I', which is essentially imageless, corresponds with the perception of space unfolding in the continuous present. The 'me', a retrospective constituent, parallels the mode of object perception. Objects are obviously experienced in memory as well as in the present. Their apprehension, however, is a relatively instantaneous, all-at-once experience. The object is moreover the image par excellence of memory: static, edited to generalities, independent of the surroundings. The distinction is a thoroughgoing one dividing modern consciousness into binary modes: the temporal and the static. The distinction holds true whether consciousness is representing itself, the world, or its division, the self (177-181).

My reasons for quoting Morris at length here rest with the implications embedded within this formulation of a distinction between these two types of perception for the types of 'transformative representations' to which he turns his attention towards the end of the essay. It is probably immediately obvious that the real-time interactive experience which characterizes the sculptural work that Morris is interested in, and which is bound to a consciousness of an "I" existing in an ongoing present, could broadly be aligned by him to the 'filmic'. Correspondingly, the collapsing of real space-time into the instantaneous moment in which modernist sculpture is made available immediately and completely to a single viewpoint but which can only be grasped by fragmentarily and retrospectively and gives rise to the alienated consciousness of "me", clearly invokes direct comparison with photography. Indeed, it is photography that emerges from 'The Present Tense of Space' not only as the natural accomplice to the experience of modernist sculpture in its ability to seize and stabilize the object as a static image, it is also, for the principal reason that it is incapable of accessing the experience of real time-space, cast as the most common enemy of the sense of the 'continuous present'. In an assault that clearly goes beyond the immediate concerns of his essay, Morris writes:

> It would seem that photography has recorded everything. Space, however, has avoided its cyclopedian evil eye. It could be said that the work under discussion not only resists photography as its representation, it takes a position absolutely opposed to the meaning of photography (Morris, 1993a, 201).

Yet Morris recognizes that the nature of such work makes it especially dependent upon photographic documentation and he continues, with a marked tone of resignation:

> There is probably no defence against the malevolent powers of the photograph to convert every visible aspect of the world into a static, consumable image. If the work under discussion is opposed to photography it doesn't escape it. How can I denounce photography and use it to illustrate this text with images I claim are irrelevant to the work proper (202)?

Morris was not alone amongst his generation to advance a critique of photography on the basis that it was antithetical to the concerns of contemporary sculpture. His antagonism towards photography was shared amongst others by Carl Andre, who similarly took the view that the only proper experience for the viewer of three dimensional work was one that took place in actual space and real time. Yet, as Alex Potts has argued, both artists were equally adept at using photography to stage their work in particular ways for the camera (Potts, 1998). If the irony of this may not have been lost on Morris, his prejudice towards photography nonetheless obscures the more complex issues that had been raised by artist's use of the camera beyond the notion of mere documentation. Commenting, for example, on Robert Smithson's *Mirror Displacements* (fig. 9.1) in which a number of small mirrors were temporarily arranged in various locations, photographed and then dismantled, Morris noted that these pieces:

> ...defined a space through which one moved and acknowledged a double, ever-changing space available only to vision. There was an exactness as well as a perversity implied by his photographing and then immediately dismantling these works. Exact because the thrust of the work was to underline the non-rememberable 'I' experience; perverse because the photograph is a denial of this experience (Morris, 1993a, 204).

However, whilst seemingly fitting his argument, what Morris's account of Smithson's *Mirror Displacements* ignores is precisely the uncertainty as to what constitutes 'the work'. As others have noted of his practice, Smithson—far from preserving the integrity of the sculptural object or protecting the 'presence' of work that exists in real space-time—explored the uses of photography to suggest the dissemination and fissuring of the work in both spatial and temporal terms (Owens, 1979). One example would be the series *Site/Nonsite* begun in 1968. These consisted of various kinds of earth samples, sand, rocks and so forth, placed in welded steel containers and exhibited in the gallery alongside photographs and maps of the location from which they had been taken. These 'nonsites' in the gallery refer back to an actual 'site' outside of it in a manner that disrupts our expectations of traditional sculpture. But more than merely using unconventional materials as the means of making sculpture, these works were concerned with a more complex concept of space involving a dialectic between what is here and elsewhere, and between ideas of presence and absence. In this way the photographs that formed part of the 'nonsite' acted as more than mere records, they were structural elements of the work itself.

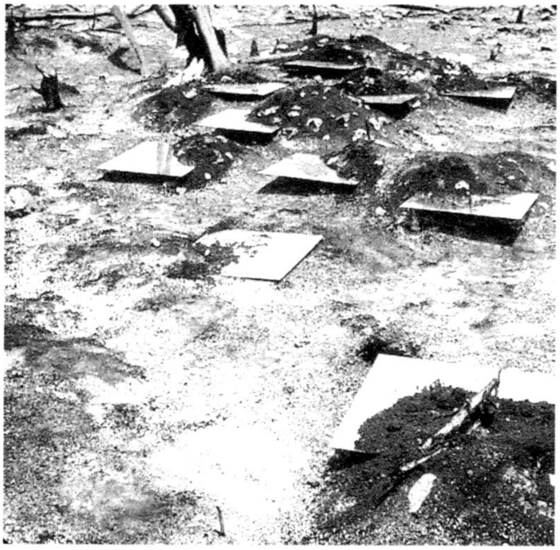

Fig. 9.1 Robert Smithson, *Yucatan Mirror Displacements (First Mirror Displacement)*, 1969. Nine locations on a trail, Yucatan, Mexico. © Estate of Robert Smithson/DACS, London/VAGA, New York 2009. Courtesy James Cohan Gallery, New York. Collection Solomon R. Guggenheim Museum, New York.

Smithson later extended this use of photography in a number of ways, most notably in the series of *Mirror Displacements* already referred to, and also in a closely related series of photographic 'displacements' that involved returning large black and white photographs to the place in which they were taken and then rephotographing them *in situ*. Like most of Smithson's work these 'photo-markers' left the status of the art object ambiguous (fig. 9.2). The play of physical displacements in the 'photo-markers' rendered problematic the notion of a work's 'presence' in a particular space at the same time that it opened the way to a temporal aporia. One was left wondering not only *what* it was and *where* it was, but also *when* it was.

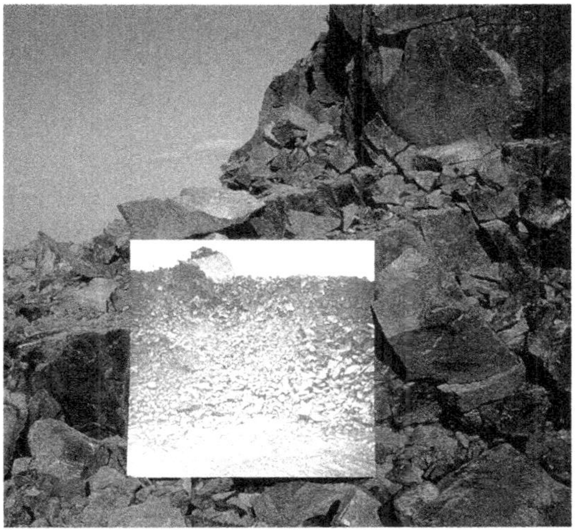

Fig. 9.2 Robert Smithson, *Photo-Markers (from Six Stops on a Section), Laurel Hill, NJ*, 1968. One of six original 35mm transparency slides. © Estate of Robert Smithson/DACS, London/VAGA, New York 2009. Courtesy James Cohan Gallery, New York.

In an essay called 'Photos within Photographs' Max Kozloff argued that if the photograph is understood and experienced as the freezing of a particular moment in time—one that continuously recedes from the present—then the phenomenon of a photograph appearing within a photograph would appear as 'a doubling of that regression inwards. It marks off at least two instants in time, contained and containing. And sometimes the contrast between them, intentional or not, can be nostalgic, even poignant (Kozloff, 1979, 91).'

Yet, as Kozloff notes, we continually encounter photographs of photographs in the form of reproductions that appear on the printed page. However, unless the edges or margins of the original photograph are shown we remain unaware of it. To all intents and purposes the photograph which is the reproduction of a photograph remains invisible, failing to establish any difference between itself and its subject. 'The field', Kozloff notes, 'simply snaps flat (91).' In pulling the camera back to reveal the margins that surrounds the image, and the empty space between the two surfaces, a complex interchange between the two images, and the two distinct moments in time they embody is set play. Certainly our first impression is that the photograph that is photographed takes on the character as an object; something which we now look 'at' rather than through. Moreover anything that might surround it and caught within the frame carries the same obdurate materiality, occupies the same sense of the 'real'. But precisely the same movement that reveals the first photograph as material artifact, contrives to conceal the materiality of the second photograph, thereby retaining its 'transparency'.

What Kozloff goes on to argue, however, is something more complex than this. Unlike the instance of paintings that contain representations of other paintings and which may (and often do) differentiate—through the dissimulation of a fractured surface—the painting within the painting, photography is incapable of this. Photographs of photographs cannot 'quote', Kozloff argues, they can only reproduce. As such

> they do not disrupt the surface, for no matter what they will, the surfaces tend circumstantially to be the same as their subjects. In fact, the esthetic of photos within photographs depends precisely upon the constant fictitousness of photographs as substance. Take away the 'transparency' of the surface, and one also removes the magic of their image substitutions (Kozloff, 1979, 92).

The fact that the photograph within the photograph is indistinguishable in terms of its surface has implications in terms of the temporality of the image, an issue that Kozloff returns to at the end of the essay. Going beyond the idea of a simple temporal recession he suggests that what may be involved in the phenomena of the re-photographed photograph is a fracturing of any such simple narrative structure by one in which 'past and present are often scrambled (98).' What may have once been 'situated in specific places at specific times' are potentially rendered 'homeless' (98). Drawing a comparison to the split images and replays, the cut outs and scale jumps, that are a staple ingredient of television, the photograph within the photograph, he remarks, 'blurs even as it alludes to the continuity of events in time. The photographer might be aiming, in fact, to bestow upon you the faculty of being in two related situations simultaneously (99).'

Kozloff's arguments converge with Craig Owens's account of Smithson's 'photo-markers'. Cited as an example of the phenomenon of *mise en abyme*, Owens suggests that Smithson's photographs of photographs 'gives rise to commentary on the conditions of the photograph itself (Owens, 1997, 28).' Moreover, their reflexive nature not only precludes any simple notion of the photograph as record, by the same token it also problematizes our assumptions as to the time to which they relate. As such, Owens asks,

> ...can we seriously regard any Smithson photograph simply as documentation? It is impossible to experience these double images as such. We are wrong to resume that the 'work' in this case consists of an action performed (the placing of the photograph in the landscape) and that the photograph is transparent to that action, which it preserves in the tense peculiar to photography, the 'having-been-there'. However, these photographs are distinguished from documents by the relationship of the internal photograph to the photograph that contains it. Not only does this relationship exist at present only within the photograph, it has *never* existed elsewhere. So that the action Smithson preformed was simply an instrument, and not the object, of signification. The photograph *is* the work (28).

Clearly such a reading of Smithson's work, and the significance of the use of photography within it, directly opposes that offered by Morris. Yet, whilst 'The Present Tense of Space' is implacable in its opposition to photography and insistent upon its antinomy to the concerns of sculpture, the irony is that Morris himself had once produced a number of works that used photography in such a fashion as to suggest an equally complex relationship to the medium that his essay would later seek to deny.

In the later 1960s Morris moved away from the predominantly geometrical and fixed forms, by which he had become associated as a noted proponent of minimalism, towards the use of non-rigid materials and combinations of materials that placed emphasis on process over product or, what Morris called, 'anti-form'. Morris's notion of 'anti-form' clearly involved as central a concern with temporality; one inscribed primarily in the idea of change, contingency and indeterminacy. Whilst most of Morris's 'anti-form' works never quite escaped being objects of some description, one project in particular attempted to embody impermanence in both the manner of its production and reception. *Continuous Project Altered Daily* took place over a three week period in March 1969 at the newly acquired uptown warehouse space used by the Castelli Gallery in New York. Morris visited the gallery space on each morning of the exhibition and proceeding to work with a heterogeneous range of materials he had assembled, including clay, earth, lengths of timber, asbestos, grease, cotton, wood, plastic, felt, threadwaste, and a few large trestle tables. At the end of the morning session the gallery would be

Figs. 9.3 - 6 Robert Morris, *Continuous Project Altered Daily*, 1969. © DACS, London/VAGA, New York 2009. Courtesy Leo Castelli Gallery, New York.

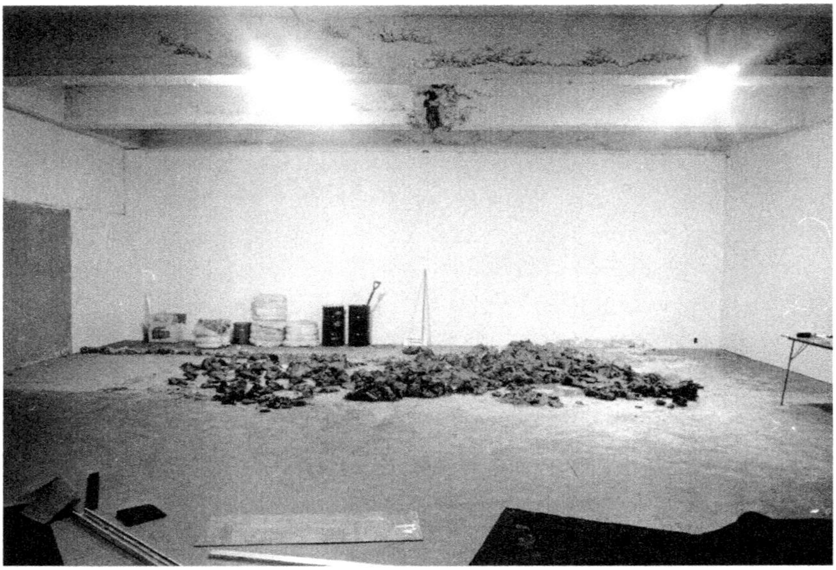

Fig. 9.3

opened to visitors. What those visitors encountered most closely resembled a kind of building site, replete with the various tools—spades, shovels, containers and brooms—that were integral to the on-going process of construction. The next day Morris would return to the gallery, re-work the materials, producing a different configuration and the gallery would again be open to visitors.

The diary that Morris kept during this event makes clear that what he did with the assembled materials was 'experimental, exploratory, non-directed (Morris, 1994, 234).' In other words, most things were left to whim or chance. On the first day he notes: 'Dumped out 2000 pounds of wet clay out of 50lb cans onto floor. No idea of what to be done with it. Began aimlessly—throwing it around (ibid.).' There was no one in attendance to record these aleatory actions but Morris did employ a photographer to record the result at the end of each session. The photographs that exist of *Continuous Project Altered Daily*, therefore, do not picture a process but are a record of residues, traces of traces. Shot from exactly the same position, the series of images showed the work in its various states of development (figs 9.3-9.5). At the end of exhibition, Morris cleared the gallery space of all of the materials with which he had been working and pinned up on the wall eight of the photographs that had been taken. Another photograph of the virtually empty gallery was made (fig. 9.6). This shows the eight photographs in situ together with

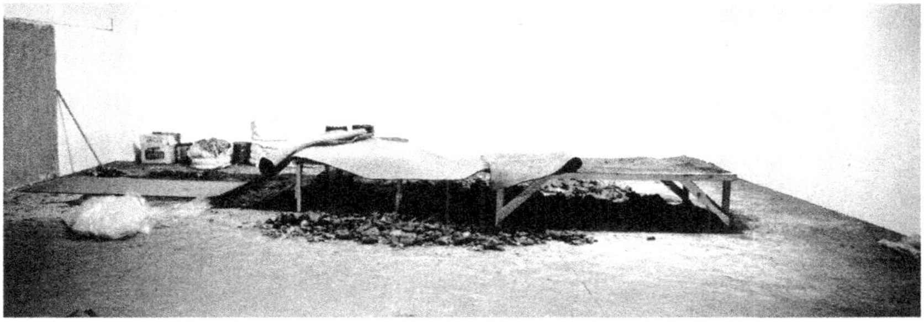

Fig. 9.4

the tape recorder which was placed on the floor in the middle of the space and which replayed the sounds of Morris clearing the space, sweeping up the debris, prior to the final day's viewing.

In an interview conducted at the time that *Continuous Project Altered Daily* was taking place, Morris was asked by Paul Cummings about the role of the photographs in the exhibition.

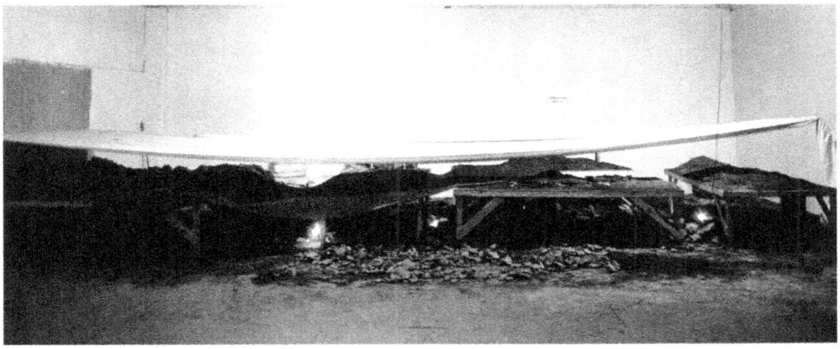

Fig. 9.5

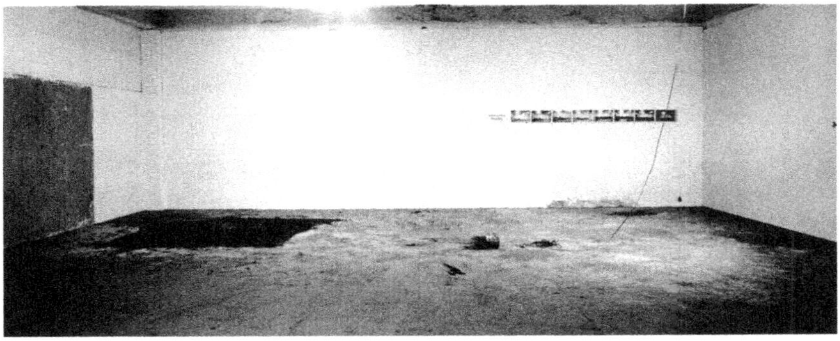

Fig. 9.6

> PC: At the end of the exhibition, you will have, what? A series of twenty photographs or something?
>
> RM: Yes.
>
> PC: That will be what?
>
> RM: That will be the record of the piece. Just a record.
>
> PC: So there will no longer be any piece? There'll just be the record of the piece?
>
> RM: That's all.
>
> PC: Information of a kind?
>
> RM: Yes.
>
> PC: And an image of a kind?
>
> RM: Right.
>
> PC: But it's an image of an image in a way?
>
> RM; Yes, but seen differently. I mean it's spectacular whereas you don't see rectangularly. So it's very removed from the piece. I'm doing a piece in California. Did we talk about this one—the heat, hot and cold air?
>
> PC: No.
>
> (Cummings, 2009)[2]

Seemingly impatient with the line of questioning the artist brings this somewhat terse exchange to an abrupt end by switching the subject. And on other occasions too, when probed about the place of 'documentation' within his practice, Morris remained indifferent to the suggestion that his use of photography might amount to something more than 'just a record' (Alberro and Norvell, 2001). Yet, Paul Cummings' comment that the photographs that form part of *Continuous Project Altered Daily* might be thought of in terms of 'an image of an image' (something which Morris felt partially obliged to agree with) begins to sully any simple distinction between the work, on the one hand, and it's documentary record, on the other.

Thus, whilst the final photograph taken of *Continuous Project Altered Daily* may be deemed as holding a different status from the photographs it shows, since this single photograph lies outside the spatial and temporal frame of the exhibition and acts as a record of its final state, the photographs that are pinned to wall certainly have a more ambiguous role.[3] Even if Morris considered them simply as documentation, their effect must have exceeded such a function. Drawing attention to—by virtue of its absence—what had once been there, the series of photographs would seem to stand as a desultory residue to the presumed plenitude of an experience that had previously been on offer, functioning as an expedient but ultimately inadequate supplement to the work itself. Certainly this was how the use of photography in relationship to the more ephemeral forms of contemporary art practice at the time was largely understood and the way in which Morris apparently regarded them. Yet, following Derrida, it needs to be noted that the 'logic of supplementarity' is never a simple affair. Caught in a series of paradoxes, the supplement is both additional *and* integral, both marginal *and* central, both outside *and* inside, both superfluous *and* necessary. Thus, the supplement is never *merely* a supplement. Placed on display—although in a rather rudimentary fashion—in the gallery space and whilst the exhibition was still in progress, the series of eight photographs existed within the physical and temporal parameters of the installation; more a part of, rather than apart from, the work itself.

Turning the logic of supplementarity to one's own ends was always a possibility and one explored by many artists at the time. As I have briefly suggested here—and others have explored in detail—Robert Smithson's work, in particular, was always difficult to locate; there seemed to be no centre, no one thing that you could point to and say this is it, this is the work, only a sense of continual deferral borne out of a calculated and conscious indeterminancy. Indeed, I want to suggest that Morris himself—despite all his protestations to the contrary—was well aware of the potential ambivalence that surrounds such forms of photographic documentation and made full use of it.

In the same year as *Continuous Project Altered Daily*, Morris employed the camera in several other works, the most ambitious being an installation at Finch College that involved both photography and film. The work evolved from a process whereby a 16mm cine camera, erected on a revolving stand and placed in the middle of the gallery, filmed Morris and an assistant, as they first set up and then took down, in sequence, a grid of mirrors on one wall and, directly facing it on another wall, a large photographic image of a 1940s movie audience watching a film. Subsequently the film of the installation and deinstallation of the mirrors and the photograph was projected back in the same space, the projector itself placed on a turntable in the middle of the gallery and rotating at the same speed as the original filming. As Chrissie Iles has noted in *Finch College Project*:

> Several doublings occur: real and filmed time; space and surface; and the reflection of the movie audience's faces back to themselves in the mirror, positioned where the film screen would be. A further doubling occurs in the appearance of the simulation of an art work within a real art work. The enlarged found photograph of a movie audience is both part of the art work and an abstraction of the original photograph and of cinematic spectatorship...In the darkened gallery, we are able neither to observe a stable object on the wall, nor to absorb a central, fixed image on a conventional cinema screen. Morris has detached both the art object and the film image from their moorings. Instead, on an elusive film image rotating around the walls, we see traces of an exhibition in process, whose content records a fragment of another kind of viewing space (Iles, 2002, 39).

It could be added to this account that the repetitious revolving of the filmic image of the space, and around the space that it re-presented, involved not only a sense of spatial displacement but one of temporal displacement as well. Above all else *Finch College Project* confounded any simple attempt to fix the place and time in which the work existed through the uncertainty as to whether what the audience encountered was either the work itself or its documentation. In truth it was probably both. Though less spectacular, and perhaps less obvious, I am suggesting that the eight photographs pinned to the wall in the empty space of the Castelli Gallery at the end of *Continuous Project Altered Daily* are to be considered in the same way.

It is worth briefly recalling one other piece that Morris made during this period, although it had little coverage at the time and has virtually disappeared from all more recent accounts of his work. The *Shotgun Project,* as it was known, was a work conceived for a touring exhibition that circulated between Canadian galleries in late 1969. To make the work Morris fired a shotgun at a blank wall and then photographed the result. An enlarged print was sent to the first galley, where a second shot was fired at the photograph. Another photograph was taken of this, then enlarged and sent to the next gallery, and so on. The culmination of the process was a photograph that contains within it the image of another photograph, which contains within it the image of another photograph and so on; each photograph having been blasted with a shotgun. Like a hall of mirrors, each image recedes in space and, of course, in time. As far as I am aware Morris never used photography or film in his work after 1969 and it is possible that *Shotgun Project* was the last of his works to make use of the camera. Perhaps this was the turning point in Morris's attitudes towards photography; the point where he began to take revenge on what he later came to regard as the 'malevolent power' of the medium through an iconoclastic act that would hopefully reassert the authority of the 'here and now'. The fact is, however, that as mere traces of an event, the scars left by the shotgun had as much 'presence' as the photograph itself. Or, we could say, that both were equally as present to the viewer.

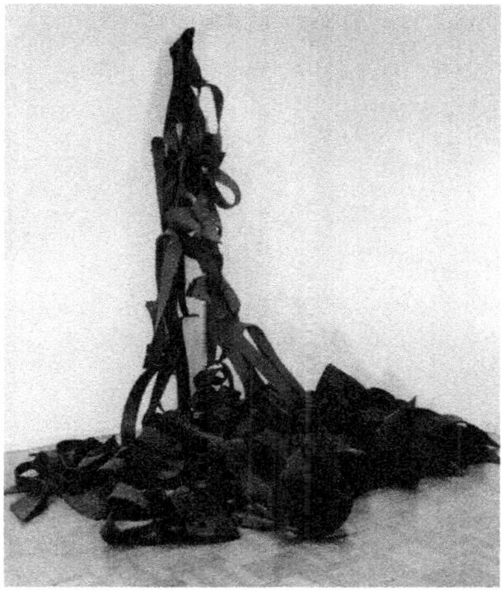

Fig. 9.7 Robert Morris *Untitled*, 1967-68. © DACS, London/ VAGA, New York 2009. Courtesy Leo Castelli Gallery, New York. Photo: Rudolph Burkhardt.

Thus perhaps the greatest irony is that even with those works through which Morris hoped to engage the viewer in a direct interactive experience of something existing in real space and real time and in the perception of an ongoing present tense, the encounter was nonetheless one marked by a sense of temporal alterity. Despite his insistence upon phenomenological basis of 'anti-form', an emphasis upon the fact of making and direct physical engagement with materials and their properties, and the importance of process, all of this remained invisible to the viewer. Whether conducted in the artist's studio or the gallery space itself, whatever the means of making or processes involved, the work was confronted by the viewer as a *fait accompli*. Whatever the rhetoric of process suggested, the work remained for the spectator an object to be viewed; an indexical trace of an event that had taken place. Moreover, despite Morris's later theorization of this work as involving a mode of 'the perception of space unfolding in the continuous present' it is equally possible to see it as one in which time has been arrested. Works such as the *Felt* series from1967 onwards—large pieces of industrial felt casually dumped upon the floor or hung from the gallery wall—exploited notions of randomness and impermanence but it is perhaps their static nature that impresses itself most directly on the viewer; they appear as if frozen, like a snapshot (fig. 9.7). And perhaps this was the truth behind Paul Cummings suggestion that the photographs of *Continuous Project Altered Daily* were 'an image of image'.

I'm reminded of that passage in Smithson's essay 'A Tour of The Monuments of Passaic':

> Noon day sunshine cinema-ized the site, turning the bridge and the river into an over-exposed *picture*. Photographing it with my Instamatic 400 was like photographing a photograph. The sun became a monstrous light bulb that projected a detached series of 'stills' through my instamatic into my eye. When I walked on the bridge, it was though I was walking on an enormous photograph that was made of wood and steel, and underneath the river existed as an enormous movie film that showed nothing but a continuous blank (Smithson, 1996, 70).

Smithson's account of his journey through an area of industrial wastelands of his home town in New Jersey, where reality appears as an image, where the photograph is encountered even before it is taken, radically undermines Morris's distinction—posed in his essay 'The Present Tense of Space'—between the experience of the 'continuous present' of real space-time, on the one hand, and that of a 'retrospective', 'static and consumable image', on the other. But as I've suggested here Morris was once, perhaps, less assured about the distinction himself.

In his early writings Morris had envisaged 'a viewer who is an integral participant in the work not a passive beholder, a viewer who exists in time rather than one merely who witnessed its passing (Meyer, 2001, 162).' It was precisely this interrelationship between the viewer and the work of art, and its embedded experience of temporal duration, that Fried took issue with in his critique of minimalism. In the later 1960s with *Continuous Project Altered Daily*, together with other of Morris's 'anti-form' pieces, Morris attempted to secure any even stronger bond between the viewer and the work by reducing or eliminating, as the artist put it, 'the existential gap between the studio preparation and the formal presentation (Morris, 1993b, 91).' As Alex Potts has argued this attempt to elide the distinction between the moment of the work of art's production and the viewer's encounter with it carried with it a utopian ambition:

> Morris now sought a situation for his work where the taming effects of the public arenas for the presentation of art would be completely abolished, and where there would be no aesthetic or ideological framing of the viewer's access to this work. His new pieces were to be apprehended as identical with his performance of them, so there was as he saw it no artificial separation between ends and means. Any framing or insulation of the work would take place in the viewer's head, and would not be imposed from outside, the viewer Morris had in mind occupying the same psychic space as the artist through a total identification with the artist's activity of making... Morris took his conception of process art to the point where he came close to advocating the late Romantic idea that the essence of art lay in some unmediated transfer between the inner spirit of the artist's creative act and the inner imaginative world of the viewer (Potts, 2000, 251-252).

Ultimately it would seem that, for Morris, the idea of a 'presentness' that marked the encounter of the viewer and the work as being both immediate and direct, testified to the desire to overcome any kind of mediation whatsoever between the artist's intention and the viewer's experience. In this context, Morris's views on photography can be seen as bearing witness to a more pervasive anxiety as to the possibility of a directness of vision on the part of the viewer, as to whether the work of art could retain a sense of its own immediacy and whether the object and the viewer could remain as equally present to each other. Choosing to present photography as cause rather than symptom, Morris perhaps merely allayed his own fears as to the insufficiency of the work of art's 'presence'.

Notes

[1] It needs to be noted here that whilst Fried uses the terms 'presence' and 'presentness' to signify two different and opposing concepts of the viewer's experience, Morris uses the two terms interchangeably.

[2] The Smithsonian website that reproduces this interview dates it as having taken place on March 11 1968. However, it is clear from references in the interview to the current exhibition at Castelli Gallery that this is incorrect and that the date should read March 11 1969.

[3] Morris produced an eighteen page folded card booklet containing sixteen photographs of *Continuous Project Altered Daily*, recording twelve 'stages' of the work. The final 'stage' is the photograph of the

empty gallery containing only the other photographs and the tape recorder. Insofar as this photograph was now included in an 'artist's book', its status becomes equal to that of the other photographs, that is, equally ambiguously poised between document and work.

Bibliography

¬ Alexander Alberro and Patricia Norvell (eds), *Recording Conceptual Art* (Berkeley and Los Angeles: University of California Press, 2001).

¬ Paul Cummings, *Interview with Robert Morris*, Smithsonian Archives of American Art, Found at http://www.aaa.si.edu/collections/oralhistories/transcripts/morris68.htm. Accessed 23 May 2009.

¬ Michael Fried, 'Art and Objecthood', *Art and Objecthood: Essays and Reviews* (Chicago/London: University of Chicago Press, 1998a), 148-172.

¬ Michael Fried, 'An Introduction to My Art Criticism', *Art and Objecthood: Essays and Reviews* (Chicago/London: University of Chicago Press, 1998b), 1-74.

¬ Chrissie Iles, 'Between the Still and Moving Image', *Into the Light: The Projected Image in American Art 1964-1977* (New York: Whitney Museum of American Art, 2002), 33-69.

¬ Max Kozloff, 'Photos within Photographs', *Photography and Fascination* (Danbury, New Hampshire: Addison House, 1979), 91-100.

¬ Pamela M. Lee, *Chronophobia: on time in the art of the 1960s* (Cambridge, Mass./London: MIT Press, 2004).

¬ James Meyer, *Minimalism: art and polemics in the sixties* (New Haven/London: Yale University Press, 2001).

¬ Robert Morris, 'The Present Tense of Space', *Continuous Project Altered Daily: The Writings of Robert Morris* (Cambridge, Mass./London: MIT Press, 1993a), 175-207.

¬ Robert Morris, 'Some Notes on the Phenomenology of Making', *Continuous Project Altered Daily: The Writings of Robert Morris* (Cambridge, Mass./London: MIT Press, 1993b), 71-93.

¬ Robert Morris, *Robert Morris: The Mind/Body Problem* (New York: Solomon R. Guggenheim Museum, 1994).

¬ Craig Owens, 'Earthwords', *October*, 10 (Fall, 1979):120-130.

¬ Craig Owens, 'Photography *en abyme*', in *Beyond Recognition: Representation, Power and Culture* (Berkeley: University of California Press, 1997), 16-30.

¬ Alex Potts, 'The Minimalist Object and the Photographic Image', in Geraldine A. Johnson (ed.) *Sculpture and Photography: Envisioning the Third Dimension* (Cambridge: Cambridge University Press, 1998), 181-198.

¬ Alex Potts, *The Sculptural Imagination: Figurative, Modernist, Minimalist* (New Haven/London: Yale University Press, 2000).

¬ Robert Smithson 'A Tour of the Monuments of the Passaic', in Jack Flam (ed.) *Robert Smithson: The Collected Writings* (Berkeley and Los Angeles: University of California Press, 1996) 69-74.

Notes on the Authors

Jan Baetens is Professor of Cultural Studies at the K.U.Leuven and Editor of Image [&] Narrative (www.imageandnarrative.be). His main field is literature and French poetry. Despite this special background, he has also published widely on interart comparison, mainly in so-called minor genres (comics, graphic novels, photonovellas, novelizations).

Victor Burgin is an artist, writer and Professor Emeritus of History of Consciousness at the University of California. His theoretical works include *Situational Aesthetics* (2009), *The Remembered Film* (2004), *In/Different Spaces* (1996), *The End of Art Theory* (1986) and *Thinking Photography* (1982). Monographs of his visual work include *Components of a Practice* (2008), *Relocating* (2001), *Victor Burgin* (Fundacio Antonio Tapies, 2001) and *Between* (1986).

David Green is Senior Lecturer in the History and Theory of Contemporary Art at the University of Brighton. His published writings have been concerned primarily with the place of photography and video in contemporary art practices. He is the co-editor and contributor to *Stillness and Time: Photography and the Moving Image* (2006).

Louis Kaplan is Associate Professor of History and Theory of Photography in the Graduate Department of Art at the University of Toronto and Director of the interdisciplinary Institute of Communication and Culture at the Mississauga campus. He is the author of numerous books including *The Strange Case of William Mumler, Spirit Photographer* (Minnesota, 2008) and *American Exposures: Photography and Community in the Twentieth Century* (Minnesota, 2005). In the spring of 2010, he co-edited a special issue of the *Journal of Visual Culture* entitled 'Regarding Jean-Luc Nancy'. His current projects include essays on Patrick Clancy's photoscroll *365/360* and Wallace Berman's Verifax collages.

Joanna Lowry is Academic Programme Leader for Photography, Moving Image and Sound and MA Photography Course Leader at the University of Brighton. She has written widely on contemporary photographic practices for academic publications, the art press and exhibition catalogues. She is the co-editor of *Stillness and Time: Photography and the Moving Image* (2006).

Susana S. Martins graduated in 2004 with a Diploma in Art History from the Faculty of Social and Human Sciences of the Universidade Nova de Lisboa (Portugal). After her graduation, she joined the Sintra Museum of Modern Art – Colecção Berardo, working as education responsible and as assistant curator for two years. In 2006, she became a member of the Lieven Gevaert Research Centre for Photography (Belgium), where she is currently conducting her PhD research on photography and national identities at the K.U.Leuven.

Andrea Nelson is an assistant curator in the Department of Photographs at the National Gallery of Art in Washington, D.C. and teaches at the Corcoran College of Art + Design. Her publications include articles on László Moholy-Nagy's *Malerie Fotographie Film* and 1930's mass media photography books. She is currently working on a project that examines the narrative structure of modern photography books.

Maren Polte is an art historian trained at Cologne and Berlin universities. In Berlin, she completed her PhD with a thesis on the Düsseldorf 'Becher School', Germany's leading group of photographers. Until 2007, she taught Art History at Humboldt-University. She is a specialist in contemporary art and photography and was a guest lecturer at the K.U.Leuven in the winter term 2009/2010.

Chitra Ramalingam recently completed a PhD in History of Science at Harvard University, and is currently a Mellon/ACLS Postdoctoral Research Fellow at the Research in the Arts, Social Sciences, and Humanities (CRASSH), University of Cambridge. Her research broadly explores connections between science and visual culture in the nineteenth century. She is working on a book on visual observation and imaging practices in Victorian physics.

Graham Smith is Professor Emeritus in Art History at the University of St Andrews and a Fellow of the Royal Society of Edinburgh. He has been Editor of the international quarterly *History of Photography* since 2001. His most recent publications include *'Light that Dances in the Mind': Photographs and Memory in the Writings of E. M. Forster and his Contemporaries* (Peter Lang, 2007) and '"Latent Preparedness": Literary Association and Visual Reminiscence in "Daisy Miller"', in *Illustrations, Optics and Objects in Nineteenth-Century Literary and Visual Culture* (Palgrave, 2010).

Alexander Streitberger is Professor of Modern and Contemporary Art History at U.C. Louvain and Director of the Lieven Gevaert Centre for Photography Research (www.lievengevaertcentre.be). His PhD thesis on the influence of language philosophy on 20th-century art has been published under the title *Ausdruck - Modell - Diskurs. Sprachreflexion in der Kunst des 20. Jahrhunderts (Berlin : Reimer).* His photographic research is focused on the relationship between the still (photographic) and the moving (filmic) image, and the photographic discourses of modernity and modernism.

Hilde Van Gelder is Associate Professor of Contemporary Art History at the K.U.Leuven. She is Director of the Lieven Gevaert Research Centre for Photography (www.lievengevaertcentre.be). Editor of *Image [&] Narrative* (www.imageandnarrative.be) and Series Editor of the Lieven Gevaert Series (Leuven University Press). Her research focuses on the critical potential of the photographic in contemporary art.

ISBN 978 94 6270 147 2

D/2010/1869/15

NUR: 652

Series editors: Alexander Steitberger and Hilde Van Gelder

Final editing: Jan Baetens, Esther Rosser, Alexander Streitberger and Hilde Van Gelder

Proof reading: Esther Rosser

Lay-out: Rein Deslé

Cover image: David Claerbout, *Shadow Piece* (2005), video stills. © David Claerbout

Lieven Gevaert Research Centre for Photography
Arts Faculty K.U.Leuven
Blijde-Inkomststraat 21 pb 3313
B-3000 Leuven
Belgium